CAMRA'S
GREAT
BRITISH
PUBS

Published by the **Campaign for Real Ale Ltd.**
230 Hatfield Road
St Albans
Hertfordshire AL1 4LW

www.camra.org.uk/books

ISBN 978-1-85249-265-6

A CIP catalogue record for this book is available from
the British Library
Printed and bound in China by Latitude Press Ltd.

Head of Publishing: Simon Hall
Project Editor: Katie Hunt
Editorial Assistance: Emma Haines
Design/Typography: Linda Storey
Cover Design: James Hall
Proof Reading: Simon Tuite
Mapping: iStockphoto/johnwoodcock
Head of Marketing: Tony Jerome

ry effort has been made to ensure the contents of this book are
ct at the time of printing. Nevertheless, the Publisher cannot be held
nsible for any errors or omissions, or for changes in the details given
uide, or for the consequences of any reliance on the information
by the same. This does not affect your statutory rights.

and opinions expressed in this guide are those of the author
t necessarily those of the Campaign for Real Ale.

aphy
to right: Alan Perryman; Hawkshead Brewery; Astrid
flap: Margaret Stranks. Back cover: Sheffield Tap

CAMRA'S
GREAT
BRITISH
PUBS

Adrian Tierney-Jones

CAMRA

BOOKS

Acknowledgements

Thanks are due to everyone who suggested a pub, while a hand across the north/south divide goes to 2010 Beer Writer of the Year Simon Jenkins for writing the Adelphi review; I also direct an affectionate salutation to my wife and fellow journalist Jane Alexander who many a time saved the day at times with soothing words and the odd not-so soothing word that would bring me down to earth as I rhapsodised about pubs and beer (and to James who has to put up with his dad's pub obsessions, it's a helluva job but someone has to do it…). Thanks also goes to Tim Hampson, Bob Steel, Arthur Taylor, Sophie Dorber, Sue Nowak, Sebastian Vanoni – and to anyone else I have missed out thanking; I apologise, but you know who you are. Cheers to CAMRA's Simon Hall who shared faith in the book and Katie Hunt who kept things running smoothly. Thanks also to Linda Storey who has done a magnificent design job. This is a book that I have wanted to write for years and for that I salute all the licensees who keep Britain's pubs afloat in the roughest of seas – can you buy me a drink? Or should that be the other way around?

Dedication
To Jane and you know why…

Picture Acknowledgements

With thanks to all the pubs and breweries who allowed us to use their images. Specific thanks go to:

p3 Katie Hunt; p4 Cath Harries; p7 (t) Maria Hiles (Flickr); (r) Jon Howard; (b) Cath Harries; p12 David Conniss (Flickr); p14 Adrian Tierney-Jones; p16 Ewan Munro (Flickr); p17 John Law (Flickr); p18 Bob Steel; p19 Ian Bayliss (Flickr); p20 Adrian Tierney-Jones; p21 Richard G. Hilsden (Flickr); p22 Katie Hunt; p23 Ewan Munro (Flickr); p24 Andrew Head (Flickr); p25 & p26 Cath Harries; p28 Alan Crawshaw (Flickr); p29 Neil Lloyd; p30 Stan Stephens; p32 Kelvin Barber (Flickr); p33 Cath Harries; p34 www.sastaylor.co.uk; p35 Gary S. Crutchley (Flickr); p36 Adrian Tierney-Jones; p43 Terry Doran (Flickr); p44 Andy Davison (Flickr); p45 Tom Stainer; p47 Dan Augood (Flickr); p49 Kelvin Barber (Flickr); p51 Adrian Tierney-Jones; p52 Mark Wheaver (Flickr); p54 John D McDonald (Flickr); p56 Mark Bolton; p57 Mark Bolton; p58 Adrian Tierney-Jones; p60 Mark Wheaver (Flickr); p61 Mark Bolton; p62 Adrian Tierney-Jones; p64 Hazel Munro (Flickr); p66 Chani McBain; p67 Adrian Tierney-Jones; p69 Alan Perryman; p70 Adrian Tierney-Jones; p71 Warren Wordsworth; p73 Katie Fortney (Flickr); p74 Manox Photography; p75 Adrian Tierney-Jones; p76 John Whitehead; p79 Adrian Tierney-Jones; p80 Will Salt (Flickr); p81 & p82 Adrian Tierney-Jones; p83 Cris Bartlett; p85 John Whitehead; p86 Nigel Mullender; p91 Andrew Howe (Flickr); p92 Nigel Cheffers-Heard; p93 Michael Carøe Andersen (Flickr); p94 Vikki Nuttall/ Dulverton Folk Festival; p96 Nick Robinson (Flickr); p97 jayneandd (Flickr); p98 Spyke Golding; p99 Cath Harries; p104 Adrian Tierney-Jones; p105 Chris Hunt; p108 Colin Anderson; p109 Tim Green (Flickr); p110 Maria Hiles (Flickr); p111 Keith Laverack (Flickr); p112 David Glaves (Flickr); p113 Bob Vipond; p116 John Law (Flickr); p117 John Law (Flickr); p118 John Law (Flickr); p119 Adrian Tierney Jones; p120 David Bayliss (Flickr); p121 David Bearstow (Flickr); p124 calflier001 (Flickr); p126 Stephen W Conaty (Flickr); p127 Ewan Munro (Flickr); p128 Ben Coulson (Flickr); p129 Ian Hadingham (Flickr); p130 Adrian Tierney-Jones; p131 Tom Stainer; p132, p133 & p134 Adrian Tierney-Jones; p135 calflier001 (Flickr); p139 Bob Steel; p140 Zoltan Galsi; p142 Adrian Tierney-Jones; p146 Cath Harries; p148 Katie Hunt; p149 Elliott Brown (Flickr); p150 Bob Steel; p151 Nigel Cheffers-Heard; p152 Paul Olivant (Flickr); p153 Adrian Tierney-Jones; p154 Steven Foers; p155 Cath Harries; p156 Katie Hunt; p157 Helge Nareid; p158 Adrian Tierney-Jones; p159 Cath Harries; p160 Adrian Tierney-Jones; p161 John Law (Flickr); p162 Nigel D Nudds (Flickr); p163 Jim Lock (Flickr); p164 Alan Perryman (Flickr); p166 Anthony Seminara; p167 Karen Roe (Flickr); p168 Matthew Wilkinson (Flickr); p170 Kelvin Barber (Flickr); p171 Chris Sapey (Flickr); p172 Mark Rutley (Flickr); p177 Bob Steel; p178 Adrian Tierney-Jones; p179 Ewan Munro (Flickr); p180 Claire-Michelle Pearson; p182 Ian Heath (Flickr); p183 David Kirkby (Flickr); p184 Bob Steel; p185 The Quaffer (Flickr); p189 Adrian Tierney Jones; p190 John Law (Flickr); p191 Mark Hillary (Flickr); p194 Adrian Tierney-Jones; p195 J.J. Myers (Flickr); p196 Richard Bysouth (Flickr); p197 Adrian Tierney-Jones; p199 Matt Yarsley (Flickr); p202 John Law (Flickr); p208 Adrian Tierney-Jones; p209 travelswithbeer.com; p210, p212, p213 & p214 Adrian Tierney-Jones; p215 Colin Anderson; p217 www.heatheronhertravels.com; p218 Katie Hunt; p220 Hayley Wincott (Flickr); p221 Lacey Glanville (Flickr); p222 & p223 Katie Hunt; p224 Margaret Stranks (Flickr); p225 Simon Cox; p226 Katie Hunt; p227 Scott Ferguson (Flickr); p228 Katie Hunt; p230 Jim Linwood (Flickr); p231 Katie Hunt; p234 Chris Hunt; p235 Adrian Tierney-Jones; p236 Tom Stainer; p237 Colin Anderson; p240 Matt Stewart (Flickr); p241 Katherine Nagl (Flickr); p242 Adrian Tierney-Jones; p244 Cath Harries; p245 Thorskegga Thorn (Flickr); p246 Adrian Tierney-Jones; p247 Richard Breakspear (Flickr); p248 © English Heritage. NMR; p251 Bob Steel; p253 Tim Warnett (Flickr); p254 Colin Wootton; p255 Mick Slaughter; p257 Adrian Tierney-Jones; p258 Tom Stainer; p260 Smart Community Fife (Flickr); p261 Andrew Mawby (Flickr); p262 Kelvin Barber (Flickr); p263 Rob Oliver (Flickr); p264 Warren Wordsworth; p265 Cath Harries; p268 Adrian Tierney-Jones; p269 Bill Boaden (Flickr); p270 Jon Howard; p272 Ewan Munro (Flickr); p274 Adrian Tierney-Jones; p275 Andrew Fogg (Flickr); p276 Bob Steel; p277 Adrian Tierney-Jones; p278 Jon Howard; p279 David Kirkby (Flickr); p280 Mike Forsyth (Flickr); p281, p284 & p285 Cath Harries.

Contents

▲ Brewery Tap, Peterborough

The best

Features

▲ Ship Inn, Red Wharf Bay

▲ Square & Compass, Worth Matravers

▼ Black Friar, London

About this book

As the title might suggest *Great British Pubs* is a celebration of the great British pub; one of the most magnificent things that this country has given to the world. In this book you will discover over 200 pubs, in places ranging from deepest Cornwall all the way up the Highlands, with stopovers in rural villages, northern cities, London hotspots and coastal districts where the beer is poured to the sound of waves in the background. The book's expansive profiles of the pubs offer a chance to place each establishment within its context: what it's like; what you can expect when you pass through its doors; the beer, cider and food on offer; the ambience; the music; the games; the history; and the people who step through its doors day after day. In addition, dotted throughout the pages are a variety of features dwelling on aspects of the brewing industry, beer, pub history and culture.

▲ Pubs featured within a category are listed at the start of each section. Others to try are listed as 'See also'.

Great British Pubs helpfully places all the pub entries into different categories, such as the best pubs for food, beer range, music, gardens etc. – it is both a traditional pub guide book and a travel book; a book that fits just as well into the glove box of a car as on the arm of a comfortable sofa.

Every profile, I hope, will make you want to visit the great British pub and play a part in ensuring its survival. For make no mistake, these are desperate times for many pubs, with more than 25 closing every week. The pub is the perfect environment in which to enjoy real ale at its best and CAMRA has been campaigning hard at national and local level to help Britain's struggling pubs. CAMRA's campaigning has secured the appointment of a Minister for Community Pubs, to help support pubs, while ongoing campaigns are seeking to address high levels of beer tax and supermarket below-cost alcohol promotions and to deliver a fair deal for pub landlords tied to the large pub-owning companies. If you would like to lend a hand to saving a local pub, see the feature on p276 for advice or, if you would like to help by joining CAMRA, see p296 or visit **www.camra.org.uk**.

Special pubs everyone should visit

Great British Pubs is a travel book with the beer- and pub-lover in mind, for whom a good pub is a destination in itself. If you would like to find a pub that is a survivor from the golden age of Victorian pubs then it will be within these pages; pubs that serve good food are lauded for their dishes; there are pubs that offer a stunning selection of cask beers and that brew their own beer; pubs that sit at the heart of the community, within inspiring landscapes or on the coast; pubs that act as a mirror for the buzz of the city in which they lie.

Easy to find pubs that you like

Great British Pubs features over 200 pubs from across the country; from old to new, rural to urban, multi-handpumped to a single cask beer. So how do you know what to look for? For a start, the pubs are organised into categories – beer ranges, brewpubs, cider pubs, country pubs, family pubs and so on. You'll get the full list on the contents page. So, if you're in want of a pub with more than the usual quota of beers then 'Beer ranges' is the category for you. At the beginning of the section you will see that the opening spread has a list of pubs which have been profiled, with a map of their locations; you will also see a list of pubs featured elsewhere in the book – they might be in the cider, food or family pubs section but they are also worth looking at if you want a pub with a good beer range. Within the entries themselves, where it states underneath for example, **Also great for:** Cider, the pub is also worthy of consideration for that category.

▶ Features give more detail about aspects of pub life.

◀ Each pub entry has contact details and a beer list at the top, and opening hours below.

Straightforward, useful information

This is very much a symbol-free book, but at the end of each review we have included the most up-to-date opening times. However, in the same way financial investments can up and down, the pub world can be a fluid one at times so, if you are travelling some distance to visit a pub, it might be worth a call to make sure that nothing has changed. Following on the theme of fluidity, if a pub has changed totally since I wrote about it please let me know at **tierneyjones@ btinternet.com**. As for finding your desired pub, where they exist we have also included a pub's website – most will have details (or even maps) of their location. There are also indexes at the back of the book enabling you to find a specific pub either by name, or by location.

In the **Best Heritage Pubs** section you will see that many of the pubs are noted as being listed buildings and/or as being on the National Inventory of History Pub Interiors – the latter is maintained by CAMRA. Part One of the Inventory includes interiors that have remained virtually intact since before the Second World War, while Part Two pubs have features of exceptional historic or architectural importance. For more information go to **www.heritagepubs. org.uk**.

Introduction

Pub. Boozer. Tavern. Local. Rub-a-Dub. Public bar. Village inn. Gin palace. Home from home.

We call the British pub many things, always with affection in our hearts and rarely with anger (save that for those who give a bad name to this uniquely British institution or places where the beer is bad) – the pub is where we meet and greet friends, neighbours, strangers (friends in the making) and (on occasion) future lovers. Some pubs are gloriously and stubbornly old-fashioned: dark, cloistered places dedicated to the arcane art of drinking, where the snug has survived the attentions of those eminent Victorians who thought it a home to vice. A sense of continuity and history resonates from the pictures and prints that cover the walls. Other pubs are fresh and bright, upbeat and eager with light pouring in; all the better to appreciate the bright hoppy chatter of a golden beer in its glass. Cosy sofas comfort, stripped pine furniture soothes, while beers from home and abroad and food with an accent on the unusual offer sustenance.

Whether old, middle-aged or new, a good pub is a comfort, a crossroads of social mobility, a centre of communications and a place where the reward of a great beer sustains during the long working day. There are town pubs, city pubs, suburban pubs, seaside pubs, village pubs, in the middle-of-nowhere pubs, pub pubs, and brew pubs where the beer is freshly brewed on the premises. Each will be quite different and each will have its own unique atmosphere. But one thing that binds all good pubs together is that they are the heartbeat of a community, as well as being a home of good beer.

So what is a great British pub? That's the question I've been asking myself all throughout the writing of this book. And the only answer I have been able to come up with is that there is no easy answer. There are pubs in this book that excel in food, have a history going back almost to the days of the Ark (well not quite the Ark, but to the Crusades), are good places to take the family without being subjected to the enforced jollity of kids entertainers, stay overnight at and enjoy a breakfast omelette infused with jalapenos, or use as a pit-stop on a country walk.

A pint & a pork pie

We like muddy boots & dogs!

I suppose the only real thread that binds them is that they all serve good cask beer, whether it's just a couple of well-kept regulars or a plethora of hand pumps at the bar dispensing exotic and exciting brews from near and far. Some of them also serve beers from around the globe.

Beer. Beer is the currency with which we spend our time in these pubs, the rich seam of gold that makes British pubs such a valuable part of our national heritage. We are a beer nation, a beer country and we are part of the beer belt of northern Europe (the German speaking lands, the Czech lands, the Nordic countries, the Low Countries, even the northern part of France where beer always takes its rightful place on the table); we are the sons of John Barleycorn, who according to the old poem must die every harvest before being reborn in the following spring – the golden promise of resurrection.

People. Then there are the people as well, the people who tell stories (for what is the pub but a place where stories are told), the people that define the local neighbourhood, the people who make the jokes that lighten up the pub and lest we forget the people who serve behind the bar and keep the whole show on the road. The pub is a public house where people gather. Yes they gather to drink beer but they also gather to pass the time of day, to celebrate their good fortune, their marriages, their birthdays, a winning steak on the horses, to meet their friends, to remember old friends. I go to the pub to meet people and drink beer.

This has been a great book in the making, a thoroughly enjoyable one, a book that will leave me with many happy memories and I hope that you, the reader with a love of pubs, will enjoy it as well. I have to say that I have managed to visit the majority of pubs in this book, but not all of them; for the ones I have not visited I was aided by colleagues, friends and CAMRA members. Your favourite pub might not be within these pages or you might disagree with my choices (please let me know at tierneyjones@btinternet.com), but for me the pubs in this book are truly Great British pubs and I for one am happy to commend them to the nation.

Adrian Tierney-Jones

◀ Queens Arms, Corton Denham

TIMOTHY TAYLOR - LANDLORD	(LIM)	4.0	
TIMOTHY TAYLOR - GOLDEN BEST	(LIM)	3.5	2.50
THORNBRIDGE - JAIPUR	(L)	5.9	2.80
THORNBRIDGE - WILD SWAN	(L)	3.5	2.30
FULLER'S - GALES HSB	(M)	4.8	2.70
GADD'S - COMMON CONSPIRACY	(LIM)	4.8	2.70
DURHAM - APOLLO	(L)	4.5	2.60
MARBLE - LAGONDA IPA	(L)	5.0	
BREWDOG - TRASHY BLONDE	(L)	4.1	2.60
DARK STAR - AMERICAN PALE ALE	(L)	4.7	2.40
1 GREEN MILL - CITRUS TWIST	(L)	3.8	2.50
2 ROOSTER'S - CITRA	(L)	4.3	2.60
3 BARTRAMS - MARLD	(D)	3.4	2.50
4 GADDS - DOUBLE I.P.A.	(L)	9.0	2.10 per ½
5 THORNBRIDGE - MERRIE	(M)	5.9	2.00
6 WENTWORTH - WOPPA	(L)	5.1	2.80
7 BUNTINGFORD - IMPERIAL BALTIC STOUT	(D)	7.0	3.30
8 BUNTINGFORD - XXX	(M)	5.0	2.80

NEW IN
IPA is DEAD
BRAMLING
X
£3.40 per pint

AGOSTINI PERRY
7.5 £3.50 (pint)

TRADITIONAL:
BROADOAK PERRY
7.5 £3.50 (pint)

PERMANENT/FIZZY:
ASPALL'S SUFFOLK CYDER
5.5 £3.40 (pint)

DRAUGHT
CIDER

The best
beer ranges

There are hundreds of breweries in the UK, which means that there are plenty of beers to choose from – from home-grown English bitters to the new wave of more exotic flavours coming from many breweries – providing you pick the right pub, which is the purpose of this section.

These pubs offer up a scintillating choice of handpumps. You might be in Cheshire, in which case hasten along to the Bhurtpore Inn in the village of Aston, where a dozen cask beers plus a stunning array of bottles will on display. The Somerset countryside provides a magnificent backdrop to enjoying the well-established cascade of ales in the Halfway House in Pitney.

Spending time in London? Then pay your respects to the magnificent White Horse in Parsons Green, which has long been a place where beer is king – or research your chosen subject at the newer breed of craft beer pubs such as the Southampton Arms or The Rake. Cambridge, Leicester and Huddersfield also offer a full deck of beery cards for city slickers.

Whether country or city, the pubs here offer the beer connoisseur a reason to step into their confines and study the beers within. The only problem? You might not have enough time…

See also
Anchor,
Walberswick (p194)
Brewery Tap,
Peterborough (p42)
Bunch of Grapes,
Pontypridd (p209)
Cock Hotel,
Wellington (p183)
King's Head,
Norwich (p71)

◀ Grove, Huddersfield

Bhurtpore Inn

Wrenbury Road, Aston, Cheshire, CW5 8DQ
01270 780917
www.bhurtpore.co.uk

🍺 Beer range varies

. . . .

There's a nice sense of homecoming about the history of the Bhurtpore Inn. Originally called the Red Lion, it received its current name after the siege of Bhurtpore in India. In 1849 one of the George family took over the place and ran it until it was sold to a Crewe brewery in 1901. When Simon and Nicky George came looking for a pub in 1991 it was shuttered up. Now the Bhurtpore Inn has been brought back into the George family fold – and it has prospered ever since.

It's not hard to work out the immediate reason for its success – walk into the big open front bar and you're immediately face to face with an array of hand pumps alongside some seriously good continental beer taps. Follow the bar into the back room (complete with pool table and locals chatting) and there are more pumps.

The Bhurtpore Inn is a true temple of beer, offering up to 11 cask beers at any one time, from the likes of Thornbridge and Summer Wine. There's also a bottled beer menu that wouldn't be out of place in a Belgian beer cafe. Single malt whiskies and artisanal ciders are also on sale for those who want a break from beer.

This is an Aladdin's cave of drink for cask beer lovers, but what makes it slightly different is that all the ales are guests. There is not one single beer that is always on, although Simon George always listens to locals' requests for their favourites; the pub also runs two beer festivals annually.

There's a lot to admire while you drink: the Bhurtpore Inn has a sense of architectural style. Its solid red-brick Victoriana structure is pleasing and engaging; and it has grown over the years with several rooms being added. Inside the main bar several photos show the pub's development over the last century or so. There's also framed memorabilia: most poignantly a series of letters from a Battle of Britain fighter pilot who fell during the summer of 1940.

And when you want something to eat then the curries come highly recommended. Bravehearts will plump for the scorcher of a tindaloo, whilst others looking for less spicy fare will enjoy perusing a menu that features local produce from venison right down to the pork pies. Thank goodness the George family returned.

Opening hours: 12–2.30, 6.30–11.30;
12–midnight Fri & Sat; 12–11 Sun
Also great for: Community

Cambridge Blue

85–87 Gwydir Street, Cambridge, CB1 2LG
01223 471680
www.the-cambridgeblue.co.uk
🍺 Nethergate Dewdrop; Woodforde's Wherry; guest beers

I first visited this pub back in the late 1970s when it was called the Dewdrop Inn and owned by Tolly Cobbold, though its history goes back to the late 19th century when Gwydir Street was being built. It was an old-fashioned backstreet boozer with two rooms, one of which had a jukebox, and I seem to remember the landlady being very tolerant of a noisy bunch of lads, some of whom were in fancy dress. The Tolly Cobbold beers also made a change from those of Greene King, which dominated the city's pubs.

I returned in 1987: the Tolly Cobbold was gone, the name changed to the Cambridge Blue and the big garden at the back opened up. A gloriously sunny lunchtime was spent outside.

Since then, the Blue (named after the colour worn by sports teams from Cambridge University) has gained an enviable reputation as a lively community pub offering a great and grand selection of beers alongside a robust parade of snacks and meals. It's also an essential stopover for anyone planning a triangular pub crawl off Mill Road – the Kingston Arms is in the next street and the Live & Let Live (both old haunts) a few minutes away in Mawson Road.

The pub still maintains the basic two-roomed structure at the front though it's now more open-plan, while the light and airy conservatory at the back also offers a comfortable drinking space –

however, those in search of a mite more privacy can still find the odd nook and cranny. The garden remains a welcoming spot for lunch and a pint.

If you have a thirst for beer then this is the right place to come – up to 16 cask beers are often available (10 during quieter times); the house beer Dewdrop is produced by Nethergate and the Blue also always aims to have a stout and a mild available most days. There's an exhaustive list of bottled beers from all over the world, including Belgium, the US and Germany. The new kitchen serves up a pub menu that includes home-made favourites such as chilli con carne and fish pie, or cider sausages served with mash and gravy. If that's not enough there is also a regular summer beer festival and an Oktoberfest. It's not a surprise that this is a place I keep returning to.

Opening hours: 12 (11 Sat)–11; 12–10.30 Sun

*The best **beer ranges***

Cask Pub & Kitchen

6 Charlwood Street, Pimlico, London,
SW1V 2EE
020 7630 7225
www.caskpubandkitchen.com

🍺 **Dark Star Hophead; guest beers**

. . . .

It's a room. A very large room, granted, a spacious room even, but it's still a room. It's lit by the tall assembly of windows looking out to the street. Elsewhere there's a tongue-and-grooved ceiling, a long bar at the back with a silver forest of fonts, and square pillars holding up the sky. Chairs and tables are dotted about and the hum and buzz of conversation is like the wind through the trees.

Enter Cask for the first time and you might feel what I felt: it's a room, yet it doesn't take long for you to realise that it's no ordinary room. From the outside, it's nothing special either, a corner pub built as part of a redbrick housing estate, perhaps sometime back in the 1980s. Flats rise in layers above the pub, while the sign 'CASK pub & kitchen' appears almost as an afterthought.

Yet, back in 2009 there was a buzz about Cask – its devotion to beer (new cask beers, hard to find German and Czech beers, 'meet the brewer' nights), while its transition from losing boozer to a vital stopping point on the London beer trail was also a great story (it belongs to a major regional brewer who leased it out). Now, it's a success story, at last a reason for the beer lover to go to Pimlico, this most unsung of London areas when it comes to beer (it wasn't always so: in the early days of craft brewing, Pimlico was home to the Orange Brewery brew-pub).

At the bar 10 hand pumps dispense cask beer, with the likes of Otley, Thornbridge, Dark Star and BrewDog all firm favourites; other taps give witness to some of the best global craft breweries including Mikkeller and Rothaus. The wall behind the bar is lined with glass-fronted coolers, where hundreds of bottled beers rest waiting to be picked out. Ask for the beer menu and you'll probably find something you've never had before. And as you sip at your glass of Dark Star Hophead or Mikkeller's Breakfast Beer Geek, take another look around. It's a room, but rather a special one. First impressions are not always right.

Opening hours: 12 (4 Mon)–11; 12–10.30 Sun

The best **beer ranges**

Cloisters Bar

26 Brougham Street, Edinburgh, EH3 9JH
0131 221 9997

🍺 **Cairngorm Trade Winds; Stewart Pentland IPA, Holy Grale; Taylor Landlord; guest beers**

• •

Religious seclusion may be one of the aims of those that dwell in a cloister, but you're unlikely to find much seclusion in this popular Edinburgh ale house. It used to be a manse – the home of a minister – although it is not known whether its former occupant took the pledge or enjoyed a dram, so whether or not he would approve of the building's current occupation is unknown. What can be reported though is that Cloisters Bar (to give it its full name) does inspire a devotional-like following amongst both the students of the Tollcross area in which it stands, and the city's beer fans. It's not hard to see why.

For a start, even though it's just one room (though several alcoves add a bit of variety), there's a cosy and comfortable feel to the bar that helps to encourage the art of conversation. Décor is minimal (taking its cue from the austerity of the divine again?): the whitewashed walls are dotted with brewery mirrors, while there's a small bookcase elsewhere. Then there's the beer. There are usually up to nine cask beers on offer, from both the growing number of Scottish craft breweries and further afield. Caingorm Trade Winds is a regular at the bar, light and spritzy, fragrant and floral, an elderflower-infused speciality beer that almost drinks like a wheat beer. House ale Holy Grale is an eminently drinkable bitter brewed just outside of the city by

Stewart brewery. Food is traditional pub grub and all the better for it – fish and chips, and chicken breast stuffed with haggis for a start.

Edinburgh is a magnificent city for the pub-goer and beer drinker (after all, its nickname 'Auld Reekie' referred to the smoke from the city's many breweries and other industries in the 19th century) and Cloisters Bar is an ideal place to pay homage to the city's beery heritage.

Opening hours: 12–midnight (1am Fri & Sat);
12.30–midnight Sun
Also great for: City

Start at the Tourist Information centre on Princes Street, at the top of Waverley Steps. Cross Princes Street by the lights in front of the Balmoral and look for narrow West Register Street opposite the clock tower, just to the left of the National Archives of Scotland. A short stroll up West Register Street you'll see the handsome sandstone exterior of the Café Royal (p66).

Returning to Waverley Steps turn left to walk along Princes Street, crossing at the junction with Waverley Bridge. Steps lead down into the eastern part of Princes Street Gardens. Pass under the Scott Monument and walk along to the Royal Scottish Academy and the adjacent National Gallery on the Mound.

Crossing the Mound re-enter the gardens, strolling past the bandstand and St Cuthbert's Kirk with its pretty steeple, and climb up towards St John's Church above it where there is a little Fairtrade shop and café which might appeal.

Reaching the end of Princes Street head southwards along the busy Lothian Road. Take Castle Terrace which leads off on the left after about 150 yards and follow this road with excellent views of the Castle towering above you. At the end of this street bear right at the T junction into Spittal Street and walk along to its junction with Bread Street where on the corner you will find the Blue Blazer.

Retrace your steps to the junction with Castle Terrace, but this time continue straight ahead, again with the castle dominating the view, into Johnston Terrace. Below you but well hidden is the Grassmarket which if you have the time is well worth a detour. Access it either down the Patrick Geddes Steps on the right along here, or walk down Victoria Street beyond the Bow Bar.

Just past St Columba's church, a small alleyway leads off to the right and brings you in about 20 yards to a narrow terrace looking down onto the street below. Don't worry if you miss it because you can take the wider lane, Upper Bow, beyond it, immediately short of the junction with Castle Hill. Below you is Victoria Street, and the effect of one set of high buildings perched on another is quite sublime; only enhanced by being able to look down on the very attractive Bow Bar (p140). To reach it continue along the terrace to take the steps downwards at the end of Upper Bow.

Adapted from *CAMRA's Edinburgh Pub Walks* with the kind permission of Bob Steel

Grove

2 Spring Grove Street, Huddersfield,
West Yorkshire, HD1 4BP
01484 430113
www.groveinn.co.uk

🍺 **Empire Grove Grog; Fuller's London Pride; Taylor Golden Best, Landlord; Thornbridge Jaipur IPA; guest beers**

So many beers, so little time. There can be up to 18 cask beers available at the Grove and if that's not enough there's also a trio of draught ciders and nearly 300 bottled beers from around the world. Not bad for a sandstone-built corner pub that's been around since the 1850s.

The Grove was originally a group of terraced houses that were knocked through – if you look closely you can see the joins. As you would expect from a pub that stocks such an ambitious range of beers, there's a liveliness about the atmosphere, much of which is orchestrated by general manager Chloe. Music nights and the slightly bizarre wall murals all add to the mix.

This is a pub that bridges the divide between the emerging new craft breweries and the more established family firms. There are permanent rotating pumps for the likes of BrewDog, Thornbridge, Marble and Dark Star, but Fuller's is also represented while Taylor Golden Best and Landlord are always available; a mild, stout and strong beer also have regular pride of place. 'Even in a pub with a range as wide as ours,' laughs the Grove's Brian Dickson, who is in charge of the majority of guest beer orders, 'Landlord is still the biggest seller. Yorkshiremen know what they like, though Thornbridge's Jaipur is catching up, which is quite something for a 5.9% beer!'

Another talking point for the Grove is the fact that – unusually for a northern pub – the handpumps all have short necks and beer is not served through sparklers. Dickson freely admits that this caused some comment amongst their locals, 'but we have total faith in the quality of the beer we sell and like it to speak for itself. Most customers now share our faith and are happy to drink it as it comes. A sparkler is available if requested though!'

Some would say that food gets in the way of beer, and while the Grove doesn't do meals, there are plenty of snacks for the hordes of geeks that find their way to its doors (as well as locals out for a pint of something unusual). Snacks in this case encompass a variety of foodstuffs that includes crisps, cockles, mussels, beef biltong and – most notoriously of all – some dried crickets and larvae worms. Drink carefully or after a couple of pints of Jaipur you might find yourself being egged on by friends to eat something out of the ordinary.

Opening hours: 12–11 (midnight Thu–Sat)
Also great for: Community

The best beer ranges

The best **beer ranges**

Halfway House

Pitney Hill, Pitney, Somerset, TA10 9AB
01458 252513
www.thehalfwayhouse.co.uk

🍺 **Butcombe Bitter; Otter Bright; Teignworthy Reel Ale; guest beers**

. . . .

Like many a good country pub, the Halfway House is a place for all seasons. Come spring and summer when the urge to go outside appears, the pub's pleasant garden is a sun trap where the sound of birdsong alternates with the sudden whoosh of passing vehicles. When the wind blows and a fall of snow is imminent, you can snuggle up by the roaring log fire, glass in hand, and toast your good fortune to be indoors.

This is a place where the mood music of British pub life plays in the background: the chink of glasses, the scrape and clink of cutlery against plate and the murmur of conversation. The interior of the pub is rustic with well-worn stone slabs on the floor and sturdy wooden furniture. A side room features a medieval crook beam over its fireplace, above which hangs a collection of sepia-toned black and white photographs. The décor is both sparse and comforting.

Then there's the beer. Above the small bar, a chalkboard offers between eight and 12 West Country cask beers, all of them drawn straight from the barrel in a cool room at the back. Exmoor, Butcombe, Hop Back, Red Rock and Moor (which brews up the road) are some of the breweries whose beers get an airing in a pub that was one of the first in Somerset to offer such a heady choice. Food is not forgotten with a menu of home-cooked favourites including the justly lauded curries plus good honest yeoman's dishes such as goose egg, ham and chips.

Originally a pair of cottages, the Halfway House started offering alcoholic sustenance in the 1790s, and up until 1962 was owned by local brewers Hambridge of nearby Curry Rivel. It then went through the ownership of Bristol-based George's (whose logo can be faintly seen at the entrance of the pub), Ind Coope and Courage. Cask beer would have probably been a mystery on the bar in the early 1990s, though this all changed when local social worker Julian Ditchfield bought the freehold. He had a vision of his perfect pub, which included building up the beer range. This decision paid dividends when the Halfway House was made CAMRA's National Pub of the Year in 1996; other awards have followed. Ditchfield has now moved on (though it remains his local) but his ethos and idea of what a public house should offer still survives to maintain the Halfway House as a remarkable institution in this part of the world. No halfway measures here.

Opening hours: 11.30–3, 5.30–11; 12–3.30, 7–11 Sun

The Pub

12 New Walk, Leicester, LE1 6TF
0116 2552150
www.thepubleicester.co.uk
🍺 **Beowulf Dragon Smoke Stout; Oakham Inferno, Bishops Farewell; guest beers**

. . . .

There are just three pubs with this most minimal of names in the UK. 'It does exactly what it says on the outside,' laughs The Pub's licensee Paul Summers, 'we were looking for a name and a friend said why not call it The Pub, after all it's a pub; it's concise and doesn't muck about.'

The Pub has only been open in its current incarnation for a couple of years. The building dates back to Edwardian times when it was a pub and then went through several different names such as the Wig & Pen and the Courthouse. When Summers got hold of it, the building was home to an Indian bar called Pause. His track record on the Leicester real ale scene was pretty impressive – he'd run the award-winning city pub the Vaults,

which offered 12 beers on hand pump. When that closed he went looking for a new venue and The Pub is the result of this search.

Whilst the Vaults was very much a spit and sawdust kind of place, The Pub has a more modern and quirky feel, with plenty of light and air. The beer range is pretty beguiling as well, with up to 15 hand pumps on, plus a goodly selection of beers from across the world, both in bottle and on draft. Craft breweries predominate at the bar, including the likes of Beowulf and Oakham, whose light and zesty Inferno is a regular. Other breweries whose beers turn up include Abbeydale, Fernandez, Saltaire and Nottinghamshire – the beers change all the time.

Even though beer seems to be king, food has a place, and you might want to place an order for The Pub's much-loved 11-inch sausage baguettes (the meat is sourced from a Lincolnshire farm), while there is also room on the menu for what seems like a real East Midlands pub favourite – homemade fish fingers (also on parade at the Kean's Head in Nottingham, p70 and the Brewery Tap in Derby, p142). Handcut chips are – you'll be glad to hear – on the plate.

All these choices and the incongruity of The Pub's design makes for an eclectic drinking base, featuring students, beer hunters, morris men, rugby fans and the occasional rock star (it's been said that members of Kasabian pop in for the odd jar and there are also occasional gigs, while the walls feature a display of famous ska musicians).

The Pub might have the most minimal name in British pub culture, but there's nothing sketchy or meagre in what it offers the good people of Leicester. The Pub? I like it.

Opening hours: 12–11 (midnight Fri & Sat); 12–6 Sun

The best **beer ranges**

The best **beer ranges**

The Rake

4a Winchester Walk, Borough,
London, SE1 9AG
020 7407 0557
www.therakeblog.wordpress.com
🍺 **Beer range varies**

• •

The Rake. Named after a gardening implement or a dissolute man of fashion? After an evening spent in this small bar at the heart of Borough Market, you're more likely to be inclined towards the latter – there's a swagger and devil-may-care feel to the place that sets it apart from other bars that major in beer (and this is a place that certainly majors in beer with up to 200 bottles from across the globe plus a trio of constantly rotating casks).

For a start, the most visual manifestation of the Rake's beer worship is the wall in the bar covered with the scrawls of visiting brewers from all over the world – Doug Odell, the BrewDog lads and Purple Moose (in Welsh of course) are just some who have left their mark. Meanwhile at the bar, it's not uncommon to be roped into an impromptu cheese and beer tasting with morsels and advice offered to any curious bystander.

The Rake is Lilliputian in size, a single room that was once a greasy spoon caff. Such is its popularity that you can be squeezed for space at the bar. Relief comes with an outside drinking area with umbrellas to keep off the rain. No food is served, as there isn't room for a kitchen, though gourmet crisps from the Yorkshire Crisp Company are available for the peckish (and with the multitude of Borough Market's stalls on the doorstep does the lack of a menu really matter?). Cask beers from all over the country can be found on any given day: Dark Star, Otley, Hardknott and Rudgate for instance. There are also special festivals showcasing beers from various regions of the British Isles. Then there's the choice of Belgian beers, German Pilsners, American craft beers – you name it, there's a chance that The Rake has it.

The Rake opened in 2006, when the owners of the Utobeer stall in the market wanted a shop window for their business. It was a hit on its first day with a queue snaking round the corner waiting to get in. The awards and plaudits then followed and the pub is now a regular stopping place on London's beer tourist trail, a place where young hipsters and more mature cask beer fans congregate.

The Rake was also the first pub to specialise in craft beer, a trend now joined by the likes of the Euston Tap (p127), the Southampton Arms (opposite) and Cask (p16) in London while the Port Street Beer House (p74) and North Bar (p72) make up the northern contingent. The Rake might not have the tradition and heritage of a classic London pub, but it is a trailblazer and as such is somewhere that anyone with a love for beer needs to visit before they shuffle off this mortal coil.

Opening hours: 12 (10 Sat)–11; 12–8 Sun

Southampton Arms

139 Highgate Road, Kentish Town,
London, NW5 1LE
07958 780073
www.thesouthamptonarms.co.uk
🍺 **Beer range varies**

. . . .

'ALE CIDER MEAT' says the sign on the side of this old school lookalike boozer that stands on the border of Kentish Town and Gospel Oak. Don't be fooled though, the beer offering is anything but old school and the last few years have seen the Southampton Arms become one of London's most vibrant craft beer celebrators.

It certainly stands out on the road with its glass pane frontage set in a solid wooden framework – Dickens' Old Curiosity Shop meets Dublin perhaps? Inside, there's a long narrow room with the bar on the right hand side, and plain sanded floorboards. Take your glass and sit upon weathered wooden chairs at large tables, or try the compact garden at the back.

According to those in the know, the Southampton Arms was once a failing pub: cask beer was a stranger as was anyone whose face didn't fit, no matter how many times they came in. Then one day it was boarded up and done over in the aforementioned style. What was even more unique was the appearance of 10 hand pumps for cask beer, while artisanal cider got eight.

There is no regular beer so expect all manner of treats. Local and independent brewers are favoured, so you'll get the likes of Sambrook's rubbing shoulders in the cellar with Redemption, Brodie's, BrewDog and Otley. The latter chose it as one of the pubs for the London launch of their guest beer Saison Obscura (full disclaimer: I collaborated in the brew and the launch). Ciders come from their traditional heartlands and include the likes of Gwatkin and Burrow Hill.

Tradition (or is it tongue-in-cheek archness) sees the genial bar staff pull the pints into handled dimpled mugs unless the drinker asks otherwise (which I always do – I have a horror of handles). Oh and meat? You get a robust platter of pork baps here, an offering that goes down equally well with the scuffed Chelsea boot and dusted denim-wearing young professionals as with older seen-it-alls that live in the area and now visit the pub they once gave a wide berth to.

Opening hours: 12–11 (11.30 Fri & Sat)

p/shop out hand

Tom Cobley

Spreyton, Devon, EX17 5AL
01647 231314

🍺 **Cotleigh Tawny; St Austell Tribute, Proper Job; guest beers**

• •

Back in the 18th century farmer Tom Cobley plus several pals set out from Spreyton for Widecombe Fair, all of them sitting on one poor old mare that perished at the end of the journey (try that nowadays and you'll have the RSPCA round faster than you can say donkey sanctuary). Fast-forward to now and Tom Cobley and pals are remembered with a famous song. Oh and there's also an excellent free house that a canny landlord in the 1950s renamed as he decided to cash in on Spreyton's only claim to fame.

The Tom Cobley has become famous for reasons other than a misconceived lads' day out – it's a serial CAMRA award-winner and in 2007 won the biggest accolade of them all, CAMRA National Pub of the Year. It is, as you might suspect, a haven of cask beer, with a brewer's dray of beers being served at any one time. Up to 14, yes that's 14, cask beers are often available, most from the West Country, either served by handpump or drawn straight from the barrel in the cellar. And I can testify that every time I pitch up here and taste several of the beers, they're all in tip-top condition, whether it's a pristine pint of St Austell's Proper Job or something a little stronger like Wizard's rich and dark Druid's Fluid; there are also 10 artisanal ciders available.

It's received beer wisdom that country pubs should keep their taps down but the pub's ebullient landlord Roger Cudlipp begs to differ. 'It's a load

of rubbish that you only have to have a couple of ales on if you run a pub in the countryside,' he says. 'When I took on the pub in 2003 I started off with two cask beers, then I added another, then another and I kept going up. I was giving the punter what they couldn't get in other pubs, but I also have a good turnover for all my other ales.'

Beyond the beer the Tom Cobley also has a sense of cosiness. Take your ale in the comfortable front parlour with the thatched gantry above the bar, old black-and-white photos, solid wooden chairs and tables – and the pub cat. In the winter months there's a glowing log fire. Have an appetite? Then stock up on the honest pub grub that soaks up the ale – trenchermen can plump for a series of suet puddings (including steak and kidney, chicken and leek) served with grand helpings of mash and veg. If they ate like this in the 18th century, it's a wonder the poor grey mare even made it out the village.

Opening hours: 6.30–11 Mon; 12–3, 6–midnight (1am Fri & Sat); 12–4, 7–10.30 Sun
Also great for: CAMRA award-winners

The best **beer ranges**

White Horse

1–3 Parsons Green, London, SW6 4UL
020 7736 2115
www.whitehorsesw6.com

🍺 **Adnams Broadside; Harveys Sussex Best Bitter; guest beers**

A pub of sorts has sat on this patch of West London for several centuries, but it's only in the past 25 years that it's acquired the status of temple of beer. For many a beer connoisseur the White Horse is first stop on any grand tour around the capital's pubs.

After he took on cellarmanship duties in the early 1980s, city slicker Mark Dorber was the man who steered what was then a straightforward, street corner boozer into something then novel for London – a pub where beer was celebrated. He also caused a stir by pairing beer and food. The great and late beer writer Michael Jackson was an early fan of the place. Dorber now runs the Anchor in Walberswick, where he continues to thrive (see p194), while his replacement Dan Fox has built on the White Horse's reputation.

Cask beer? Six to eight are usually on offer, with regulars Harveys and Adnams joined by beers from across the nation. There are also beer festivals throughout the year with the most famous being the Old Ales one at the end of November – this has been going strong since the 1980s and features a fabulous selection of old ales, strong porters, barley wines and other strong beers that warm the cockles of the heart as winter starts to take hold. Then there is also a massive selection of beers from around the world – this is the sort of place where you will find a rare American Imperial Stout or a Belgian Triple served as the brewer intended back in their home town; just don't ask for them in a pint glass.

As mentioned above, the White Horse is also a place where the gastronomic possibilities of beer and food have long been explored. The menu offers a choice of beer alongside most dishes, with the beer battered haddock and chips accompanied by Harveys Sussex Best Bitter being a particular favourite according to Dan Fox. During the summer, the pub also hosts popular daily barbecues in its beer garden.

When it comes to pubs, iconic is a term that tends to be pitched and thrown about with easy abandonment. However, when it comes to the glorious White Horse, iconic is exactly the right word to use.

Opening hours: 11–midnight (12.30am Fri & Sat)

THE
BRUNSWICK
INN

·

A TRUE
ALE HOUSE
& BREWERY

The best
brewpubs

Beer brewed here. There it sits in a corner of the pub, within a glassed in partition, on show and on parade; or it might be found at the end of a narrow corridor or out at the back up a flight of stairs or hidden in the basement, a mysterious provider of beer, the only clue to its workings a providential plume of steam on brewing day.

Take a look – a gleaming, shining, well-polished stainless steel assembly of brewing kit promising beer brewed here, food miles nil, the journey from brewer to bar brief and untroubled. It was a common enough sight in the 19th century, when thousands of pubs made their own beer – some good, some not so good – but the onset of big breweries and the pubs that they bought seemingly sounded the death knell for beer brewed here.

Not now though. Brewpubs are a growing attraction for those who love the pub and love the idea of beer brewed just yards from where they drink it. In this section savour the best of British brewpubs from the Cornish Brigadoon that is the Blue Anchor in Helston to the magnificent monument to classic pub design that makes the Brunswick in Derby such a magnet for pub-lovers.

See also
New Inn,
Cropton (p198)
Old Brewery,
Greenwich (p159)
Victory,
Hereford (p60)
Watermill Inn,
Ings (p87)
Florence,
Herne Hill (p231)

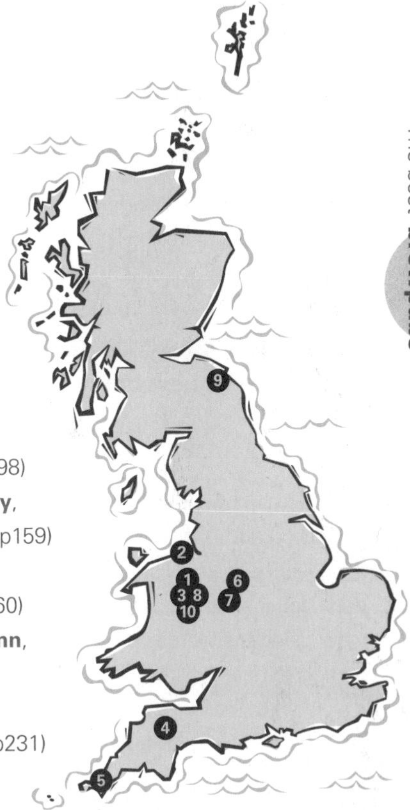

All Nations

20 Coalport Road, Madeley, Telford,
Shropshire, TF7 5DP
01952 585747
www.shiresbrewery.co.uk

🍺 **Shires Coalport Mild, Dabley Ale,
Dabley Gold; guest beer**

There are two ways in which you can view the adjective 'basic' when it refers to a pub. You can shudder and pass on by, imagining all manner of depredations, or you can take a more benevolent view, using the word to conjure up a place with no frills but plenty of integrity. For the All Nations, it's the latter 'basic' that comes into play when this remarkable survivor of 19th century industrial life is first visited – whitewashed walls with old photos, wooden beams, simple banquettes lining the walls, solid tables and a small booth-like bar, almost confessional in its simplicity. And that's before you've even had a mouthful of beer.

Built in the 1830s, it began life as a beerhouse for miners at neighbouring Blists Hill – now an open air museum. It seems that from the start, the All Nations brewed its own beer – possibly a dark strong mild that might have gone up and down in its quality (brewing science being what it was in the 19th century, especially in small brewhouses). As for the name, a couple of suggestions have been put forward: one that All Nations was the name of a local tobacco blend and secondly that it reflected the hospitality offered to all by the pub (in his 1988 book *Classic Town Pubs*, Neil Hanson mentions faded Allied flags hanging outside).

By the early 1970s, the All Nations was famous for being only one of four brewpubs left in the country. At the time and until it temporarily closed in 2001, it was also noted for producing only one beer: the 3% Pale Ale. Reopening again at the end of 2002, brewing also returned when Shires brewery moved into the back of the pub (the brewery was initially known as Worfield). The days of the single ale were long gone as Shires offered a variety of beers of varying strengths. Meanwhile the All Nations also maintained its class act of offering good beer, simple food (the black pudding and cheese toastie is a favourite) and an historic ambience that many probably thought would be lost during its brief closure. With 'basic' meaning good here, the mood music is conversation and the contemplation of beers such as Coalport Mild, with its light touch of hazelnut and chocolate on the palate, and the ever-popular Dabley Ale (pale and bittersweet). Occasionally, international rugby union matches are shown on the TV (the landlord is a big fan), but this is probably as far as the modern world intrudes into this classic pub gem.

Opening hours: 12–midnight

Baltic Fleet

33 Wapping, Liverpool, Merseyside, L1 8DQ
0151 709 3116
www.wappingbeers.co.uk
🍺 **Wapping Bitter, Baltic Gold, Summer Ale, Stout, seasonal beers; guest beers**

. . . .

The Baltic Fleet stands all alone; alongside a busy road, across the way from the Albert Docks, its front end tapering to a prow, giving it the appearance of a ship cleaving its way through the waves. All around Liverpool's redevelopment continues full steam ahead, leaving this imposing Victorian-era pub to carve out its own passage. Which it does: the Fleet prospers, a traditional pub with its own brewery in the cellars below (allegedly the haunt of smugglers and loose women in the early part of the 19th century – naturally there are a couple of ghosts). It's also the sole brewpub in the city and its Wapping beers are no strangers to awards.

There's a single bar in the front, marble topped and dominated by handpumps for the fine Wapping beers brewed here. A back room offers food, which includes the traditional hearty Scouse stew, which some say is the best in the city (further pub grub includes fish and chips, omelettes, sandwiches and toasties). You can also enjoy your beer at the front of the pub (the bow, so to speak) and upstairs. The ambience is spartan and robust: bare wooden floors, exposed brickwork, stools and big open windows that let in light and also offer views of the race track outside. On the walls, a reminder of the area's mercantile past (there's a Scandinavian church from the 19th century just up the road, popular no doubt with those who sailed in from the Baltic), with a collection of wooden plaques recalling ships gone by, while a model of an old sailing ship hangs over the main door entrance. The pub gives a real sense of Liverpool's sailing past – it's not hard to imagine the rough and tumble of sailors as they waited to go to sea whilst sinking a few pints.

This is a place for chat. Football and beer, or subjects that drift in from left-field and take everyone by surprise. For instance, what to do with an excess of Stilton cheese – on the latter dilemma someone suggests Stilton and broccoli soup, while another muses about making pork and Stilton sausages. 'Great,' comes the reply, as quick as a dart, 'all I need is a load of sausage skins and an industrial mincer.'

The beers are well-crafted and pleasing, veering from Liverpool Wit, a spicy and refreshing take on a Belgian wheat beer, through to Wapping Bitter and a strong Winter Ale with spices in the mix (there are also occasional beer festivals). The Summer Ale is light and refreshing and its year-round availability can be a handy morale-booster if you're in the Fleet on a winter's day watching the rain coming down outside. And at least you won't get seasick...

Opening hours: 12–11 (midnight Sat); 10–10.30 Sun

The best **brewpubs**

Beacon Hotel

129 Bilston Street, Sedgley,
West Midlands, DY3 1JE
01902 883380
www.sarahhughesbrewery.co.uk
🍺 **Sarah Hughes Pale Amber, Surprise,
Dark Ruby; guest beers**

• •

Beacon Hill stands above the West Midlands town of Sedgley and was once the place where fires were lit to warn local people that invaders were on their way. Nowadays, the only invaders approaching the town will be those aiming for the Beacon Hotel. Built in the 19th century, this solid-looking building is also the tap for the Sarah Hughes brewery, a redbrick tower brewery behind the pub that was reopened in 1987 by John Hughes, grandson of the eponymous Sarah Hughes (brewery trips can be booked). Famously, its earliest beer was a recreation of Dark Ruby, a strong mild that Hughes had begun brewing in the 1920s (it only stopped being produced in 1951 when this enterprising brewster and landlady died).

Yet there's more to the Beacon than a retro beer style (and the brewery does produce other beers). Once inside you'll find one of the best-preserved pub interiors in the country, a place that almost acts as a time capsule in the way it recaptures the mood and ambience of late Victorian pub life. There are four rooms, all of which are served by a unique, centrally placed island bar where the beers are handed out through hatches. There is a snug, a tap room, a large main bar and a family room; seating consists of comfortable benches and banquette-style seating lining the walls, while winter warmth is provided in the tap room by an old cooking range and a marble fireplace in the comfortable snug. Food is undemanding and simple: cheese and onion cobs. For lovers of the pub, coming upon the Beacon is like coming home, though there's also a sense of theatre about its ambience. Such is the spell cast that as you sit there with your glass of mild you half expect men with mutton-chop whiskers to wander in and ask for their pint with a twirl of a moustache. If you want to return to modern day life then the light and airy conservatory at the side of pub is just the job.

'Come far?' asked a genial chap in the tap room as I sipped the delicious Dark Ruby and looked about the equally genial surroundings. I replied yes, but really wanted to say that distance was relative: a visit to the Beacon is a journey through time as much as space.

Opening hours: 12–2.30 (3 Fri), 5.30–11; 12–3, 6–11 Sat; 12–3, 7–10.30 Sun

Beer Engine

Newton St Cyres, Exeter, Devon, EX5 5AX
01392 851282
www.thebeerengine.co.uk

🍺 **Beer Engine Rail Ale, Silver Bullet, Piston Bitter, Sleeper Heavy, seasonal beer**

• •

'Derek been in?' asks an elderly gentleman to the barman. 'No? Can you tell him when he comes in that I've got some plants for him.' That's the great thing about a true community pub: locals use it as a sort of community centre, while visitors can watch the democracy of the British pub in fully functioning action.

And visitors do come to the Beer Engine. Solid and silent, this onetime railway hotel overlooks the Tarka Line, a pretty little journey that connects Exeter and Barnstaple while offering the chance of stopping at several good pubs along the way. It's the route to Henry Williamson country, though such is the shyness of local otters, you'd have to be very lucky to spy one.

Still, there's always the consolation of visiting the Beer Engine. Sure of itself as it stands by the line, it's a pleasing village pub whose origins lie at the start of the Victorian railway age, when it provided refreshment and sustenance for weary travellers. Move on to the 21st century and the same applies now, though for the past three decades travellers have had an added motivation to make a visit: the Beer Engine's beers are brewed on the premises.

In 1983 teacher Peter Hawksley felt he'd had enough of his nine-to-five job and decided to take up the life of a publican. The Beer Engine (then the Barn Owl) was purchased, a small three-barrel brewery installed and Devon's first brewpub of the modern era was underway. Hawksley sold the pub in 2005, but the Beer Engine still remains a worthy destination for beer-travellers in the West Country.

Entering the seductive interior with its dark wood fittings, patches of distressed brickwork and old photos dotting the wall, you might be reminded of an old neighbourhood pub in the north of England. The bar stands in the centre of the L-shaped room, while there's more space on a decking area that overlooks the line, as well as a garden in which to spend long summer days.

And the beer? When Hawksley left, his brewer remained, giving a continuity that's all too rare in pubs (and even breweries) these days. Rail Ale is a crisp and dry session beer with a grainy, biscuity character and a dry bittersweet finish, while those in search of something stronger might like the 5.4% Sleeper Heavy, a fruity bittersweet delight. Food is not forgotten with regular favourites being confit of duck legs or the Sleeper Ale steak pie. And if you miss your train there's time for another: the pub is open all day.

The best **brewpubs**

Opening hours: 11–11; 12–10.30 Sun

Blue Anchor

50 Coinagehall Street, Helston,
Cornwall, TR13 8EL
01326 562821
www.spingoales.com

🍺 **Blue Anchor Spingo IPA, Spingo
Middle, Spingo Special; seasonal beers**

• •

Back in the 1970s, the Blue Anchor was just one
of four brewpubs left in the country. Beer lovers
flocked to the no-nonsense, former mining town
of Helston to drink deeply of Spingo Middle,
a strong and distinctive ale with a reputation
for taking no prisoners. In the years since, the
Blue Anchor has been joined by a multitude of
brewpubs, but it still remains a venerable fixture
on any beer lover's tour of the West.

Built in the 15th century as a rest house run
by monks, after the Reformation it became a
tavern and has been that way ever since. The 19th
century saw the wages of the local tin miners
paid out from the bar, a canny if cynical move –
thirsty miners would have been sorely tempted
by a few glasses of Spingo, a move guaranteed
to cause family dissent when they returned home
with empty pockets.

For the uninitiated stepping through the low
doorway of this stone-faced, thatch-topped legend
can be a life-changing event. Inside is a cool
flagstoned corridor with cosy rooms on either side.
In the winter, coal fires merrily burn away in the
rooms. Around the bar locals and Spingo-lovers
congregate, laugh and gossip. Time can be elastic
here. You pop in for a quick pint and discover, when
you wander out, that night has fallen.

The brewery is at the back of the pub, up
a flight of stairs. The mash tun is made from
oak and apparently fell off the back of a boat
sometime in the early years of the 20th century.

Back in the pub, a pint of Spingo Special is
a hefty draught of 6.5% beer, though Middle,
at a more manageable 5%, is popular. Come
Christmas and Easter, a Special is brewed to
7.6%, a beer that has been known to stretch
festivities on for several days. All this beer
needs some food. Carnivores will opt for the 8oz
Cornish Angus sirloin steak or its wild venison
cousin, while for something lighter and less red
in tooth and claw, there's the homemade soup
of the day. It's good grub, but if truth be told, this
is a place where beer and conversation rule the
roost. As I wrote earlier, time is elastic here so
make sure you keep an eye on the clock…

Opening hours: 10.30–midnight; 10.30–11 Sun

Brunswick

1 Railway Terrace, Derby, DE1 2RU
01332 290677
www.everards.co.uk

🍺 **Brunswick White Feather, Triple Hop, Porter; Everards Beacon Bitter; Marston's Pedigree; guest beers**

• • • • • • • • • • • • • •

If you're changing trains at Derby then pray your connection is delayed or even better get a later one. The Brunswick is a brisk short stroll from the station and it would be a crime to miss this monument to good beer and classic pub design.

Built in 1842, it stands at the end of a red-brick row of railway workers' terraced houses. Stepping into its confines is akin to a bout of time-travel, as you are reminded of a time when pubs offered warmth, comfort and space to contemplate the day's labours with a glass of the finest beer.

There's certainly plenty of space. Once inside the word warren springs to mind. To the right is a room with the words 'family parlour' etched onto a brass plate. Turn left in the direction of the bar

and you pass a couple of snugs, glass fronted and cosy. The walls in the stone-floored corridor feature ornate wood panelling and a collection of framed newspaper cuttings about how the pub was saved from demolition in the 1980s through the joint efforts of the Derby Civic Society and the Derbyshire Historic Buildings Trust.

The main bar is open and welcoming, offering stools, robust pub tables and a couple of long leather-topped sofas. A ledge below the ceiling is home to a row of empty beer bottles that march in a line above drinkers' heads. The substantial bar occupies a corner of this room, a fastness of handpumps – there are 14, seven of which offer beer from the in-house brewery, whose gleaming stainless steel can be seen at the end of the corridor. Those in the know plump for the bittersweet and refreshing Triple Hop or the dark and coffee-like Rockin' Johnny's Derby Pride, both of which are brewed on the premises. Beers from Everards (who bought the pub but didn't change a thing a few years back), Burton Bridge and Thornbridge are amongst those who also appear, while decent cider can be found (no ice here!).

Even though this is definitely a place for those with a penchant for good ale, food is also offered at lunchtimes, home-cooked and substantial, nothing fancy, just good honest pub food: hands up who fancies lamb and mint pie with gravy mash and peas or a turkey and cranberry hot jumbo cob? Meanwhile, those with a yen for something a bit more sophisticated will note with glee that the pub often does special food and beer nights, offering more sophisticated dishes such as wild boar haunch with chestnut and juniper stuffing. This is a pub with surprising and unexpected depths.

Opening hours: 11–11; 12–10.30 Sun

The best **brewpubs**

Coach & Horses

Weatheroak, Alvechurch,
Worcestershire, B48 7EA
01564 823386
www.coachandhorsesinn.co.uk

🍺 **Hobsons Mild, Best Bitter; Holden's Special; Weatheroak Hill Icknield Pale Ale, Bitter; Wood Shropshire Lad; guest beers**

• •

Brum is eight miles to the north, the M42 roars by just a mile away. Recipe for an urban pub? Hardly. You could say that the pub drives a coach and horses through the idea of what a country pub needs to be.

Despite the apparent proximity of the city and motorway, you'd be amazed how tranquil and rural the location of the Coach & Horses is. Gentle countryside surrounds this serial award-winner of a brewpub and the views drift over towards the Vale of Evesham. Hidden away perhaps, but it's a popular place, possessing a magnetic appeal

for both beer lovers and those who enjoy the traditional ambience of the English pub.

It's been in the same family since the late 1960s and started its first in-house brewery in 1998 – Weatheroak Brewery. Growth followed and the brewery moved to a new site in 2008, but undaunted the Coach & Horses unveiled a new brewery in the same year. This time it's called the Weatheroak Hill Brewery, brewing its beers in the old stables (the pub sits on an old coaching route). Come in and try a beer. Maybe a glass of WHB, a bitter best bitter that charms and chimes with delightfully orangey fruity notes. Other beers sold include offerings from Woods, Hook Norton, Hobsons and Malvern Hills Brewery. Hale and hearty could be the description for the food – how does a slow-cooked shank of lamb sound? There are also regular beer festivals, usually with a theme. It's simple: sit in the quarry-tiled bar with its church pews and old tables and just enjoy life.

Opening hours: 11.30–11; 12–10.30 Sun
Also great for: CAMRA award-winners; Motorway

Olde Swan (Ma Pardoe's)

89 Halesowen Road, Netherton, Dudley,
West Midlands, DY2 9PY
01384 253075

🍺 **Olde Swan Original, Dark Swan, Entire, Bumble Hole Bitter; guest beer**

. . . .

You have to admire the person responsible for decorating the outside of the Old Swan. He or she was either short of paint or not very good in calculating the size of letters. 'Pure Home Brewd Ales' is the legend that calls out to the world from this old school West Midlands pub that has long pulled in beer drinkers from all over the country.

History clings to the Old Swan with the ferocity of a limpet to a rock. It was first licensed in 1835, but the current pub and brewhouse date from the 1860s. In 1974, it was famously one of the four surviving brewpubs left in the UK. Seen from outside, it's part of a redbrick terrace, a pub that you could easily miss if it wasn't for the slogan across its top. There's a sense of the Old Swan having long settled into its surroundings,

organically becoming part of the road. To miss it would be to miss a fine pub experience.

The classically Victorian front bar features an amazing ceiling of ceramic tiles, in which the mural of a swan is set. It's a public bar in the best traditions: grab a pint of the light-coloured, sweetish Original along with a cheese cob and you're ready to blend into the environment. People talk, read their newspapers and contemplate their beer. There's also a snug and the restaurant upstairs has a cast iron fireplace and old pictures on the wall. Unsurprisingly, the building is Grade II listed and on CAMRA's National Inventory of Historic Pub Interiors.

For years it was known as Ma Pardoe's (and still is by many) after a long-serving landlady who spent half a century behind the bar until her death in 1984. As for 'home brewd', the ales in the Old Swan are made at the back. In the past, only one beer was brewed, but these days there are several, which occasionally get out into the free trade. Brewd or brewed, it doesn't matter – the Old Swan gets full marks for everything else.

Opening hours: 11–11; 12–4, 7–11 Sun
Also great for: Heritage

The best **brewpubs**

Ship Inn

Newton Square, Low Newton,
Northumberland, NE66 3EL
01665 576262
www.shipinnnewton.co.uk

🍺 **Ship Inn Sandcastles at Dawn, Sea Coal, Sea Wheat, Ship Hop Ale, Dolly Daydream; guest beers**

• •

If you're passing through this gorgeous part of the Northumberland coastline and someone murmurs Sandcastles at Dawn to you, don't worry – it's not some arcane challenge issued to outsiders, but one of the beers brewed in the garage next door to this lusty-hearted brewpub.

Originally built in the 18th century, it's situated in a small former fishing village, a picture perfect National Trust-owned place complete. And if you don't want the aforementioned Sandcastles, then why not try a glass of Dolly Daydream or Sea Wheat? The latter is a superb English wheat beer that shimmers with lemony and tropical fruit notes that are kept in line with a bitter twist.

Brewing started in 2008, after landlady Christine Forsyth purchased a second-hand brewing kit and brought in Michael Heggarty as her brewer. Given that the pub's reputation for food rests on sourcing local ingredients, especially from the fishing boats that land in the bay just below the pub, producing beer was the logical next step.

This is a pub for all seasons: come in the summer when the sun shines on the millpond-calm sea and grab yourself an outside seat. During a visit in more inclement times, the Ship is a bulwark against the weather. Sit at the window and enjoy the sight of waves crashing on the beach below. The pared back interior of the Ship Inn provides an equally rugged accompaniment to the elements – bleached wood flooring, bashed about furniture and bare stone walls.

It's a popular place and its reputation for food and beer brings in both locals and visitors, which means that finding a seat during the early evening and lunchtime can be difficult. Fish and seafood are bought in from local boats; while the meat comes from an award-winning butcher in nearby Alnwick. It's a small menu veering between simple pleasures such as Craster Kippers with brown bread or fresh crab sandwiches, and the more sophisticated choice of locally-caught lobster (which must be ordered a day in advance).

Is it a gastro-pub? Well, there is a hint of it, though the menu is free from the usual pan-fried clichés that can clog up pubs with pretension. On the other hand, with its own brewery and assured place in the local community the Ship Inn is simply a good pub that brews beer and serves good food. You can't ask for more than that.

Opening hours: 11.30–11
Also great for: Food

Six Bells Inn

Church Street, Bishop's Castle,
Shropshire, SY9 5AA
01588 630144
www.sixbellsbrewery.co.uk

🍺 Six Bells Big Nev's, Ow Do!, Cloud Nine,
seasonal beers

. . . .

What is it about Bishop's Castle? It's a small
Shropshire market town on the border with
Wales, with a long street leading up a hill, quirky
shops, and several pubs, but it also finds room for
two breweries. The Three Tuns (p49) is featured
in the brewery tap section, but it's the Six Bells
that's rightly celebrated here – a vibrant 17th
century coaching inn set at the bottom of the hill,
next to the town's church.

History shows that there used to be a brewery
on the pub's site until 1920 when it became
just a pub. However, by the time it was bought
by Neville Richards ('Big Nev' to all and sundry)
in 1997, it was operating as a hippy commune.
A brewery was set up at the back and the bar
opened once more, taking the Six Bells from
strength to strength.

A lot of this is down to the exuberant
personality of Big Nev, whose grandfather once
had a brewery. I first met him in 2001 during a
trip to Shropshire and when we visited his pub
at 9.30 in the morning his first words were:
'Breakfast beer gentlemen?' How could we
resist? Another memorable visit was when a
group of folk musicians were gathering in the
bar and during an interlude a man next to me
broke into song, plaintive and poignant. After he'd
finished I asked what he had sung. 'I go around

the area collecting the old agricultural songs,'
came the reply. This was the sort of chance
meeting that only pubs can produce.

Music doesn't seem to play as big a part at
the Six Bells now (though there's the annual Nev
Fest), but it remains a place where conversation,
beer and food (curry nights a speciality) are justly
celebrated by the mix and match of of folk that
Bishop's Castle seems to collect. The ambience is
laid back and comfortable (bare wooden boards,
exposed stonework) with a smallish and sparse
front bar and a bigger room next door.

The brewery is out at the back and can be
visited if it's not too busy and you ask nicely
(there are three regular beers brewed plus a
'calendar ale' produced every month). The pub is
also part of the two beer festivals that the town
has every year. So it seems to me that the only
dilemma you'll have on a visit to Bishop's Castle
is whether you start your pub crawl at the top or
the bottom of the hill!

Opening hours: 12–2.30 (not Mon), 5–11; 12–11 Sat;
12–3.30, 7–10.30 Sun

The best **brewpubs**

The best
brewery taps

The brewery tap is the place where a brewery likes to showcase its beers. Some taps are an integral part of the brewery building such as Batemans' magnificent visitor centre in the small village of Wainfleet All Saints – an ivy-covered windmill that can be seen as soon as you arrive at the railway station. Or it might be the glorious Vine, an architectural pub marvel that acts as the tap for Batham. In these places the smell of brewing as you enter will sharpen up your appetite for the ales.

Many taps are like this, or sit in close proximity to the brewery where the ales are made, but some stand across the road or in the next street, or even further afield; such as Barrels in Hereford, which acts as a glorious platform for the beers of Wye Valley brewery. Others, such as the Evening Star in Brighton, offer an historical perspective to a brewery (in this case Dark Star), which once brewed within their walls; the brewery moves on but the spirit remains.

Wherever they are, these taps are not just where a brewery's beers should be at their very best quality, but also places in which drinkers can identify with the brewery – with signage, posters and even souvenirs on display.

See also
Beer Hall,
Staveley
(p138)
Brewery Tap,
Chester (p141)
Brewery Tap –
Derby's Royal
Standard,
Derby (p142)
Kirkstile Inn,
Loweswater (p225)
Old Crown,
Hesket Newmarket
(p184)
Triangle Tavern,
Lowestoft
(p189)

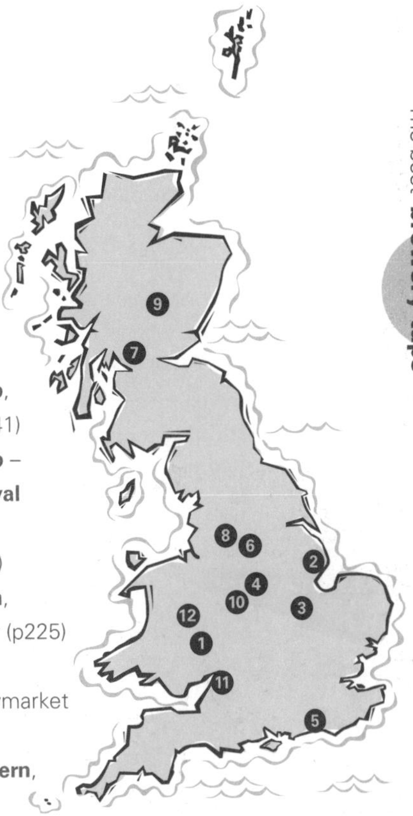

◀ Brewery Tap, Peterborough

Barrels

69 St Owen Street, Hereford, HR1 2JQ
01432 274968
www.wyevalleybrewery.co.ukl
🍺 **Wye Valley Bitter, HPA, Dorothy Goodbody's Golden Ale, Butty Bach, Dorothy Goodbody's Wholesome Stout; guest beer**

• •

Some pub names are a mystery, but you don't need to be Sherlock Holmes to deduce how Barrels got its handle. Just go into the bar on the right of the porch-like entrance (the old Jug and Bottle area perhaps?), and it's immediately apparent – the bar counter rests upon seven well-varnished wooden casks. In a neat complement to the pub's name they are 36-gallon containers, or a barrel in brewing parlance. Here in this opened out space, when lunchtime comes, friends gather and tell their stories and jokes – on my visit the barman dropped a handful of ice cubes with an accompanying clatter and the cry of 'Sack the juggler!' came from one of the drinkers.

Barrels was once the Lamb Hotel and owned by West Country Ales, whose colourful enamel plaque is still embedded in the wall (there are several such relics dotted about Hereford on the fronts of both current and former pubs). It sits in a historic area – part of the city walls were sited here, while the busy street is lined with Georgian and Victorian houses and shops as well as the Gothic fantasy of Hereford's Town Hall.

The Lamb became Barrels in 1985 when the recently opened Wye Valley brewery moved in and began brewing at the back – this was its home until it moved to its current location in 2002. Nowadays, Barrels remains a popular tap for Wye Valley beers such as Hereford Pale Ale. With the regulars providing a soundtrack, I enjoyed its light dusting of lemony sugar on the nose, the appetising palate with its dry grapefruit/lemon sweetness and crisp cracker-like mouth-watering balance, and the grainy dry finish.

There are four separate drinking areas. The room to the left of the bar is smaller and cosier. Those in search of a quieter pint naturally gravitate into a space that provides a contrast with the bar on the other side. It is devotional in its ambience – bare floorboards, exposed brickwork, banquette seating and benches and a shelf of books. In here, unless the TV is on, people whisper or contemplate their beer with the patience of monks, though I suspect that the clack of pool balls in the adjoining games room might intrude on their thoughts more often than not. In this bar, I studied Dorothy Goodbody's Wholesome Stout, a voluptuous and vinous stout that has more than a nod to the former Dublin-based employers of brewery founder (and Barrels' landlord) Peter Amor. As I leave the men are still talking and laughing and telling their tales. For what is the pub but a place for stories?

Opening hours: 11–11.30 (midnight Fri & Sat); 12–11.30 Sun

Batemans Brewery Visitor Centre

Salem Bridge Brewery, Mill Lane, Wainfleet All Saints, Lincolnshire, PE24 4JE
01754 880317
www.batemans.co.uk

🍺 **Batemans Dark Mild, XB Bitter, GHA Pale Ale, XXXB, seasonal beers**

. . . .

The wide horizons of the south Lincolnshire fens are broken only by the sight of church towers calling good people to prayer, but when you disembark from the train at the small stop of Wainfleet All Saints the landmark you'll see is a building celebrating John Barleycorn rather than the Almighty. A couple of hundred yards away from the station, Batemans old redbrick, ivy-covered windmill stands as a symbol of the enduring appeal of the company, one of the best loved of family breweries.

Batemans is at the heart of its community, and arriving in Wainfleet will bring a sense of excitement and anticipation to all but the most cynical of beer lovers. The Visitor Centre is based in the windmill and at the circular bar within there is the chance to enjoy the whole series of Batemans great beers, including the rich and creamy Salem Porter – a rare sight outside its home territory. Some brewery visitor centres can be clinical and clean, devoid of the sort of atmosphere that beer lovers revel in. Not this one. Even though it only opens during the day (hours vary during the winter), there's a warmth about the bar – people use it, talk and drink beer, and keep coming back. The menu offers hearty dishes made with local produce and there's a games room where traditional pursuits such as Ring the Bull can be played. Opened in 2000, it also features a whole range of old brewery artefacts, including ancient brewing books, plus a massive collection of bottled beers that were collected by the late George Bateman, who put so much effort into saving the brewery when it nearly closed in the 1980s. There are also regular tours of the brewery where the scintillating aroma of the mash tun will sharpen anyone's appetite for a pint or two afterwards.

Opening hours: 11.30–4.00 (2.30 Oct–March); closed Jan and Mon & Tue except bank holidays
Also great for: Pub games

Brewery Tap

80 Westgate, Peterborough,
Cambridgeshire, PE1 2AA
01733 358500
www.oakham-ales.co.uk/brewerytap
🍺 **Oakham JHB, Inferno, White Dwarf,
Bishops Farewell; guest beers**

People used to come to the Brewery Tap in search of work when it was an unemployment office, but now they arrive looking to find good beer, Thai food and a lively buzzing atmosphere.

Oakham Ales opened their award-winning brewpub in 1998 and have continued to brew their ales here ever since, though they have also opened a larger site elsewhere in the area (the Tap has spent several years at risk of being demolished due to the local council's redevopment plans).

Stop and look at the Tap before entering; it's not the most beautiful building. It was built with pink-tinged red bricks, a common feature of postwar municipal buildings, while a selection of long plain windows point to the functionality of a place more used to processing people than pleasing them. There's a blandness about the design, electrical sub-station chic perhaps? However, Oakham has added a quirky touch to the outside with a well-burnished copper dome and its chimney (originally a brewing kettle) at the entrance – which should get you in the mood for a beer or two.

Inside the Tap is achingly modern with an open-spaced, two-level bar (light wood, stone floors and iron pillars), while the stainless steel brewing kit stands behind a long glass panel. Beer is king in this place, with Oakham specials brewed on site. There are usually up to 12 cask beers available, including ones from Oakham as well as guest beers (bottled Belgian beers also make an appearance). This celebration of beer is allied to a pub ethos that marries a large upstairs dancefloor, freshly prepared Thai grub, and a more restful space where drinkers can lounge about in large leather armchairs.

This is not your average pub and it all means that the Tap attracts a mixed clientele of young and old, male and female, all intent on having a good time, in the company of Oakham's fresh and fruity beers. Hopes are high that the Tap survives the council's plans and continues to plough on in its own unique way – Peterborough would be a lesser place for its disappearance.

Opening hours: 12–11 (late Fri & Sat)
Also great for: Beer range

Burton Bridge Inn

24 Bridge Street, Burton upon Trent,
Staffordshire, DE14 1SY
01283 536596
www.burtonbridgeinn.co.uk

🍺 **Burton Bridge Golden Delicious,
Bridge Bitter, Burton Porter, Festival Ale;
guest beer**

• •

As I approached the Burton Bridge Inn, opening time imminent, I saw a rare sight. A coal lorry was parked outside out the pub and a grimy looking man passed backwards and forwards, hefting a sack of coal on his shoulders. The coalman. A striking remainder of a character common 30 years ago, but now a rare sight. Yet, here he was, his presence completely in company with the time warp atmosphere that pervades the Burton Bridge tap.

It's hard to escape the past in Burton: walking towards the pub, which stands next to a bridge over the River Trent, the brewing heritage of the town is omnipresent. Plaques and signs commemorate long lost breweries, while if you take a glimpse over the shoulder en route to the Bridge you'll catch sight of the massive conditioning tanks of Molson-Coors.

The Burton Bridge Inn is a redbrick, three-storey building, with the name of the brewery owners emblazoned across its front; followed by the legend: 'Brewers and bottlers of traditional beers, ales and porters'. A bold statement of purpose.

The pub's origins are as a 17th century coaching stop, which makes sense given its proximity to the bridge over the Trent. Traffic continues to flow fast past its door, though once you're inside there's a quieter and more tranquil world to discover.

There are three rooms, all comfortable in their own way. The traditional interior of wooden tables and stools, old scenes of Burton breweries and whisky ads on the walls, adds a sense of homeliness and also of community. This is old style pub décor and no doubt the light brown colour of the ceiling appears in a pub fittings catalogue somewhere as nicotine. In the winter coal fires add to the comfort (hence the sight of the coalman). People sit and chat, say hello to each other, enjoy the beers on tap. The Golden Delicious has an orange marmalade tang and leaves the world with a dry, bitter finish, while those with a penchant for darker beer can plump for the rich and dry Porter. Food is basic, and why not? Michelin stars can be handy, but sometimes a plate of faggots and chips or bangers and mash (both staples on the menu) go marvellously with a beer.

Outside in the road, the cars whiz by and at the back on brewing day there is the occasional clang of barrels, as a reminder of the self-contained world of the Bridge. While I contemplate my pint and wonder whether to go for the faggots or the bangers, the coalman comes in to settle his bill. The sense of timelessness is now complete.

Opening hours: 11.30–2.30, 5–11; 11.30–11.30 Fri & Sat; 12–3, 7–11 Sun

The best **brewery taps**

Evening Star

55–56 Surrey Street, Brighton,
East Sussex, BN1 3PB
01273 328931
www.eveningstarbrighton.co.uk

🍺 **Dark Star Hophead, seasonal beers;
guest beers**

. . . .

There might be a romance about the thought that the beer you're drinking has been produced beneath your feet, but there comes a time for every successful brewery to move on if they want to get more people to drink their beers. This is what happened to Dark Star.

The brewery started off in a cellar at the Evening Star, the output measured in gallons as opposed to brewers' barrels, but people liked their beers and they had to move in 2001. They have shifted home once more since then, and who knows when this might happen again, as the brewery's beery reputation continues to grow. However, Dark Star retained the link with the Evening Star and the pub always has four of their beers on, including Hophead, which drinks as it sounds.

Alongside this you might find their jingly jangly Espresso Stout, the smoky Export Stout or one of the brewery's jazzy takes on Belgian or US beer styles. You will also find three guest beers that change all the time: perhaps Thornbridge, Windsor & Eton or breweries closer to Brighton. Music happens once a month as well (it used to be more regular until the licensing act changed in 2003).

The Star sits in the midst of a mid-Victorian terrace built for railway workers – the station is mere minutes away, ideal for a swift one on the way home. So what's the vibe of the Evening Star? Wood in one word. Much of the furniture is made from reclaimed wood, the tables from railway sleepers and the bar from Merrydown cider casks. It's a comfortable ambience, though pretty sharp and modern in its take on the traditional pub.

The pub first appeared in the 1850s starting in one of the dwellings, before taking over its neighbour in the following decade. It's the type of town pub, when seen from outside, you want to go into. There's a bold wash of red on the front of the ground floor, while a couple of panels on each side feature a host of beer labels. The message is: come in and celebrate beer. No ghosts I'm afraid, but the pub sheltered Daisy and Violet Hilton in 1909. Who, you might ask? They were babes in arms at the time, but also conjoined twins and in the spirit of the times found fame in the USA on the vaudeville circuit.

Opening hours: 12–11; 11.30–midnight Fri & Sat; 12–11 Sun

The best **brewery taps**

Fat Cat

23 Alma Street, Sheffield,
South Yorkshire, S3 8SA
0114 249 4801
www.thefatcat.co.uk

🍺 **Kelham Island Best Bitter, Pale Rider;
Taylor Landlord; guest beers**

• •

Down a backstreet, close to the River Don,
the Fat Cat is an enduring example of a classic
redbrick Victorian tavern. Built in the first half of
the 19th century as the Kelham Tavern, it was an
unremarkable boozer owned by Stones Brewery
by the time economics lecturer Dave Wickett
came along in 1981 and made a bid for it.

Wickett, who has a passion for cask beer,
renamed it the Fat Cat and started majoring in
beers from regional breweries and the emerging
micro-brewing scene (legend has it that opening
night saw a queue of discerning drinkers waiting
to get in). Without a doubt, the Fat Cat was the
pioneer pub that would lead to Sheffield's current
position as one of the UK's best beer destinations.

Step through the door and it's immediately
apparent that this is a place where beer is
celebrated. The walls are covered with all manner
of beer memorabilia, including the multitude of
awards the pub has won. There's a hatch in the
corridor from which beer is served.

In the cosy main bar, which has the feel of an
old fashioned sitting room, the beers are served
through what seems curiously like a confessional
booth – mahogany-coloured wood with a clock
atop. The day's beers and dishes are chalked up on
a blackboard – given that Wickett is a vegetarian,
the menu is strong on imaginative meat-free and
vegan choices such as spinach and red bean stew
or savoury mushroom pie, although meat-eaters
are also catered for. A further side room features
a cheery coal fire during the winter.

In 1990, Wickett added a brewery at the back
of the pub and named it after the local area: the
Kelham Island Brewery. Fame came the brewery's
way in 2004 when Pale Rider – a light-coloured
strong bitter with plenty of tropical fruit notes on
the nose and palate – was elected Champion Beer
of Britain. So it's no surprise that the best place to
study this award-winner is on draught at the Fat
Cat, not that there is any shortage of beer choice
– up to nine cask beers (including several from the
brewery next door) are available, as well as bottled
beers from around the world. The eclectic nature
of today's beer world is justly celebrated here.

In a city of special pubs, this is an extra-special
pub, a refuge from the hurly burly of the outside
world, as well as a showpiece for Wickett's
foresight all those years ago in 1981.

Opening hours: 12–11 (midnight Fri & Sat)
Also great for: City

The best **brewery taps**

Fox & Hounds

South Street, Houston,
Renfrewshire, PA6 7EN
01505 612448
www.houston-brewing.co.uk

🍺 **Houston Killellan Bitter, Peter's Well,
Texas, Warlock Stout, seasonal beers;
guest beers**

. . . .

Sometimes just selling beer is not enough and the urge to try your hand at brewing your own gets too strong to ignore. Having run the 18th century Fox & Hounds since the late 1970s, the Wengel family had felt the itch throbbing for some time and finally installed a brewery in 1997. It's proved a success, and the pub's onsite brewery, Houston, is a dab hand at picking up awards. You can see the brew kit through a window in the Fox & Vixen bar.

This trend towards triumph has also found some unlikely fans. Back in 2008 both the pub and the beer it brews hit the headlines when crooner Neil Diamond dropped by for a pint and a bite to eat (he enjoyed it so much that he came back two nights in a row – double Diamond works wonders?).

Adding extra strings to one's bow obviously comes to mind when there's a brewery attached to a pub. It's a given that the beer you brew has to be good, but the surroundings also need to be congenial. It's all very well to brew good beer next door, but serving it in a room that has the ambience of a morgue is not conducive to good cheer. No fears about this here.

At the Fox & Hounds there's no lack of congeniality with its homely trio of bars plus a comfortable upstairs restaurant. Red is the theme, whether by design or accident. The carpets are a warm red, dotted with multi-coloured spiral designs, while the settle-style seating and banquettes also feature a raspberry jam-like shade. The lounge is the place to sit and chew the fat over the day's events, but for a sparser and livelier feel (and less crimson mood), move to the bare wood floorboards of the Stables Bar. This is aptly named as it looks like it was converted from a former stables: high ceilings and beams give it a sense of space. This is one of those places where there's room for everyone, whether you want to have a quiet chat or hang out with your pals and shoot a game of pool. Houston, we do not have a problem.

Opening hours: 12 (12.30 Sat)–10; 12.30–9 Sun

Marble Arch

73 Rochdale Road, Manchester, M4 4HY
0161 832 5914
www.marblebeers.co.uk

🍺 **Marble Pint, Dobber, Manchester Bitter, Ginger, Lagonda IPA, Chocolate Marble, seasonal beers; guest beers**

• •

On a corner on the busy Rochdale road, 10 minutes from the hustle and bustle of the Arndale Centre, stands the Marble Arch, a survivor from the late Victorian/early Edwardian age of pub splendour. Inside, there's a mosaic floor, which slopes gently down towards the door, while the walls are exposed brick with the words ALE, PORTER, RUM, WHISKIES, BRANDIES picked out on a stone frieze running just below the ceiling. Apparently the pub's interior impressed Nikolaus Pevsner, he of the exhaustive postwar survey of the buildings of England. Did he stop for a pint while he took a look around?

This is a pub whose interior encourages further exploration, an adventure that starts at the bar in the corner of the room: an old wooden Bathams 18-gallon cask sitting on top of its gantry. On it are eight handpumps, many of which dispense Marble brewery beers such as the exquisite session beer Pint, whose nose bursts with juicy, citrusy aromas (there are also guest beers and the bottled beer menu features an exhaustive list of world classics). The five-barrel brewery is situated at the back of the pub (there's a larger kit elsewhere in Manchester) and on brewing days the aroma of mashed grain hangs around outside beckoning you to enter. This is the sort of pub where you want to linger – a lunchtime drink with a roll and paper, or on an evening with friends.

As well as beer, food stakes a place here. The dishes are imaginative and hunger inducing. Try these for a start (rather than starters): fish, chips and mushy peas; battered poached egg with purple broccoli; smoked haddock and colcannon. Then there's the cheese list – chalked above the bar, a selection of artisanal cheeses including Stinking Bishop, French Epoisses (its rind washed in Marc de Bourgogne brandy), and Cropwell Bishop's rich and salty Stilton. Try a selection of four with a glass of the marvellous Chocolate Marble.

This is a humdinger of a pub that attracts a real mixture of people: men in flat caps talking about buses, hip couples discussing the day's work, beer geeks after a Marble speciality, sports lads and women out for a beer. The democracy of pub life is alive and well here.

Opening hours: 12–11.30 (12.30am Sat); 12–midnight Sun
Also great for: Food

The best **brewery taps**

Moulin Inn

11–13 Kirkmichael Road, Moulin,
Perth and Kinross, PH16 5EH
01796 472196
www.moulininn.co.uk

🍺 **Moulin Light, Braveheart, Ale of Atholl, Old Remedial**

The Moulin Inn had been serving drinks and offering beds for several decades when Bonny Prince Charlie raised his standard of revolt in the 1740s. It was also probably brewing its own ale as well. This history of brewing was a strong motivation when the owners decided to establish a small brewhouse back in 1995 (on the 300th anniversary of the inn opening its doors). Now the Moulin Inn can offer a trio of pleasures: home brewed beer, an adjoining hotel with restaurant and the inn itself, a cosy set-up full of charm and tradition. Think ancient wooden beams, pub memorabilia, roaring log fires and plenty of nooks and crannies, all the places and spaces of the pub where both locals and visitors can take their ease with a glass of something fresh. For summer eating and drinking there's also a courtyard.

Moulin is less than a mile away from Pitlochry, a town that has always been seen as the 'gateway to the Highlands', so establishing its brewery made good sense for the inn; after all, this is a touristy area and many of the visitors' first words on coming through the doors will be 'What's the local beer?'. The flagship ale is Ale of Atholl, a roasty, nutty, copper-coloured drop that has plenty of depth in its flavour, though those with a penchant for Hollywood's kind of history might go for the lighter and fruitier Braveheart.

Time has a terrible habit of eroding and displacing the attractions of the British pub or inn. But the Moulin Inn, even though successive centuries have seen its frame added to, remains at its heart a venerable Highlands inn featuring good beer and cheer. As well as the beer, the food looks to local produce to make its mark, offering such Scottish pub favourites as mince and tatties, and haggis, neeps and tatties (not on the same plate of course). Yet, the menu isn't just a Caledonian theme park of food, with dishes of lamb shanks and grilled salmon also making an appearance.

Those with an historical temperament might want to visit the battlefield of Killiecrankie, where in 1689 (six years before the Moulin Inn opened) a body of Highlanders loyal to the deposed King James II gave a good account of themselves against government troops. It might have all ended happily if there had been an inn here where they could settle their differences.

Opening hours: 11–11 (11.45 Fri & Sat); 12–11 Sun

The best **brewery taps**

Three Tuns

Salop Street, Bishop's Castle,
Shropshire, SY9 5BW
01588 638797
www.thethreetunsinn.co.uk

🍺 **Three Tuns 1642 Bitter, XXX,
Cleric's Cure; guest beer**

. . . .

I first visited the Three Tuns in 2001 as part of a
marathon 24-hour British Guild of Beer Writers
trip to eight microbreweries in Shropshire.
At the time the pub and the adjoining Three Tuns
brewery were part of the same business, and
the beer writers showed much interest in the
resolutely low-tech Victorian tower brewery at
the back of the pub.

However, the history of the Three Tuns goes
back a bit further than when Queen Victoria sat
on the throne. A pub and brewery have been
on the site since 1642, with some claiming that
the Three Tuns Brewery (or the John Roberts
Brewery as it has been known a couple of times)
is the oldest in the UK, predating Shepherd
Neame by over 50 years. In the early 1970s it
was only one of four pubs that
brewed their own ale. Naturally,
both pub and brewery have
gone through several changes
through the centuries.

The brewery was reorganized into the much
admired tower system towards the end of the
19th century, while more recently the pub had
a light and airy dining space added on; lots of
glass gives it the feel of a conservatory. Another
change is that the brewery and pub are now two
separate businesses, but both work in accord and
harmony with each other.

The Three Tuns is very much a pub that
belongs at the heart of its community, sited in
an individually exceptional town (spend some
time here and you'll soon discover Bishop's
Castle's sense of uniqueness). Music nights
get toes a-tapping, the film club meets here,
no doubt exchanging jokes about reel ale, and
as soon as the weather becomes clement the
morris men hove into view.

In the comfortable public bar, black beams,
flagged floors, a low ceiling and old-fashioned
handpumps at the bar suggest a sense of
timelessness, a feel that the pub is just carrying
on what it has been doing down the ages:
providing a home from home for locals (plus good
beer of course – a glass of XXX is a floral delight).
Food is served in the lounge bar and glass-sided
dining area from a menu that offers a thoroughly
modern eating experience: the beef is well-hung,
the chips hand-cut, while the starters are multi-
cultural in their theme (piri-piri chicken salad, satay
king prawns, fishcakes).

Just like the brewery, it's not always been
plain sailing for the pub. It shut in the mid 1990s
and was rescued after being bought by a group
of canny locals. A couple of decades later, it still
thrives, which just goes to show that there is
room for a happy ending in the pub trade.

Opening hours: 12–11; 12–10.30 Sun

The best **brewery taps**

Three Tuns

78 St George's Road, Bristol, BS1 5UR

0117 907 0689

www.arborales.co.uk

🍺 **Arbor Ales Single Hop, Brigstow; guest beers**

• •

Even though there's not a 48-inch flat-screen in sight at the Three Tuns, it does share something with TV culture – it's yet another example of the pub trade's version of home improvement shows. Once upon a time the Three Tuns was run-down, to say the least. In 2010 it was taken over by Bristol microbrewery Arbor Ales and since then has been totally made-over, following in the footsteps of a trend occurring in other towns and cities.

Standing on a corner in an area close to the Cathedral and its choir school, the Three Tuns is a single room pub with a large alcove at the rear. Its simplicity is engaging and one of its charms. Painted dark mustard yellow on the outside, there's a fresh and vibrant sense of rejuvenation about its interior. The bar is light and airy, helped by the two large windows at the front – it's on a busy street, nothing is hidden from passers-by here. Meanwhile, even though the weathered, distressed wooden floor, plush red-coloured, mock-leather sofas and scrubbed pine tables suggest gastro-pub, the Three Tuns' sensibility is more that of a modern brewery tap, where good beer, both in cask and in bottle, rules the roost. Food of course is also available (bangers and mash, chilli, rolls, baps), while a proper coffee machine behind the single bar gladdens the heart, but first and foremost you go to the Three Tuns to drink beer – and what a choice there is.

The single bar has seven handpumps (there are plans to increase it to 10). Even though Arbor Ales run the joint, they are generous in their guest ale allowance. Generous, but also confident in a belief that their own beers can speak for themselves without swamping the bar top. On my visit their Oyster Stout certainly was a superlative representative of brewing prowess, producing a beer that mixed and merged fruity hints with more traditional roast and bitter notes associated with stout (was that a briny undercurrent at the back of the palate?). Guests come from the likes of Dark Star, BrewDog and Thornbridge, while the bottled selection includes some of the more esoteric offerings from BrewDog (including the 18% Toyko) as well as the likes of Anchor from San Francisco.

The Three Tuns has rapidly put itself on the Bristol beer trail, which is no mean feat considering that the city is one of the best in which to drink beer (and cider). Even though the building is old, the Three Tuns has a young and eager feel and a sense that its journey to pub greatness is just beginning. Join it on this voyage.

Opening hours: 12–11

Vine (Bull & Bladder)

10 Delph Road, Brierley Hill,
West Midlands, DY5 2TN
01384 78293
www.bathams.co.uk

🍺 **Batham Mild Ale, Best Bitter,
XXX (winter)**

On a nondescript road leading away from the
Black Country town of Brierley stands a row of
1960s terraced houses, the drivers passing by
heedless of what they are missing: the Vine. Or
the Bull & Bladder, as it's known locally.

The Vine has the calm air of Victorian
architecture. Squat and solidly built, it stands
out from the rest of the neighbourhood with its
cream coloured exterior; though what strikes you
first is the quote 'Blessings of your heart, you
brew good ale', which is emblazoned across the
front of the pub, a Shakespearian exhortation to
enter and cast the cares of the day behind.

Next door, the reason for the hearty quote
is revealed: this is the site of Batham brewery,
which moved here in 1877 when the family
bought what was then a slaughter house and
went onto to convert it into a pub and adjoining
brewery (hence the bull and bladder name
by which the pub is known). Now, the Vine
is a priceless and prestigious piece of pub
architecture and pub life that beer drinkers from
all over the British Isles (and the world) flock to.

Inside there's a snug front bar to the right of
the tiled corridor, a lounge to the left, warmed
by a coal fire in the winter; then a family room
and a large back bar in which music is often
played. In the front bar the walls are coated with
framed newspaper reports about the brewery.
Come on Saturday lunchtime (as I did) and you'll
discover a chatty, lively spot for locals seeking a
pint of Batham's crisp and creamy Mild or their
sprightly, lively Best Bitter. It might be a local but
newcomers won't find any sense of exclusion as
they stand at the front bar (which is backed by a
massive wooden back-bar and mirrors) waiting to
be served. With your glass in hand, take the time
to roam around the wall to read the newspaper
reports from a pre-social networking age.

In the sofa-lined lounge, the space colonised
by round tables, there's a sense that this a good
place to talk, to exchange gossip, to discuss local
matters. Like the rest of the pub it's a homely
place. In the lounge as in the snug front bar
Batham are not shy either – framed awards for
beer and the pub can be seen wherever you look.
And why not? Batham has every right to be proud
of this exquisite treasure of a pub.

Opening hours: 12–11; 12–10.30 Sun

The best
cider pubs

A celebration of Britain's great pubs wouldn't be complete without a nod to those that major in Britain's other national drink, offering a scintillating selection of ciders and perries.

Some run their cider range in parallel with a boisterously good selection of cask beers – the down-to-earth Penrhyn Arms in North Wales has won awards for both its beers and ciders (as has its near neighbour the Blue Bell Inn), while the Victory in Hereford offers Westons ciders alongside beers brewed at the back of the pub (the county is famous for apples and hops and both are rightly celebrated here).

However, there is also a very small elite of cider-only pubs in this section, ranging from the Cider House in Worcestershire to the unique Apple in Bristol, where you drink your cider on a barge moored in the centre of the city. And lest not we forget, there's the venerable Olde Cider Bar in Newton Abbot, a famous fixture for Devon-based lovers of the apple. These are survivors of a tradition of cider houses that once marked the cider-growing areas and which has sadly declined over the years – take your time to visit these gems as you never know how long they will stand...

See also
Barton Inn,
Barton St David
(p79)
Cumberland Arms,
Newcastle upon
Tyne (p242)
Old Fire House,
Exeter (p246)
Ring O'Bells,
Ashcott (p256)

The Apple

Welsh Back, Bristol, BS1 4SB
0117 925 3500
www.applecider.co.uk
🍺 **Cider range varies**

. . . .

And now for something completely different – a barge in the middle of Bristol that majors in cider and perry, both on draught and in bottle. Forget all notions of cider houses stuck in the middle of the countryside, The Apple sees cider served in a totally different environment, an urban one of cutting edge coolness – and ever since it was launched into the placid waters that flow through Bristol it's been a roaring success.

The Apple is situated in the waterfront area of Welsh Back, so named because this is the area where slate from South Wales was once delivered. At the water's edge, having passed through the group of tables and chairs that form The Apple's terraced area (for cider-loving land-lubbers no doubt), you cross the gangplank and are welcomed aboard the converted Dutch barge. Upstairs in the top lounge there are views of the surrounding area (newish developments jostling for space with riverside remnants). Downstairs is where the drinks are served, a dark and wintry space that is perfect for the cooler seasons, though warmer times also see people ascending to sit down there. On my visit, a group of people arrived and one of them queried why they were going to sit below. 'Sofas!' came the reply. It is very comfortable down in the basement.

At the bar seven ciders are dispensed from handpump, served by knowledgeable young staff who take their time to explain the various ciders on display to novices. I noticed a marked trend towards Somerset with the likes of Sheppy's, Wilkins and Thatchers on show. Those with a stronger constitution often make for Broadoak's medium-sweet Old Bristolian – it can veer between 7.5 and 8.4% abv, so take it easy! I, however, opted for that rare beast, a West Country perry from Hecks in the Somerset town of Street. This was fragrant on the nose with toffee and pear notes on the palate. It's an elegant drink.

The Apple may be a legendary cider boat, but it has also won awards for its food, notably the ploughman's. Those wishing for some grub along with their cider are offered the choice of 25 ingredients to build up their ploughman's with, including seven different cheeses. There are also pork pies, home cooked ham and plenty of pickles. If it wasn't for the gentle rock of the barge on the water, you could imagine yourself in the depths of the cider heartlands of Somerset – in some ways you are; despite Bristol's beery heritage, the city's heart also beats to the rhythm of the cider drum.

Opening hours: 12–midnight; 12–10.30 Sun
Also great for: Riverside

Blue Bell Inn

Rhosesmor Road, Halkyn, Flintshire, CH8 8DL
01352 780309
www.bluebell.uk.eu.org

🍺 **Facer's Blue Bell Bitter, Dark Blue Porter; guest beers; cider range varies**

• •

Three handpumps are available for cider and perry at the family-run Blue Bell Inn, which was CAMRA's Cider Pub of the Year for 2010. They're joined at the bar by four cask beers. This old-fashioned, edge-of-village pub started life as a pair of cottages in the 1700s, and is a popular place for walkers. Some of them have even gone as far as organising their own club based at the Blue Bell; well it does make sense as the pub produces a selection of recommended walks in league with the Ramblers Association.

There's also Sunday afternoon jazz sessions, Welsh lessons for those who want to learn the local tongue and games nights and quizzes. A blackboard is covered with punning film and song titles – those familiar with the Radio 4 show *I'm Sorry I Haven't a Clue* would understand all.

The busy nature of the pub is complemented by the depth of its beer and cider choices: the beams above the bar feature the information that 700 cask beers have been served since 2003 when Steve Marquis took over. On the cider and perry front the score is climbing well above a century; all served from polypin bags that keep them fresh and delectable. They include superstars from the new wave of Welsh cidermakers such as Gwynt y Ddraig and W.M. Watkins & Sons, as well as ciders and perries from over the border, such as Gwatkin.

The Blue Bell Inn is also in a beautiful location on the slopes of Halkyn Mountain. On a summer's day this makes for a stunning vista with your pint in hand. Food is only served at weekend lunchtimes (when the pub is open all day – it's evenings only during the week), with the same dedication to quality and choice as is shown with drink. A local buffalo farm provides meat for stews, a nearby butcher for other animals, while fish is pole caught. A lot goes on here – the pub is definitely the hub in Halkyn.

Opening hours: 5–11 (midnight Fri); 12–midnight Sat; 12–11 Sun
Also great for: Family

The best cider pubs

Cider House

Woodmancote, Defford,
Worcestershire, WR8 9BW
01386 750234

🍷 **Westons Medium, Woodmancote Dry, Country Perry**

• •

Or the Monkey House as this gem of an old cider house is affectionately known by its many fans. The Monkey House? The tale told is of a farm worker who spent some time imbibing here and when he arrived home was covered in scratches. When asked what had happened, he swore blind that a monkey had attacked him and then dragged him through a hedge… make of that what you will. However, whether you call it the Monkey House or Cider House, there is no doubting the unique flavour of this establishment. For a start it is one of a small, almost vanished, handful of cider-only pubs left in the UK (Newton Abbot is home to another, see page 61). Then there's the fact it has no bar.

Cider is dispensed through a hatch in a stable door, poured from a jug, and you either drink outside or, when the weather is inclement, go to the old bakehouse where there's a log burner. Bulmers used to make the cider, based on an old recipe (the House has been in the same family for over a century), but now Westons make it – and very refreshing and moreish it is too. There's no food, but people bring their own while locals sometimes leave out vegetables for other drinkers to take home with them.

The Cider House looks the part as well – thatched, black beamed, drooping eaves, plus a real sense of venerability in the bakehouse. It's hidden away from the road: go down a lane, past the Royal Oak and there it is. Since the death of the husband of landlady Jill Collin a couple of years ago opening hours are rather limited so it's wise to check. However, for any lover of the original English tradition of cider, the Cider House is an essential visit.

Opening hours: Wed & Sat 6–10; Fri & Sun 12–3; Mon (summer) 12–2

Cider is simply the fermented juice of the apple, but not just any old apple. Supermarket favourites such as Granny Smith and Golden Delicious are out; instead, cider apples with gloriously evocative names such as Sweet Alford, Tremlett's Bitter, Kingston Black and Somerset Redstreak are used. These apples have more in common with the bullet-like, unpalatable crab apple than anything found in the supermarket. Bite into a West Country cider apple (or a Three Counties perry pear for that matter) and chances are that your mouth will go on strike, such would be the harsh tannic attack and sly slosh of acidity.

Cider apples in the West Country are chosen for their levels of tannins, acids and sweetness. Further east in Kent and East Anglia cooking apples are blended with dessert apples to help to balance the underlying sweetness. Apples harvested early on in the season are the ones with the tannins and acids, while later ones are sweeter. The trick is to get the right blend of apples, which means that each cider-maker has their own unique mix.

Hi-tech is not a word that comes into play when discussing craft cider. The collection of apples from the orchard is a laborious process sometimes involving a long ash pole to knock down the fruit. After this the apples are crushed in a mill and the pulp is layered between steel plates in a cider press. Traditionally, this is called the 'cheese' and is layered between hessian sacks, although steel plates are more common now. After the press is brought down several times, the pure apple juice is collected and left to ferment with added yeast. Some makers prefer to let wild yeasts play a role. The quality and taste of the resulting product depends on the apple variety and blend of apples used. The long sleep of fermentation takes a few weeks until a cider at an alcoholic strength between 6%-8% is available. Some continue to mature in oak barrels where they become stronger and drier. Farmhouse 'scrumpy' is made when yeast in the bottle continues the process of conditioning, producing a muscular, full-bodied cider.

Cider

Penrhyn Arms

Pendre Road, Penrhynside, Llandudno,
Conwy, LL30 3BY
07780 678927
www.penrhynarms.com

🍺 **Banks's Bitter; Marston's Pedigree;
guest beers; cider range varies**

● ●

A couple of miles from the bright lights and sunny smiles of the Welsh seaside resort Llandudno, the village of Penrhynside clings to the hillside overlooking Penrhyn Bay and the coast curving eastwards in the distance. At the bottom of the hill sits the ancient Penrhyn Old Hall, one of the oldest buildings in North Wales and home to ghosts, severed hands, skeletons, priest holes, and now also a bar.

Penrhynside was built as a mining village for those who worked in the local limestone quarry, a thankless, physical job that once gave the village a certain reputation amongst the more genteel folk of Llandudno. The two pubs in the village were doubtlessly popular places for the men who worked in the quarries, with the chapel sparking off the usual tension between the pub and the pulpit. No such conflict now – the Penrhyn Arms stands solid, square and respectable, twin gables on each wing and a striking colour scheme of cream laced with a black-and-white timber frame effect. Inside, there's an L-shaped bar, basic but comfortable, with one wall given over to photos of famous drinkers such as Richard Burton, Ian Botham and even the 1930s comedian Will Hay.

This is very much a locals' pub, a community asset where people know each other. There are usually four cask beers available and landlord

John Sumberland has carved out a reputation for offering beers from all over the country (this was the Pub of the Year 2010 for his local CAMRA branch). There is no food, apart from Thursday night, which is cheese night. However, just like the Blue Bell Inn (p55) further up the coast (with whom Sumberland frequently collaborates in the distribution of ciders and perries), the Penrhyn Arms offers a hearty selection of real ciders and perries from both Welsh and English producers. For this, it has won Welsh Cider pub of the Year as well as coming second in the national CAMRA competition. If you like perry from Gwynt y Ddraig or scrumpy from Westons, chances are that the Penrhyn Arms will have them and, if not, something equally fruitful – the Penrhyn Arms' core values remain intact when it comes to cider.

Opening hours: 5.30 (4.30 Thu; 4 Fri)–midnight;
12–1am Sat; 12–11 Sun
Also great for: CAMRA award-winners

Valley Bar

51 Valley Road, Scarborough,
North Yorkshire, YO11 2LX
01723 372593
www.valleybar.co.uk

🍺**Theakston Best Bitter; guest beers; cider range varies**

. . . .

Enjoy being beside the seaside? And also fancy a glass or two of artisanal cider? Then head for the North Yorkshire coast – to be exact, the Victorian resort of Scarborough, where the Valley Bar enjoys a well-deserved reputation for the quality and range of the ciders and perries it serves. Fancy a drop of Broadoak Perry from Bristol? Sweetish and strong at 7.5% it's a particular favourite with the Valley Bar's locals. When they move on to something else there's the sort of choice that would put a rural Somerset pub to shame – there can be up to eight different varieties available, with the range of dry ciders usually joined by a couple of sweet ciders and perries. Names to look out for include Gwatkins, Hewitts and Oliver's.

This devotion to the apple and the pear has not gone without notice, and the pub was awarded the title of CAMRA's National Cider and Perry Pub of the Year in 2007. You might be surprised to see drinks that seem so firmly rooted in the West Country on a bar in North Yorkshire, but then further north the Cumberland Arms in Newcastle (p242) has a similar devotion to the apple. 'We started selling ciders in 2005,' the Valley's landlady Linda Soden says, 'but really got going a couple of years later. We were passionate about having a great traditional drink here. Many locals have become cider drinkers only after drinking it here.'

The Valley Inn is a solid looking Victorian-built establishment standing on a road not far from the sea. The bar is in the basement, with accommodation offered on the floors above at very reasonable rates. The interior is choc-a-bloc with posters, clocks and enamel signs for Belgian beer (of which over 100 bottles are stocked), and it also boasts a good selection of beers. Six cask beers are usually offered, with regular Theakston's Best Bitter being joined by beers from the likes of Dark Star, Hornbeam, Durham and local brewing heroes Roosters (Soden reckons that 6,000 different beers have flowed through the pumps since she took over). No food is served so the emphasis here is on good drink and conversation, which perhaps is the reason that the Valley Bar is home to a variety of local clubs and groups who meet here. With a Victorian heritage, you'd half expect that this welcoming cellar bar might have a ghost somewhere or other. 'Afraid not,' says Soden, 'well not that'd you know as it's too exciting here to notice any.' Or maybe any ghosts just enjoy a quiet sip of Broadoak now and again.

The best **cider pubs**

Opening hours: 12–midnight (1am Thu–Sat)
Also great for: Seaside

Victory

88 St Owens Street, Hereford, HR1 2QD
01432 274998
www.herefordbrewery.co.uk

🍺 **Hereford Original Bitter, Herefordshire Owd Bull, Mutleys Dark, Best Bitter; guest beer; cider range varies**

. . . .

Pubs named the Victory often claim some connection with Nelson – a dirty weekend spent with Emma Hamilton or a glass of porter and a beef steak en route to Portsmouth and national immortality.

Nelson, sadly, didn't make it to the Victory in Hereford, but the pub has had plenty of other seafaring connotations in the past 20 years. In the early 1990s what had been the Bricklayers Arms became the Jolly Roger, named after the microbrewery set up onsite. Its interior was famously decked out in the shape of a galleon with plenty of rigging and netting plus a sort of crow's nest (a precursor of the *Pirates of the Caribbean* craze perhaps?). However, brewing stopped in 1993 and Wye Valley Brewery picked up the pub and changed the name to the Victory – but the splendid galleon remained.

In 1999 Jim Kenyon bought the Victory and set up a brewery at the back, initially calling it Spinning Dog (after his dog Cassie who provided hours of entertainment by chasing her tail). Cassie's gone and Spinning Dog is now the Hereford Brewery but one thing that has remained is the theme of a life on the ocean waves. Go into the pub and the bar pokes out of the side of a good-sized model of an old galleon, complete with bow and stern. Beer as you can

imagine is king here with at least four cask beers from Hereford Brewery on at all times. However, as a recognition of Hereford's long-term relationship with the apple, there are also four traditional ciders available from Westons, which include Old Rosie Scrumpy, Herefordshire Perry and Vintage Organic. Given that Hereford can be seen as being at the heart of both cider-making and hop-growing country, there is a pleasing symmetry about the Victory's celebration of both these drinks. Elsewhere in the pub, the spartan wooden theme continues with a galleried room at the back suggestive of a ship's stores, though without the stores. Try and make it on a Tuesday, which is quiz night – with the added bonus of a free curry for those taking part.

Opening hours: 3 (1 Fri summer)–11; 11–midnight Sat; 12–midnight Sun
Also great for: Brewpubs

Ye Olde Cider Bar

99 East Street, Newton Abbot,
Devon, TQ12 2LD
01626 354221

🍺 **Cider range varies**

• •

Newton Abbot is an unremarkable Devon town, overshadowed to the south by its seaside neighbour Torquay, while the granite playground of Dartmoor broods to the north. However, while the English Riviera has sun, sand and sea, and Dartmoor a touch of the wilderness, Newton Abbot has its own unique charm in Ye Olde Cider Bar. Stepping into it is like taking a trip back in time as this venerable institution is one of a handful of survivors of the traditional cider houses that were once dotted about the West Country.

With a name that summons up a sense of cider mystique, you would expect to find it hidden down a side-street, perhaps the sort of place where you have to rap three times on the door to gain entrance. Not so; instead it's located on the main road through Newton Abbot, a solid, no-nonsense 19th century farmhouse-style dwelling with a neon sign outside saying 'Cider bar'.

The main road might be crammed with all the nonsense of high street Britain, but once you step inside it's another world: the furniture is off-the-peg fittings from the 1970s though there is also a sense of rustic style with tables that seem to have been hewn out of gigantic cider barrels; the floor is uncompromising stone; unfashionable creams and browns swirl about on the walls; jugs and tankards hang over the bar. A wide corridor stretches away from the bar – this is called the Long Bar and has long been the home to the

Cork Club, a sort of Friendly Society for members whose history goes back to the years before the First World War.

However, it's what's behind the counter that really anchors the bar within another age: there is no ale here, just ciders, perries and fruit wines, the latter being lethal concoctions made from damsons and other hedgerow fruits. Four massive 40-gallon barrels dispense ciders from local producers Winkleigh, while smaller pins offer ciders and perries from the likes of Thatchers and Westons. There are also bottles of single-varietal ciders plus taps to dispense chilled draught ciders. Food is simple and filling – filled rolls or pasties.

Such is the uniqueness of this bar that it is rarely empty. You can visit before midday and join in with loyal locals tucking into glasses of Thatchers Gold or Winkleigh Sam's. Spend enough time here and you will discover that this Newton Abbot institution attracts a whole cross-section of drinkers. Lifelong cider drinkers call it home, while youngsters hit 18 and come here to have their first pint; the place is also popular with tourists from Canada or the US who have heard of it and want to check it out. Just don't ask for ice in your glass…

Opening hours: 11–11 Mon–Thu; 11–midnight Fri–Sat; 11–10.30 Sun

The best **cider pubs**

ROYAL OAK

HARVEYS of LEWES

HARVEYS
FOUNDED 1790

TO LET
FIELD & SONS
020 7234 9639

The best
city pubs

What makes a great city pub? The Black Boy in the genteel cathedral city of Winchester has a strange menagerie of stuffed animals and other artefacts – you might be startled by the sight of a stuffed baboon in a kilt, while the landlord was once offered a horse's head (not real of course). Meanwhile the vibrant Northern Quarter of Manchester is home to the Port Street Beer House – it only opened in 2011 and is the youngest pub in the book, but its vitality and beer choice mark it out as an essential city pub to visit.

Other city pubs listed here are architectural gems, beer palaces, or formerly rundown old boozers that have been taken by the scruff of the neck and transformed – before she took over the Bricklayer's Arms, landlady Becky Newman says that her gem of a Putney pub gained a reputation as a 'reunion place for Wandsworth nick'. The cons have long gone and beer fans from all walks of life have moved in.

Whether you're by the sea in Plymouth and witnessing the pub magic that inspired the artist Beryl Cook, in search of culture in Edinburgh or Bath, enjoying cosmopolitan Leeds or Cardiff, or just ambling along London's South Bank here is a selection of city pubs just waiting to be visited.

See also
Cloisters Bar, Edinburgh (p17)
Crown Posada, Newcastle upon Tyne (p154)
Fat Cat, Sheffield (p45)
Harp, Covent Garden (p265)
The Philharmonic, Liverpool (p160)
Star, Bath (p163)

Black Boy

1 Wharf Hill, Winchester,
Hampshire, SO23 9NQ
01962 861754
www.theblackboypub.com

🍺 Flowerpots Bitter; Hop Back Summer
Lightning; Ringwood Best Bitter;
guest beers

If the Black Boy were a Dickens' novel then without a doubt it would be *The Old Curiosity Shop* – step inside and you'll immediately see the reason. The bar acts as a hub around which a group of five rooms circle, all of them filled with bric-a-brac and clutter, arranged in the most artfully disarranged way. In one room, Victorian-era plaster hams hang, while elsewhere there's an elephant's foot (not real), a seagull in a cage, various stuffed birds on wire and a corridor filled with book shelves. And let's not forget the stuffed baboon in a kilt that stands sentry-like in a space just off the bar. According to landlord David Nicholson the displays have grown organically since he took over the pub in the 1990s. One regular bought in a horse's head – it wasn't real.

This is the pub as a museum of marvels, a place that always has something new to observe; if you're waiting for a friend who's running late then grab your pint and have a wander. You'll probably bump into someone else doing the same thing. Pubs have long been known for the landlord's collection of bits and pieces but the Black Boy takes collecting to a totally different level.

Of course, this sort of décor could all go horribly wrong, leaving a pub looking like some gimmicky palace of tat where all the artefacts have been bought by the yard. Not so at the Black Boy – it all adds a curiosity as well as warmth to this popular local; this is also helped by the fact that the beer choice has an emphasis on local breweries.

Five handpumps do their duty at the bar, offering ales from the likes of Plain Ales, Ringwood, Bowman, Hop Back and Flowerpots. On my visit I tried a glass of Bowman's Swift One, which was fruity and citrusy in a gentle sort of way. It really suited the lunchtime mood. Food is down-to-earth: robust sandwiches (try the home-cooked ham) served alongside homemade soup or chips. Those wanting something substantial can enjoy a plate of quintessential pub grub such as fish and chips or toad in the hole, all freshly cooked on the premises, but do note that food is not served Monday and Tuesdays (if you're really hungry try the biltong, which comes in several spicy flavours).

Winchester may have a reputation as a city that is trapped in aspic, but just take a trip over the river to the Black Boy and you'll see a different Winchester, a more quirky, local and definitely non-tourist one. And do say hello to the baboon.

Opening hours: 12–11 (midnight Fri & Sat);
12–10.30 Sun

Bricklayer's Arms

32 Waterman Street, Putney,
London, SW15 1DD
020 8789 0222
www.bricklayers-arms.co.uk

🍺 **Dark Star Hophead, Partridge Best Bitter; Loddon Gravesend Shrimpers; Rudgate Ruby Mild; Sambrook's Wandle Ale; guest beers**

• •

Fronting a pub and treading the boards are two very similar occupations. Both licensee and actor are on show and playing a part – anyone who can be a smiling licensee on a grey Monday lunchtime should automatically be up for a BAFTA... so running the Bricklayer's Arms made perfect sense for actress Becky Newman when she changed careers after appearing in the likes of *Casualty* and the *House of Elliot* as well as on stage and in rep.

This was back in 2005 and her debut on the pub stage saw her with her work cut out.

Not only was she changing career ('I didn't know much about ale and taking this on was a very steep learning curve,' she says), but the Bricklayer's had gained an unenviable reputation as a 'reunion for Wandsworth nick'.

Newman obviously succeeded as the former cons are long gone and nowadays the Bricklayer's is a bright shining beacon of cask beer that pays host to all manner of folk. And Newman's dedication has been rewarded with many awards.

Hidden down a small street, a few minutes from Putney Bridge, the Bricklayer's Arms is a compact early Victorian building and the oldest pub in the area; its preserved frontage sits incongruously in the shade of a neighbouring housing estate. It's a vibrant memory of when Putney was a village on the edge of London. The bar sits in the centre of the front room, while there's a long gallery leading to the back of the pub. Seating suits all tastes: wooden tables and stools, comfy chairs and a couple of settles from a Welsh chapel. The beer garden is packed on sunny days, especially during one of the pub's regular beer festivals.

Cask beer is king at the bar with up to 12 handpumps on at any one time (two of them devoted to cider and perry). The range travels the country but regulars include Sambrook's Wandle, and Hophead from Sussex brewing superstars Dark Star. A brace of beer festivals are held during the year: celebrations of the best British regional cask beers from Yorkshire and Devon and Cornwall. Uniquely for a London pub, the Bricklayer's doesn't serve food. But to be honest you come here to partake of a very special pub atmosphere and try some of the best beers in the UK. Encore!

Opening hours: 12–11; 12–10.30 Sun
Also great for: CAMRA award-winners

The best **city pubs**

Café Royal

19 West Register Street,
Edinburgh, EH2 2AA
0131 556 1884
www.caferoyal.org.uk

🍺 **Caldeonian Deuchars IPA; guest beers**

Café Royal – the name of this Edinburgh institution sounds almost Edwardian – a place where gents and their ladies once repaired to for champagne and oysters in the hope that Edward VII would turn up, latest mistress in tow, while the orchestra played the national anthem. The Café Royal has been on its spot since 1863 (it was originally on the other side of the road), and its owner – a plumber – originally planned it to be a showpiece for baths, sinks and other sanitary fittings. With its arched windows, three floors and a loft there's a hint of Paris about the building – it would have been a very upmarket shop window for sinks and basins. Whether it ever served this purpose is not known, but it's been a pub (and eating place) since 1901 – ironically enough the year Queen Victoria died and the Edwardian era started.

Inside it's a wealth of gorgeous fittings: an octagonal island bar, white marble floor, wood panels, screens, plasterwork on the ceilings and a series of exquisite Doulton tiled murals depicting various men of science such as Michael Faraday and James Watt. Inside, you get this feeling of ornateness, grandness and richness, the sense that the Café Royal is something more than a pub – a place where customers feel comfortable and special, but also a bejewelled and bedecked survivor of a long gone golden age, where Edinburgh citizens would gather and enjoy a glass or two. The ceiling with all its embellishments is alone worth your visit, while the bar counter – even though it was replaced in the 1970s – still has a sense of craftsmanship and dignity. The bar is light and airy, colourful and warm, welcoming and historical.

Seafood is a speciality of the house with oysters leading the charge (there's also an oyster bar). Scottish specialities crop up on the menu, including Cullen Skink and a haggis and whisky cream pie for those comfort eating moments. Deuchars IPA is available all the year round and joined by three other cask beers, usually from the likes of Inveralmond, Kelburn and Harviestoun. And while you're taking in the surroundings, spare a thought for the pub ghost and be aware – he's known to call out a drinker's name and vanish when the hapless person at the bar turns round.

Opening hours: 11–11 (midnight Thu; 1am Fri & Sat); 12.30–11 Sun
Also great for: Food; Heritage

The best **city pubs**

Dolphin Hotel

14 The Barbican, Plymouth, Devon, PL1 2LS
01752 660876

🍺 Draught Bass; Hop Back Summer Lightning; Otter Ale; St Austell Tribute, Proper Job; Sharp's Doom Bar; Skinner's Betty Stogs; guest beer

According to T.S. Eliot 'the women come and go, talking of Michelangelo'. In the Dolphin the women used to come and go and end up in paintings by the late Beryl Cook whose local the Dolphin was. Her regular table is to the left hand of the entrance, a place where she would sit with a gin and bitter lemon observing and capturing the vivacious, high-spirited characters that called the Dolphin their home.

Outside, the foot traffic of Plymouth's quayside Barbican district passes by. Tourists, locals and off-duty sailors, both civvies and Jack Tars, make up the vibrant mix, while this classic city pub, a survivor of both the devastating Luftwaffe raids and postwar planning, offers a bolthole from the mayhem that can sometimes erupt.

The Dolphin certainly stands out, its ground floor frontage featuring shades of both marine and sky blue; note the stained glass windows with the legend OB in their centre. This refers to Plymouth's Octagon Brewery, which ceased brewing in 1970. 'The Dolphin Hotel' is picked out in art-deco-style letters on an arch spanning the two windows. You get a sense of an older Plymouth here.

Inside the pub has been opened out, with a separate space to the right of the bar and more space at the back. Settles and banquettes line the edges of the room, though the large space in front of the bar suggests that the pub can get very busy at times.

One of Cook's paintings featuring the Dolphin is on display, as well as other bits and pieces including a large Draught Bass mirror (the southwest still harbours pockets of affection for this much-abused Burton classic, and the Dolphin is one such place). There can be up to eight cask beers on. No food is available, though if you're hungry there are several excellent fish and chip shops in The Barbican.

There's an austere, almost spartan feel to the environment, suggesting that the Dolphin is primarily a place for drinking and socialising (though there's also a large flatscreen TV showing various sporting highlights towards the back as well). It's the sort of place where you listen to the ebb and flow of locals talking. As I sit there the door opens and a group of noisy women enter, weighed down with shopping bags, cheerful and noisy in the best possible way. Even though Cook has long gone, the women that inspired her still come and go at the Dolphin.

Opening hours: 10–11 (midnight Fri & Sat); 11–11 Sun

The best **city pubs**

The Goat Major

33 High Street, Cardiff, Glamorgan, CF10 1PU
029 2033 7161
www.sabrain.co.uk/goatmajor

🍺 **Brains Dark, Bitter, SA, seasonal beers; guest beers**

Hungry? Then take a look at the menu at this venerable Cardiff pub. It hosts a superb selection of delicious and award-winning pies including lamb and mint, and venison and stout – meaty ballast that should fill the grumbling tummies of even the most hungry of pub-goers. Seeking something different? Perhaps a pie related to the pub's name? Don't. 'There would be uproar if we went down that route,' laughed the barman when I asked if the pub would ever have a goat pie.

There's a reason for this: the goat has a special place in Welsh military tradition with one of the beasts being marched into combat alongside the Royal 41st Regiment of Wales during the Crimean War. Safely back home, he was introduced to Queen Victoria and goats have acted as a mascot for Welsh regiments ever since.

The pub started life as the Goat at the start of the 19th century, before being renamed the Bluebell in 1813. It wasn't until 1995 when it got its shoulder pips and became The Goat Major (this is the title given to the soldier who looks after the regimental goat). It's an easy pub to find, standing as it does at the northern end of the High Street, a paved area that leads up to Cardiff Castle.

As for beer, this is Cardiff after all, capital of Wales and home of Brains brewery. This is one of their most popular pubs; here you can sup a pint of Brains' superb Dark, a classic mild with chocolate and coffee notes. Other Brains beers are available and the pub occasionally puts on a beer festival.

The décor? Enter this three-storied terraced gem and you're faced with a large single room, bar with a brass railing to the left; dark wood dominates with panelling surrounding the room, while settles and sofas line the walls offering a comfortable berth. There's a welcoming twilight aspect to the pub's interior lighting, that can comfort and soothe during the winter, producing a haven from the blustery wetness of the High Street. In the summer, the pub's ambience provides a shade and a coolness from the sun outside, in the same way as a taverna does on a sun-bleached Greek island amidst the sparkling blue waters of the Aegean (incidentally, a place where you will find goat on the plate…).

Opening hours: 12–midnight; 12–11 Sun

Gunmakers

Eyre Street, Clerkenwell, London, EC1R 5ET
020 7278 1022
www.thegunmakers.co.uk

🍺 **Purity Mad Goose; Woodforde's Wherry;
guest beers**

. . . .

The Gunmakers stands all on its own, hidden away off the Clerkenwell Road in an area commonly called Little Italy. It has the look of a traditional old school boozer, the sort of London pub that becomes rarer as the years pass. It's also a hardy survivor of 50 years of London development.

Traditional might be the first word that pops into the mind, but that's as far as the interpretation goes. Step through the door any lunchtime and you will discover a lively bunch of drinkers and diners (many young and achingly hip – Ben Sherman's head office is close), making for a busy, buzzy atmosphere. The ambience is added to by the jovial Geordie whirlwind that is landlord Jeff Bell in action – the very model of pro-active hospitality. Regulars get their dose of chat and newcomers are made to feel at home, while diners at the back get a refreshing draught of their host. Bell is a former lawyer and knows how to work the crowd; you could say he swapped the Bar for the bar.

The Gunmakers might be slim in size and compact in conception, but it makes up for it with a big-hearted and convivial approach in which drink and food are gobbled up with enthusiasm. Four cask beers are regularly proffered. Wherry and Mad Goose are the regulars while guests have been known to come from Dark Star, Thornbridge, Jarrow and Ascot amongst many others. On my visit I enjoyed a creamy glass of

Hobsons Mild followed by Wherry (delicate lemon and fragrant citrus notes). You also eat well here: smoked chicken and chorizo salad and seafood linguine with chilli and basil suggest that the chef likes gastro with gusto.

Comfort yourself in the unfussy and well-worn front bar, a place to pass time. Beyond the main bar a brace of rooms offer the classic retro feel of a 1950s Parisian cellar dive – you half expect existentialists and beatniks to jump out and declaim poetry at you.

However, instead of Jean-Paul and pals, the Gunmakers has a sit-com set of classic pub characters. As well as being a robust survivor, the Gunmakers is also the pub as soap opera. Ideas for a theme tune on a postcard please…

Opening hours: 12–11; closed Sat & Sun

Kean's Head

46 St Mary's Gate, Nottingham, NG1 1QA
0115 947 4052

www.castlerockbrewery.co.uk

🍺 **Castle Rock Harvest Pale, Preservation Fine Ale, Screech Owl; guest beers**

First impressions of the Kean's Head? On the ground floor of a three-storied redbrick building situated in Nottingham's Lace Market – from the front I'm reminded of a hairdressers' or even a wine bar. However, if you judge a book by its cover and move on in search of something more 'pubby' then the mistake and regret will be yours. The Kean's Head is a city pub not to be missed.

For a start it's owned by the locally-based Tyne Mill pub chain, which also own Castle Rock, makers of the shimmering Harvest Pale, 2010's Champion Beer of Britain. This is a company that majors in cask beer, serving intelligently chosen guest beers alongside its own range, while its pubs set themselves squarely in the heart of their community. Awards have been showered on both pubs and beer like applause from the Gods. The Kean's Head, named after the venerable Victorian thesp, is one of their jewels in the crown – good beer, fab food and a pleasing sense of friendliness.

Inside the Kean's Head is a roomy high-ceilinged bar in which a gaggle of sandy-coloured wooden tables and chairs stand in a line, with long-legged stools lining the wall. A thick iron pillar reaches to the sky on one side (prior to the 1970s this used to be a lace factory), while the bar is at the back. Skylights in the sloping roof above put one in mind of a hip loft conversion crossed with a ski lodge. Love at first sight this is

not, but be patient and wait a while as the Kean's Head transforms your expectations.

First the ambience: it's a relaxed place with conversation from the youngish and mixed crowd providing the mood music. Students, businessmen, couples and beer hounds all take their time out here. Six cask beers are usually on tap, including the aforementioned Harvest Pale plus other Castle Rock choices. Their Screech Owl comes highly commended, a spicy, peppery bad tempered but loveable grouch of an IPA. Guest beers include those from Thornbridge and Oakham. Belgian and American craft beers also wait their turn in the cool cabinets behind the bar.

Then there's the food – old fashioned, hearty plates of home-made Scotch eggs, bubble and squeak and corned beef hash have their fans, but the home-made fish fingers scale new heights of pub food. They were originally made for the kids' menu, but the adults started ordering them and there they ended up on the main menu. Why should children have all the fun!

Opening hours: 11.30–11 (12.30am Fri & Sat); 12–10.30 Sun

King's Head

42 Magdalen Street, Norwich,
Norfolk, NR3 1JE
01603 620468
www.kingsheadnorwich.co.uk
🍺 Winter's King's Head Bitter; Woodforde's
Nelson's Revenge; guest beers

• •

When you're waiting for a beer in the back bar of the King's Head take a look upwards and note the ancient Watneys Red font resting on a shelf; a warning from history, or a folk devil perhaps to make sure that such a beer never returns again. Not that there's any chance of seeing one of the most reviled British beers return to the King's Head (or anywhere else for that matter), as an evening in Norwich would demonstrate.

The place positively oozes great pubs; pubs like the King's Head. On my visit there were 11 cask beers on display, all of them chalked up on a blackboard, and all of them coming from East Anglia. I chose Grain's Blackwood Stout, a big mouthful of vanilla, chocolate and creamy oats – a man at the bar was also enjoying a glass of it and confided to me that he thought it like a delicious milk shake with a bite. However, I could have chosen Brandon's Rusty Bucket, Humpty Dumpty's Reed Cutter or Woodforde's Nelson's Revenge, to name but three. As well as a boisterous choice of beers there's a vibrancy and warmth about the King's Head and the people who drink there that encourages such a feeling of conviviality.

There are two bars at the King's Head. The front one is more sedate, a place to sit down and chat quietly over a pint. Pass through a short corridor to the back bar and you'll find a more vibrant and noisy atmosphere. There's the clack of balls from over at the French Billiards table, while regulars crack jokes, tell tales of old Norwich pubs and clubs and occasionally bring in vegetables from their allotments for other regulars (one man bought in a bag of spring onions as I stood there contemplating my Blackwood Stout).

Talking of onions, some people might not take to the King's Head for the simple fact that there's no food, but that would be their loss. This is the English pub as a home from home, even though most of us wouldn't want a home decorated as austerely as the King's Head – there's a 1930s functionality about the place with some framed beer related posters on the wall, while settles and stools offer austere comfort.

And when you leave have a look at the arch to the left of the pub. Just above you can see the word 'Brewery' picked out in stone. If you can find out the name of the brewery that might have been here please let the landlord know – so far he's drawn a blank and would love to know.

The best **city pubs**

Opening hours: 12-midnight (11 Sun)
Also great for: Beer range

North Bar

24 New Briggate, Leeds,
West Yorkshire, LS1 6NU
0113 242 4540
www.northbar.com

🍺 **Outlaw Wild Mule; guest beers**

• •

Appearances can be deceptive. Take yourself into Leeds city centre and seek out North Bar; from the outside it looks like it could be yet another trendy bar where bright young things sip Manhattans or champagne. However, at North Bar they're all drinking beer – and also talking about it. It's not unusual to eavesdrop on conversations about the merits of chocolate stout or Berliner Weisse between drinkers who wouldn't look out of place in happening indie bands or at the coalface of the 'creative business'. Lads in their late 20s drink beer from handled mugs; women of all ages ask about porter, while more traditional beer fans come in search of something different. Everyone is welcome here – and every beer drinker has something to say.

And what a choice of beer…

The range of stainless steel taps offer rarities from Bavaria, California and Flanders, while four handpumps present a quartet of real ales from closer to home. The chalked up menu has information on the ales including the beer miles – on my visit Abbeydale's Black Mass, a rich and strong stout, was on. According to the menu it was brewed a mere 30 miles away in Sheffield, while the regular cask beer Outlaw Wild Mule came in from Rooster's in Knaresborough. Look around North Bar and your eyes are drawn to all manner of beer memorabilia. For those in need of divine intervention, a sign commanding 'Thou shalt drink Trappist ales' offers advice. Elsewhere there are dozens of bottled beers from all over the world.

North Bar has been open since 1997. Photographs on the website show a gutted narrow space, into which has been elbowed its bar of many beers, while time has helped to develop its beery ethics (its original inspirations were the beer cafés of Belgium). The bar was also a forerunner of things to come: it is part of a company that also includes the quirky Mr Frothy, a retro ice cream van that operates as a mobile beer bar for outside events.

Beer and food? What could be simpler than the sort of snacks that beer is an ideal companion to? The day-long menu features cheese and bread, cold meats and local pies boasting such fillings as balsamic beer and potato, or beetroot with horseradish and Wensleydale. The tapas of the beer world, pork scratchings, can also be bought.

Whether craft beer from around the globe or cask ale from up the road, North Bar is a beer paradise. Appearances can be so deceptive.

Opening hours: 12–2am (1am Mon & Tue); 12–midnight Sun

The best **city pubs**

Old Green Tree

12 Green Street, Bath, Somerset, BA1 2JZ
01225 448259

🍺 **Blindmans Green Tree Bitter;
RCH Pitchfork; guest beers**

• •

I was in the Old Green Tree on the day that England won the Rugby World Cup back in 2003. The venerable old pub was crammed with excited fans and supporters, all celebrating. A couple of young women wearing Australian rugby shirts came in, looking a bit nervous. They needn't have worried – as soon as they entered the front bar, someone called out 'Hard luck,' while another voice asked them what they wanted to drink. For me this was a shining example of the pub as a democratic and charismatic place where all are welcome, even Australian rugby supporters.

Even though Rugby World Cup victories probably only come once a generation, the ambience at the Old Green Tree always has a good-natured feel. Even in such a well-visited tourist honey-pot as Bath, the pub has kept its cast of locals, while tourists looking for a genuine British pub experience rarely leave unsatisfied. For this reason alone, the Old Green Tree is a popular city centre pub for those who like to drink their cask beer in surroundings that reek of pub life before the brewing industry's version of Attila and his Huns were let loose in the 1960s.

It's been around for a long time, some say over 200 years. Looking at it, there is a hint of Dickens about its frontage: a big wide window divided into panes, almost in the style of The Old Curiosity Shop. Inside, there are three rooms – a front lounge, the bar and a back room. The décor throughout is a study in dark brown oak panels, giving the effect of a refuge from the madness of the city's shops on the outside.

Cask beer has always been a big draw here, with regulars from Blindmans and RCH being joined by beers from the likes of Butcombe and Wickwar. The latter's Station Porter is a frequent visitor, a creamy and chocolatey dark delight that's produced a few miles away. Food is traditional and fancy free, including soup, sandwiches, and sausage and mash.

Bath is a great pub city, and there are many places to choose from, but the Old Green Tree stands out because of its stubborn refusal to blow with the winds of pub fashion.

Opening hours: 11–11; 12–10.30 Sun
Also great for: Heritage

Port Street Beer House

39–41 Port Street, Manchester, M1 2EQ
www.portstreetbeerhouse.co.uk
0161 237 9949

🍺 **Beer range varies**

• •

Newly opened at the start of 2011, this is the youngest pub in the book, but it's well worth the entry and yet another reason for taking a beer holiday in Manchester (see the Marble Arch on p47 for starters). Located in the fashionably, carelessly hip Northern Quarter, the Port Street Beer House (or PSBH as devotees call it) doesn't shout or try to grab passers-by and drag them in. Instead, there's a quiet confidence that people will come. This sense of self-belief is such that you could easily walk past and miss it, which would be a shame. Big windows, a three-storeyed brick building with a bar on two floors, its name small and unobtrusive – this is not a pub with a history, you don't enter and wonder what the locals were doing in here on VE night.

Yes, it's a place that poses more questions than answers. Is it a pub or a bar? It has the architectural feel of a trendy bar but then beer is the main attraction. And yes it sells cask beer, five of them, constantly rotating – if you're lucky you might find Infra Red from Hardknott, a ruby red confection of hard-edged citrusy hoppiness, with a dryness that leaves the mouth wanting more. And wanting more beer is what PSBH is all about. There's an encyclopaedic selection of classic bottled beers from all over the world: American and Italian craft beers, a worthy selection from British beer trendsetters BrewDog, Thornbridge, Kernel and Dark Star, plus of course a few classics from Belgian and Germany.

The makeover is modern. Wooden floorboards have been sanded. The tables and chairs are without frills, but as befits something so fresh and new it has a positive sense of its youth that attracts a varied mixture of beer lovers – students in skinny jeans, rock fans and the art school crowd, confident young women, pensive looking young guys with wispy beards and glad, middle aged beer guys who start behaving like kids in a sweetshop. Visit PSBH and let the questions start: sometimes it's good to be without answers.

Opening hours: 4–midnight; 12–1am Sat;
12–midnight Sun
Also great for: Pub design

Royal Oak

44 Tabard Street, Borough, London, SE1 4JU
020 7357 7173
www.harveys.org.uk

🍺 **Harveys Sussex XX Mild,
Hadlow Bitter, Sussex Best Bitter,
seasonal beers; guest beer**

• •

The British pub is more than a place to drink beer and is also more than an eating-house. The best are a community of like-minded souls, centres of both conversation and contemplation. A trip to the Royal Oak in Borough, Harveys' sole London pub, is more than popping out for a quick one – this is one life-affirming home from home.

Down Tabard Street, supposedly close to the long-gone inn from where Chaucer's merry pilgrims departed for Canterbury, is where you will find this unpretentious street corner two-room pub. The vibrancy of Borough Market is less than a mile away, and walking down Borough High Street you will pass the old Hop Exchange – a pleasing if slightly poignant reminder of the days when Kentish hops came north and East Enders went south during the hop harvest.

Stand outside the Royal Oak, glance through the engraved glass windows and you'll see plenty of dark wood, a row of handpumps standing as straight-backed as guardsmen and ornate Victorian touches on the back bar. Once inside, the only sound is the hum of chatter and your feet as they cross the wooden floorboards. The main bar is wide and open, the ceiling a traditional nicotine colour, while decorative plasterwork circles the lights. Next door there's a smaller more compact place, the saloon; perhaps the best place to enjoy a meal with your glass, before heading back to the main bar for conversation. Given that the interior harks back to the Victorian age, it's a surprise to discover that it's not always been that way. Harveys only started trading here in August 1997, when they bought a rundown pub that no one expected they could salvage – but they did.

Unsurprisingly, this is a pub where locals gather, sometimes joined by classical musicians rehearsing at the close to hand Trinity Square. Meanwhile connoisseurs in search of Harveys ales come to pay their respects and study the refreshing and chocolatey Mild and the muscular, bittersweet bravado of the Sussex Best Bitter. During the winter months Harveys incredibly complex Porter is available: a confection of treacle toffee, chocolate, vinous fruit, saddle leather, tobacco box and even hints of dandelion and burdock. Time spent studying and appreciating this beer at the Royal Oak is time well spent.

Opening hours: 11 (12 Sat)–11; 12–6 Sun

The best **city pubs**

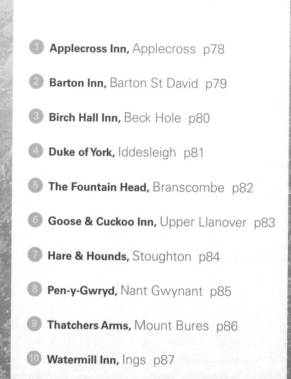

The best
country pubs

Deep in the heart of the countryside the rural inn stands as it has stood for decades (and sometimes generations), a place that sustains and nourishes the community which has grown around and about it.

Sometimes it growls at the passing world from its heartland of splendid isolation, somewhere perhaps like the Pen-y-Gwryd, in the middle of the vast mountains of Snowdonia. Or maybe it's the coastal remoteness of the Applecross Inn, whose home village can only be reached by two roads, one of which is the highest mountain road in Scotland. On other occasions the rural pub is in the heart of the village, somewhere just like the Duke of York in Iddesleigh, an aged and much loved place that that most elemental of nature poets Ted Hughes was known to drop in at for an ale.

This selection of country pubs might carry the authentic stamp of rustic life, yet the pubs detailed within are not divorced from the wider world – the Watermill Inn has its own brewery while the Thatchers Arms, which sits on a ridge overlooking both Stour and Colne valleys, organises a variety of beer- and cinema-related events. Like love, the country pub is a many splendored thing.

**See also
Barrasford
Arms**,
Barrasford (p207)
Bell, Pensax (p261)
Black Horse,
Clapton in
Gordano (p119)
**King's Head
(Low House)**,
Laxfield (p158)
Square & Compass,
Worth Matravers
(p278)
Woodman,
Wildhill (p190)

Applecross Inn

Shore Street, Applecross, Strathcarron,
Highland, IV54 8LR
01520 744262
www.applecross.uk.com/inn
🍺 **Beer range varies**

Remote is the first (and probably only) word that springs to mind when considering the location of the Applecross Inn. Embedded in the Highlands, it's hidden away on the Applecross peninsula to which only two roads offer access, one of which takes the intrepid traveller over the Bealach Na Ba pass. At 626 metres, this is the highest mountain road in Scotland, offering an Alpine-like journey of hairpin bends with breathtaking views over the Inner Sound that separates the Isles of Skye and Raasay from the mainland.

Applecross itself is a small settlement but the inn has a massive reputation. It sits amid a terrace of fishermen's cottages. Inside, the décor is laid-back and homely – slate floors, wood panelling and stone walls, while all the bedrooms face the sea.

It hasn't always been a pub. According to landlady Judith Fish, who moved in on the auspicious date of Friday January 13, 1989, 'It was formerly a Temperance House until about 50 years ago and when it got a seven-day licence the story goes that the local minister laid across the door threshold in the hope of deterring customers – obviously to no avail.'

The gorgeous location is a great draw, bringing in folk from around the world but the food its kitchen produces is no less a part of the appeal. With the nearness of the Sound, seafood is naturally a big part of the menu – perhaps a plate of fresh haddock in batter with homemade tartare sauce or maybe king scallops in garlic bread? Given that the Highlands is home to thousands of deer, it also is no surprise that venison also plays a great part in the proceedings with whole stags bought from Applecross Estate (along with beef, pork and lamb) and then butchered in house.

In such a remote place, cask beer is always going to be a delicate issue. Too many choices and the chance of beer going off is pretty high. However, the Applecross approaches the concern with due care and attention. Two cask beers are usually available, both from the Isle of Skye Brewery. 'They installed the pumps when no one else would,' says Fish, 'and it has paid off for them too, as we are nearly their best customer.' The brewery's Blaven is the bestseller, a bold blonde featuring floral notes on the nose with juicy citrus fruit on the palate before its dry, appetising finish. Red Cuillin follows closely in the popularity stakes. For devotees of malt whisky, there is pretty strong selection as well. Good food and good drink – could that be the ghost of a dismayed temperance drinker in room four?

Opening hours: 11–11.30 (midnight Fri); 12.30–11.30 Sun
Also great for: Seaside

Barton Inn

Main Street, Barton St David,
Somerset, TA11 6BZ
01458 850451
www.barton-inn.co.uk

🍺 **Beer range varies**

· ·

Quietly, in the middle of nowhere, stands the Barton Inn, a village pub on the eastern edge of the Somerset Levels, a flat land riven with myriad channels and ditches. This curious landscape is cider country, dotted with weathered apple trees grouped into orchards that have stood the test of time. The Barton Inn also has a sense of time and mystery about it. Stand outside the pub and look north: Glastonbury Tor, with all its Arthurian and druidical connections, is five miles away. However this is not a pub away with the fairies, though the sight of the pub's name upside down on the outside wall suggests a puckish sense of humour.

Inside, there's an island bar dividing the 'public bar' from the 'lounge', though there's little sense of 'us and them' between the two rooms. Both of them share the same eclectic and quirky sense of decoration, with all sorts of artefacts on the walls and lying around. The 'lounge' for instance features a piano, puppets, a surfboard, a plaster arm holding a small lantern and even cinema seats (there are regular movie nights during the winter). It's an expansive area, a space that encourages you to sit down and sprawl out, almost as if it's someone's eccentric idea of a front room, the countryside meets bohemian life.

In the public bar ales are served from barrels behind the bar (Cheddar's Potholer and Glastonbury's Holy Thorn were on during my visit

and the pub is a big supporter of local breweries). As you would expect there is also a good selection of Somerset cider, both on draught and in bottle (Orchard Pig from nearby Glastonbury).

It was also lunchtime. 'Are you doing lunch?' I asked, and the friendly woman behind the bar smiled. 'Of course. We've got baguettes, scampi and the pizza menu.' She pointed to a blackboard. 'Oh, and there might be a bit of chilli left too.' I settled for the baguette – sausage and onion. The bread was fresh and the sausages meaty and juicy – a simple dish but utterly delicious.

In the public bar, the conversation came and went: a discussion of pews in a local church and that old rural constant: the weather. 'It's not a day for sitting in a ditch with a shotgun,' opined one man with his pewter tankard full of ale. I could only agree and carry on enjoying the Barton.

Opening hours: 12–2.30, 4.30–11 (midnight Sat & Sun)
Also great for: Cider; Entertainment

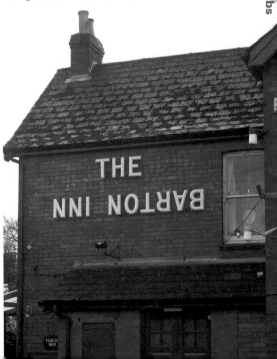

Birch Hall Inn

Beck Hole, North Yorkshire, YO22 5LE
01947 896245
www.beckhole.info

🍺 **Black Sheep Best Bitter; North Yorkshire Beckwatter; guest beers**

• •

If you've got a sweet tooth then you'll be in heaven at the Birch Hall Inn. At a small counter squeezed in between the two bars at this long-established, well-loved pub in the North Yorkshire Moors, you can buy such old-fashioned delights as aniseed balls, pear drops and the pub's own fudge. Or you can go straight to the bar and order a pint of Beckwatter, which is specially brewed by North Yorkshire Brewery; try it with one of the pub's pork pies and chutney and you'll be in another universe. Beer, sweets and pies: this all just about sums up the appeal of the pub as it mixes old style country pub ambience, robust Yorkshire ales and a quirky, slanted view of the world.

Beck Hole is a hamlet set in a wooded, steep-sided valley on a country lane north of Goathland, home of the TV series *Heartbeat*. The roads are narrow so the place is spared the tourist coaches that can cause so much chaos in many other beauty spots. It's a tranquil place today, but there was a brief boom of industralisation when the railway came in the 19th century. Miners moved to the area and no doubt the licensees of the day (there were two pubs in Beck Hole then) made the most of their opportunities.

The pub consists of a whitewashed 18th century cottage attached to a three-storeyed Victorian former shop, which also offered rooms to miners at the time. Step inside and you will find two bars. The one in the cottage is called the 'big bar' and offers wall-side seats, old photos, a wall of colourful wallpaper and a genuine sense of cloistered comfort. The 'small bar' is exactly that and features several shelves of odds and sods, while the record for the amount of people crammed into its space is 30 folk along with two small dogs.

Despite what might seem the isolation of the Birch Hall Inn, this is a rather busy place with walkers taking advantage of the gorgeous scenery and plenty of people making the journey just to visit the pub. There's even a quoits team who play in a local league.

The Birch Hall Inn is a country gem and a good beery stop. Though do go easy on the sweets.

Opening hours: 11–11 summer; 11–3, 7.30–11 (closed Mon eve & Tue) winter

The best **country pubs**

Duke of York

Iddesleigh, Devon, EX19 8BG
01837 810253

🍺 **Adnams Broadside; Cotleigh Tawny Owl; guest beers**

• •

On the walls in the bar of the Duke of York hang several framed black and white photos. One is a fading sepia-tinted photo from 1911 that shows a column of men in suits, battered bowlers and starched white collars as they take part in the Iddesleigh Club Walk (something that continues annually to this day) – three years later a line of men like this would be khaki clad and marching off to war (you can't help but see the dreadful progression). Pubs are for people and these framed photos depict those that enjoyed the Duke of York in the past, and in a fanciful moment you imagine that by some miraculous transformation their voices are ingrained in the very fabric of this old assemblage of four cottages that was originally constructed for the masons who built the neighbouring church in the Middle Ages.

This is a pub with pedigree. Ted Hughes was apparently a regular, as was, in earlier days, the famous hunting parson and dog breeder Jack Russell (dogs are much welcomed). In recent years it's also gained TV fame, appearing as the Black Bull in the BBC series *Down To Earth*. Yet this sense of celebrity has not changed the place in the years that I have been visiting it. Old bottles and pumpclips still stand above the bar, some of them mementoes of breweries that have long shuffled off the mortal coil (Wards anyone?), others from a time when they were in their infancy and design was the last thing on their mind. Meanwhile, in an interior that a pub consultant might entitle a study in brown (nicotine ceilings and wall panels, old smoke-stained banknotes pinned to the beams, the sense of the bar wreathed in a patina of age), the beer is served straight from the barrel. 'It's always been like this,' I'm told. The Adnams Broadside is full-bodied, a plump and lively pint with a full palette of flavour that would not be out of place in an artist's garret.

On both sides of the bar, separate wings almost, is where people retire for food. The space to the right of the bar is an annex, while the one to the left seems a bit more formal. Food is wholesome, good-natured and often quixotic: paroka vegetable balls curry favour with some, while a Thai red king prawn curry attracts those in need of spice. However, there's plenty for everyone.

Easy going and comfortable, as English as spring rain and cottage pie, and offering views over Devon fields towards the monolithic hulk of Dartmoor, the Duke of York is possibly one of the greatest pubs in England.

Opening hours: 11–11 (midnight Fri & Sat); 12–10.30 Sun

The Fountain Head

Branscombe, Seaton, Devon, EX12 3BG
01297 680 359
www.fountainheadinn.com

🍺 **Branscombe Vale Branoc, Summa That;
guest beers**

• •

Branscombe is the sort of place that is easy to fall in love with (and many do – this is a popular place for tourists). It's a long village, with some claiming that it is the longest in England; yet it's spread out and widely dispersed, as it trickles down to the English Channel through a beautiful steep sided valley. Thatched roofs and cosy cottages abound down these deep Devon lanes, while at the bottom of the valley the South West Coast Path passes on its way, attracting the sturdy of foot as they tramp along some of the most gorgeous coastal scenery in England.

The Fountain Head also possesses a beauty of its own: step through the door and you're in a roomy, well-worn front bar in which a massive ancient stone fireplace takes pride of place to the right. The bar is in the corner, small and

booth-like, dispensing three cask beers, all of which come from Branscombe Vale brewery who brew about a mile away in old farm buildings leased from the National Trust (you could say that the Fountain is an unofficial tap for the brewery). It's roomy and the handful of tables suggest that it is a place that attracts those who just want a drink as well as those attracted by the food (there is a comfortable dining room round to the left of the bar in a room that was once a forge). Note the well-used dartboard on the wall to the left, another sign that this is a place popular with both locals and visitors. You get the feeling that little has changed here over the years – look at the photo of the pub from the 1920s that hangs above the fireplace and it could have been yesterday.

Sit there at lunchtime and listen to the banter ebb and flow. Builders come in for a lunchtime pint, walkers greet the landlord like an old friend, while locals wander in and salute each other with a beery welcome and get down to the business in hand: conversation. This is the pub as a club, a meeting place, a forum and a discussion group. New members always welcome. The menu uses the pub's own home-grown fruit and vegetables and is compact, calm and attractive and very tempting: home-cured trout, freshly caught crab salad or beef and Branoc pie.

Life has not always been so tranquil in Branscombe. In 2007, the bay was awash with latter-day wreckers hunting down motorbikes and wine casks as booty from the beached *MSC Napoli* was washed ashore. Chances are that The Fountain Head would have provided a necessary refuge from all the mayhem.

Opening hours: 11–3, 6–11; 12–3, 6–10.30 Sun

Goose & Cuckoo Inn

Upper Llanover, Abergavenny,
Monmouthshire, NP7 9ER
01873 880277
www.gooseandcuckoo.com

🍺 **Beer range varies**

. . . .

Leafy lanes, narrow of course, lead up to
the Goose & Cuckoo Inn. Some would say
it's halfway up a hill – but this is an area with
plenty of hills. And when you arrive there's an
old farmhouse of an inn standing on the road,
painted white, with a demur kind of character,
yet confident in the time it's been standing here
offering sustenance. Drovers once used to pass
by, en route to Abergavenny, but now it's the
walker whose boots cross the threshold, along
with regulars from the surrounding farms. Inside,
as you'd imagine (or perhaps hope), it's rustic
and comfortable with original flagstone flooring,
old photos of the pub from a century ago, plus
wooden benches and a pew. *Tempus fugit*: there's
also an ancient German-made cuckoo clock.

Glass in hand? Local beers are supported with
a passion and there are normally four to enjoy.
Perhaps a glass of Rhymney's delicious award-
winning Dark or something from the Otley boys
of Pontypridd. Other beers at the bar might
come from Newmans (Red Stag goes down
well), Brecon and Bullmastiff. Accommodation is
also available while the compact menu includes
homemade soups and robustly filled rolls.

Yet the history of the Goose & Cuckoo could
have all been too different. Down below in the
valley sits Llanover, at one time home to Lady
Llanover, famous for introducing the stovepipe
hat and shawl that is nowadays seen as traditional
costume for Welsh women. She was also a
fanatical teetotaller and managed to get all the
local pubs closed. However, her plans were foiled
when it came to the drovers' pub halfway up the
hill – as it was outside her estate boundary. So
when you stand in this pub's homely if rough-hewn
interior recall this close shave with the forces of
intolerance and offer a small toast to its survival.

Opening hours: 11.30–3, 7–11; 11.30–11 Fri & Sat;
12–10.30 Sun; closed Mon

The best **country pubs**

Hare & Hounds

Stoughton, West Sussex, PO18 9JQ
02392 631433
www.hareandhoundspub.co.uk

🍺 **Ballards Best Bitter; Harveys Sussex Best Bitter; Otter Amber; Taylor Landlord; guest beer**

• •

Whichever way you head out from the Hare & Hounds you find yourself in walking heaven. Set in the village of Stoughton in the heart of the rolling South Downs, the pub has been quenching the thirsts and sating the appetites of eager walkers since the 19th century. Ancient burial grounds and ageless woodlands; rolling farmland and distant sea views; wild flowers and lilting birdsong – it's all very lovely. The Monarch's Way long distance footpath snakes through the village from west to east, for those who like a longer challenge.

The Hare & Hounds is a comfortable place, a pleasing mix of the sophisticated and the simple; the aspirational and the easy-going. All are welcome in this traditional unpretentious-looking hostelry: children will enjoy watching the cows and horses in the garden (they're also allowed in eating areas); dogs will want to stretch out in front of the welcoming log fires. Real ale lovers will sigh happily at the well-kept cask ales, of which there are at least four available – a choice that covers north, south and west. Otter's relatively new Amber is a popular choice, a sprightly bittersweet beer that dances in the glass.

Foodies will want to let out their belts as food is a big deal here, with an inventive and imaginative menu that's big on fresh tastes. Vegetarians don't get palmed off with pasta –

broad bean, feta, mint and rocket salad with lemon oil for instance, or chestnut mushroom risotto with spinach, butternut squash, parmesan and basil oil. Fish and meat eaters are done proud too – tempura squid with sticky ginger and chilli dipping sauce? Steak frites with tarragon peppercorn butter? The menu changes frequently and it's worth checking out the website if you're after something in particular.

It isn't all gastro-fare though. They do a darn fine roast beef sandwich too and a hearty honest-to-God ploughman's. And, although food figures heavily, you don't have to eat – the public bar is a drinker's haven, where you can sink a few pints and throw a few darts. Then, refreshed and recharged, you can venture once more into the landscape, suffused with that sense of timelessness that all good traditional pubs impart.

Opening hours: 11–3, 6–11; 11–11 Fri & Sat; 12–10.30 Sun

Pen-y-Gwryd

Nant Gwynant, Gwynedd, LL55 4NT
01286 870211
www.pyg.co.uk

🍺 **Purple Moose Cwrw Madog,
Cwrw Glaslyn**

• •

A solidly built 19th century pub and hotel, the Pen-y-Gwryd stands alone astride the junction on the road that cuts through the magnificent mountain scenery between Capel Curig and Beddgelert and the one that descends to Llanberis Pass. This is a land of brooding peaks and ridges, rocky outcrops, scattered scree slopes and rain-soaked moorland. If you're preparing for an assault on Snowdon itself, this is an ideal base, something that has not escaped mountaineers over the last couple of centuries. For instance, Sir Edmund Hillary's Everest expedition stayed here whilst training for their ascent of the monarch of mountains.

This connection with the men and women who spend their lives looking for the hardest way up a rock face is amply reflected in one of the rooms off the central corridor. It has the feel of a mountain log cabin, with every available space on the wall and ceiling covered with the signatures of distinguished mountaineers over the past century, including Chris Bonington, James (now Jan) Morris and Joe Brown. You can even see the scrawl of the legendary George Mallory, the man who wanted to climb Everest 'because it was there'; sadly the mountain claimed him in 1924.

The climbing theme continues throughout: another room has bundles of well-worn climbing boots, all donated by past customers, while prints, photos, memorabilia and maps offer the armchair mountaineer the chance to dream without flexing a single muscle. On a more practical note, the weather forecast for the mountains is also posted up daily.

The menu is reassuringly short and assured. The hearty filled rolls (BLT, hot sausage etc) come with a perfectly dressed salad. Smoked duck salad is delightfully zingy while the sweet potato and coconut soup is delicate and warming. Local brewery Purple Moose supplies the cask beers at the bar, including the sprightly Glaslyn Ale.

Whether you're walking, climbing or just passing by, the mountains of Snowdonia induce an appetite and a thirst for good beer – and the Pen-y-Gwryd comes up trumps.

The best country pubs

Opening hours: 11–11; 11–4 Sun Jan & Feb;
closed Nov & Dec and Sun–Thu Jan & Feb
Also great for: Sporting

Thatchers Arms

Mount Bures, Essex, CO8 5AT
01787 227460
www.thatchersarms.co.uk
🍺 **Adnams Best Bitter; Crouch Vale
Brewers Gold; guest beers**

· ·

When the railway came charging through this
beautiful piece of countryside in the late 1840s,
the owners of a recently built cottage decided it
was time to get a slice of the action. The cottage
applied for a license and set up shop as a beer
house to cater for the needs of the thirsty workers.
The doors of the Thatchers Arms have remained
open and its pumps dispensing beer ever since.

Nowadays, it's walkers rather than navvies
who step inside. After a ramble amid the gentle
delights of the Stour Valley they're ready for a
plate of locally cured ham, egg and chunky chips
accompanied by a pint of Crouch Vale's Brewer's
Gold (pale gold, passion fruit, plus banana on the
nose, a hint of grapefruit on the palate and a subtle

yet crisp cereal background). And those with an
ecological temperament will be soothed by the
fact that the pub's menu displays both the food
miles and the names of its producers.

As for natural beauty, the pub has the best of
both worlds: it sits atop a ridge that overlooks
both the Stour and Colne valleys; families, locals,
visitors and dogs all find their way here. In the
summer, you can stroll outside in the beer garden.
Inside, it's friendly and comfortable for when the
weather turns and you just have to order another
pint. A lot also goes on here: there's a golf society,
bar billiards and a quoits team. A cinema sets up
shop in the function room every Thursday, while
beer festivals are held twice a year.

Situated on the Essex-Suffolk border ('we're the
last pub in Essex,' jokes landlord Mitch Adams), the
Thatchers Arms is the sort of establishment that
encourages contemplation of the British pub at its
best amid a soothing scene of rural tranquillity.

Opening hours: 12–3, 6–11; 12–11 Sat & Sun;
closed Mon
Also great for: Entertainment

Watermill Inn

Ings, nr Kendal, Cumbria, LA8 9PY
01539 821309
www.watermillinn.co.uk

Coniston Bluebird; Theakston Old
Peculier; Watermill Collie Wobbles,
A Bit'er Ruff, Wruff Night, Dog'th Vader;
guest beers

• •

This long rambling building of natural undressed
stone, swathed in greenery with a balcony
running along one half, could simply rely on
its gorgeous Lake District location, close to
the tourist honeypot of Windermere, to bring
in the punters. But that would be lazy and the
Watermill has all the restless, exuberant energy
of a border collie.

In fact the whole place has a doggy theme.
Man's best friend is welcomed in the main bar –
the locals often moan that their dogs frequently
get served before they do. Water and biscuits
are readily available and, should you decide to
stay overnight (dogs pay £3 a night, with £1
going to the Dogs Trust), your four-legged friend
may well find an extra sausage or two on the
plate come breakfast.

The canine theme extends to the attached
brewery, which produces a range of beers, all
with vaguely doggy names. The award-winning
Collie Wobbles is a firm favourite, pale gold in
colour, citrus on the palate with a bitter finish. In
fact beer is taken very seriously here. Sixteen
handpumps cater for pretty well all tastes: the
chalk board gives a style guide to the beers
available, helping to make impossible choices a
little easier. You can even see the cellar through a
viewing window in the main bar.

It is heartening to see they don't take bookings
for food. You simply sit wherever you like and
order whatever you feel like… if you just feel like
a bowl of soup or a pudding (or two) that's fine.
Equally there are more solid platefuls on offer,
such as local Cumberland sausage on a bed of
mash or their own homemade chilli and coriander
burger. Steaks are also big here. Children are
welcome and well catered for – and walkers
staying over may request a solid packed lunch to
fortify them the next day.

Landlord Brian Coulthwaite has a formula for
a successful pub: 'Real ale + real food + real
atmosphere = real pub.' But really, you can't
reduce the Watermill to a formula. It's big-
hearted, with its tail permanently wagging; well-
disciplined yet always up for fun. There are regular
story telling nights and live music. They even
have a pirate charity day in aid of the Alzheimer's
Society. In inimitable Watermill fashion this has its
own unique event – collie wobbling. You balance
on a wobbly, spring-mounted platform and throw
a sack resembling a border collie as far as you
can. Woof woof.

The best country pubs

Opening hours: 12–11; 12–10.30 Sun
Also great for: Brewpubs

The best **riverside pubs**

A river runs past these pubs, but sometimes, as with The Bridge in Dulverton the river runs through the pub, as it did in the 1950s when heavy rain on Exmoor saw the moorland's normally benign rivers run feral and cause damage wherever they flowed (famously this was the occasion when the coastal village of Lynmouth was devastated by the Lyn). Meanwhile the Mug House in Bewdley has seen both the best and the worse of the Severn, most recently in 2000.

Rivers also mark differences. The river that passes the Bridge Inn in Kentchurch separates England from Wales while the Bounty in Cookham has no road and sees its beer being brought in by boat. Water inside the pub is not always bad for trade – at the Canalhouse in Nottingham you'll often see a brace of narrow boats moored together on the canal that sits within the pub (don't jump in though – it's not very deep). The slow and stately Thames passes the Dove in Hammersmith – just the spot for catching the action on Boat Race day.

There's nothing so tranquil or relaxing as enjoying a beer by the banks of the river and this selection offers up a goodly choice of watery pleasures.

See also

The Apple,
Bristol (p54)
Bridge Inn,
Topsham (p151)
Ferryboat Inn,
Thorganby (p223)
Waterman's Arms,
Totnes (p203)

◀ Outside the Old Bridge Inn, Aviemore

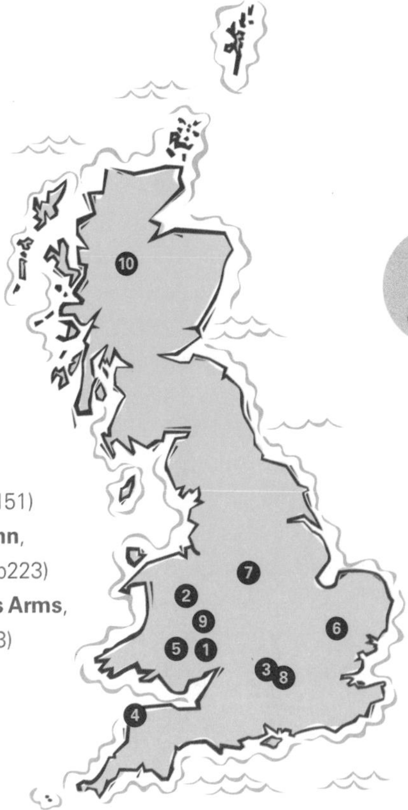

Boat Inn

The Quay, Ashleworth,
Gloucestershire, GL19 4HZ
01452 700272
www.boat-inn.co.uk

🍺 **Beer range varies**

• •

The Boat Inn is an ancient establishment that sits on the Severn where the local ferry once worked the river. The pub's a bit of a lone ranger as the rest of the village is on higher ground about a mile away (fear of flooding perhaps, something which last happened to the Boat in 2007), but this hasn't stopped this country gem from thriving and winning all manner of awards.

Is it something to do with the pedigree? The pub has been under the control of the same family – the Jelfs – for over several centuries apparently. One story has Charles II granting a Jelf the right to operate the Ashleworth ferry crossing and sell ale after he'd been ferried across when on the run following the Battle of Worcester. The family then had a farmhouse where the inn now stands. Other records talk of Jelfs in the village back during the War of the Roses. Whatever the truth of the matter, there's a wonderful sense of history and continuity when you think of such a longstanding family link. Not many pubs can boast of such a timeline.

So what to expect? The Boat Inn has the look of a redbrick farmhouse, added to and improved on over the centuries, weathered without being too battered. Look keenly at the small building to the side – it is thought that this was a brewhouse. Inside those tempting pub words 'front parlour'

spring to mind. The bar features a built in settle and flagstone floors and there's a patina of age about the bar and the back room. If it's sunny though you will want to be outside, engaging with the mood of the Severn, watching it as it travels on towards its inevitable destiny.

Four beers are always on, all served straight from their casks, which are kept in a temperature cooled room to the back of the bar. Breweries such as Wye Valley, Box Steam and RCH feature and one of the beers is always either a mild, porter or a stout. Cider lovers will be pleased to discover a selection of Westons. Rolls are served during lunchtime but beer and the fabulous location are the attractions here.

It's no secret that the Merrie Monarch liked a drop or two. He obviously had his priorities right on his passage through here all those years ago when he decided to reward the farmer that helped him.

Opening hours: 11.30–2.30 (not Wed; 3 Sat), 6.30–11 (7 winter); 12–3, 7–10.30 Sun; closed Mon
Also great for: Heritage

Boathouse

New Street, Shrewsbury,
Shropshire, SY3 8JQ
01743 231658
www.theboathouse-shrewsbury.co.uk

🍺 **Salopian Darwins Origin; Wood
Shropshire Lad; guest beers**

. . . .

The Boathouse looks magical at night, with the
soft glow of its lights reflecting on the calm
waters of the Severn. It looks equally delicious by
day sitting, as it does, on the banks of the river.
Then again, you could argue that the best view of
all comes from its large (it can seat around 200
people) garden which looks over the water towards
the Quarry Park, 29 acres of beautifully laid-out
gardens whose centrepiece, the Dingle, is a formal
garden designed by the famous Percy Thrower. The
history of this place, however, is much darker –
witches used to go to the stake here.

The pub knows its strengths and makes the
most of its riverside setting with a garden bar
and frequent barbecues when the sun shines.
However the interior has its own charm too – it's
cosy and intimate with lots of wood, including the
original oak flooring that slants drunkenly every
which way, and there are stretches of exposed
brickwork that add to the charm. The windows are
tiny so it feels smaller than it probably is. A coffee
kiosk strikes a surprisingly modern note.

The staff are friendly and cope with the frequent
inrush of giddy tourists with calm efficient
equanimity. Food is pretty standard pub fare with
the usual sandwiches, jacket potatoes, steaks
and meals in a basket. However there are some
more adventurous choices, such as salmon, sweet
potato and coriander fishcakes, nachos with salsa
and char-grilled Cajun spiced salmon. Sunday is
carvery day and very popular it is too. Then there's
the beer: cask ales tend to stay local with the
regulars being joined by ales from the likes of
Hobsons, Three Tuns and the Six Bells breweries.

The Boathouse really does have location
written large all over it. Apart from being right on
the river, it's only a short stroll from the centre
of town. Inevitably it does attract a mixed crowd
and you'd think it could get a little raucous, but
somehow the steady movement of the river
keeps everything swimming along rather nicely.

Opening hours: 11–11; 12–11 Sun
Also great for: Pub gardens

The best **riverside pubs**

The slow stately progress of a narrow boat along a stretch of canal is a romantic ideal that might make even the most hardened land lubber long for the slower place of life it invites. The waterways of Britain cover several thousand miles – pleasure boats now ply the arterial former trading routes of the Industrial Revolution that were shaken from their key place by the coming of the railway and vanquished by the dominance of the motor vehicle. It's only been in the last 50 years that they have been rediscovered, cleaned up and become an egalitarian playground for anyone who loves messing about in boats. And alongside the river there still exist many of the pubs that once watered the thirsts of passing boatmen plying their way between Leeds and Liverpool or travelling south from the Midlands to London and the Thames.

And a pub doesn't have to stand alongside a canal for its waterside location to be a natural draw. Riverside pubs have their own sense of magic, offering a sense of tranquillity or the chance to observe the comings and goings of birds on the water. With pint in hand, there's always a Zen-like sense of contemplation to be gained by watching a patient angler hooking for a catch. There is a downside to all this water of course: in 1952, The Bridge inn in Dulverton (p94) was swamped by the Barle after a torrential downpour of rain further up on the high moors of Exmoor caused havoc. Yet, this is a rare thing; the contemplation of water adds an extra dimension to enjoying a beautiful pint of beer.

Bounty

Riverside, Cookham, Berkshire, SL8 5RG
01628 520056

🍺 **Rebellion IPA, Mutiny; guest beer**

. . . .

You can't drive a car to the Bounty. There's no road. You will have to walk along the towpath from Cookham or – as the pub sits on the Thames as it falls southwards towards Maidenhead – moor your boat and step ashore. On thinking of the car-free zone of the Bounty the most banal thoughts come to mind: it must be hell doing the shopping but then everything comes in by boat; even the casks of beer from Rebellion brewery.

In the years before the Second World War a hotel called the Quarry brought in the punters to where the Bounty now sits. The patch of land to the back of the pub, now owned by the National Trust, was large enough for planes to touch down. Within the pub, there's a photo of a group of planes parked up – one with a swastika on the wing; local lore has it that this might have belonged to the Nazi ambassador Von Ribbentrop, dropping in for a meeting with those members of the English upper classes that sympathised with Hitler. The hotel burnt down in the late 1930s and the field

behind was filled with old cars during the war so as to hinder any aspiring Nazi paratroops. Then the Moorings Inn was built, followed by a teashop, which all became the Bounty, where the current licensees have been for nearly quarter of a century.

Seen from across the river, the Bounty has an element of inter-war Brewers' Tudor about the frontage with its black and white beams; the attached single storey building looks more like a Swiss chalet. Inside, there's one big room with flags covering the ceiling and a back room used for dining (the menu is pubby, homemade and substantial). The bar is boat-shaped and alongside its two regular Rebellion brewery beers, serves a guest from the same brewery. Nautical memorabilia spreads itself throughout the place, including a variety of boat name-plates. The theme continues outside as the Thames flows by – grab a glass of Rebellion's bittersweet Mutiny and just watch the world flow by.

There is a sense of individuality about the Bounty, a quirky strangeness and charm that some people might not get. Walkers in muddy boots, families out for a walk and locals with a liking for a drink by the river all make their way here: carbon-neutral beer anyone?

Opening hours: 12–11 (winter 12–dusk Sat & Sun only)

The best **riverside pubs**

The Bridge

Bridge Street, Dulverton,
Somerset, TA22 9HJ
01398 324130
www.thebridgeinndulverton.com

🍺 **Exmoor Ale; St Austell Tribute; guest beers**

. . . .

As the name of this friendly town pub suggests, it's right next to a bridge. In this case a 19th century stone bridge over the Barle which tumbles down from the heights of Exmoor.

On a summer's afternoon, the Bridge has perhaps one of the best spots in town – children splash in the shallow slow-moving waters and the pub's outside tables will be filled with contented drinkers, both locals and visitors, Exmoor Ale (or whatever the guest beer is) in hand, basking in the sun. As evening draws in, the sun vanishes behind the hill – it's time to go into the pub.

Dulverton is a mixture of tourist destination and working Exmoor town and the Bridge reflects that mix. On the local side of things it fields a tug-o'-war team during the summer fete, while the autumn carnival has seen it provide its own award-winning float. Yet, tourists will also feel at home here, whether they come in by caravan, walk in from the moor or even drop in by canoe, as is wont to happen at times. This duality of character can also affect the mood music within the pub itself – a Saturday afternoon during the winter sees a stillness and quiet within its walls as people peruse the papers or just relax with a pint, the two woodburners dispensing heat and the lucky ones sinking into the cosy leather sofa opposite the bar. Then there are the regular quiz nights or the folk festival in May when the place is transformed into a lively, vibrant meeting place (a beer festival also attracts). The menu is an accommodating mixture of crowd pleasers such as ham, egg and chips or rolls, while the pie menu offers robust examples of this great British pub staple, often with a twist – the Heidi has goats cheese, sweet potato, spinach, red onion and roasted garlic.

The Bridge was built in 1845 as a traditional two-roomed town pub. Time has wrought its change and the bar is now open-plan, though it still continues to be cosy and welcoming. Old pictures of Dulverton on the wall tell their stories, one of which is a reminder of the 1952 floods that saw debris and water come down with the Barle (Dulverton got off lightly compared to Lynmouth which was badly damaged, with several dozen deaths). Rivers, as those who live next to them will testify, can change their moods in a flash.

Opening hours: 12–3, 6–11; 12–11 Fri–Sun and summer
Also great for: Family

Bridge Inn

Kentchurch, Herefordshire, HR2 0BY
01981 240408
www.bridgeinnkentchurch.co.uk
🍺 **Golden Valley Hay Bluff; Otter Bitter; guest beers**

• •

Not many pubs can boast that their garden is a border between two countries, but the Bridge Inn can. At the back of this unassuming roadside rural establishment, the garden runs down to the banks of the Monnow as it flows to meet its destiny with the Wye at Chepstow. Across the river is Wales. Even though it's short, rising in the Black Mountains, the Monnow acts as a natural boundary between the two countries for most of its journey. Nearby there's a poignant memory of the contested nature of this part of the world – Kentchurch Court was where the daughter of Welsh rebel Owain Glyndwr retired after the end of her father's revolt (some say that Glyndwr himself went there).

Borderlands often carry with them legends. Jack of Kent was supposedly a local medieval magician in league with the Devil, who helped him build a bridge over the river. The only caveat was that the first living being over would surrender his soul to him – and of course the Devil hoped this would be Kent. As the magician approached the bridge he threw several pieces of bread over. The dog behind him raced over and the Devil, much to his anger, had his soul. Look at the pub sign standing outside the Bridge and you'll see an illustrated version of the story.

Nowadays, both Devil and marauding Welsh are gone, though the latter (non-maurauding) come in for a pint or a plate of home-cooked grub from the neighbouring village of Grosmont and further afield. Sunday lunch is the big draw, especially when the sun is shining. The crowds roll in, the clatter of plates and the chink of cutlery fill the air, while those just here for a pint grab their ale and contemplate border life.

The Inn is at least 400 years old and there's an element of cottage-cum-farmhouse about the face it presents to the world. Go through the door, and you're inside a large open bar with rural bric-a-brac setting the scene: black and white beamed décor, a handful of paintings and local photographs, and a log fire in the winter. Expect to find up to four cask beers during the summer, being scaled back to two or possibly three during the quieter winter months. Otter Bitter with its biscuity, dry, bittersweet character is the regular as is Golden Valley's Hay Bluff, while guests come from both English and Welsh local breweries such as Wye Valley and Breconshire. And when it's time to cross the bridge back into Wales, take some bread with you – just in case.

Opening hours: 12–3 (not Mon & Tue), 5–11; 12–3, 7–10.30 Sun

The best **riverside pubs**

Butt & Oyster

The Quay, Pin Mill Road, Pin Mill,
Chelmondiston, Suffolk, IP9 1JW
01473 780764
www.debeninns.co.uk/buttandoyster

🍺 **Adnams Broadside, Lighthouse, Southwold Bitter; seasonal beer**

• •

There's a black-and-white photo of the Butt & Oyster from a book on English pubs, published in the 1960s. A lone fisherman, pipe in mouth, wearing waders and a warm bobble hat, looks out over the Orwell, along which the pub stands. It's a windy day; the inn sign is off centre, swinging in the wind and the legend on the land-facing side of the pub reads 'Tolly Cobbold ales and spirits'. The fisherman might be long gone (as is Tolly Cobbold), but his like still come to the Butt & Oyster, along with weekend yachters, loyal locals and curious tourists, all eager to experience this legendary riverside hostelry (Arthur Ransome famously featured it in *We Didn't Mean To Go To Sea* and it appeared in an episode of TV's *Lovejoy*).

There it is, at the end of a lane, right up against the water, which has been known to lap below the main bar's bow window when the tide is high. Just follow the smell of the river, salty, organic even, and you'll get there.

The inn was here in the 16th century, also known as the Butt & Oyster. Various speculations exist over its name. There were once oyster beds on the Orwell and the bi-valves would have been packed into butts. However, there was also an archery butts on a neighbouring piece of land, while butt is the local nickname for the flounder, of which there were plenty in the river. Take your pick.

The pub has been added to over the years but step into the main bar and you'll get a sense of how little it has changed in the 20th century. The bow window offers views over the river to the wooded shore opposite, as all manner of boats pass by. The walls are tattooed with old photos and various other nautical ephemera, there are a couple of settles and some beers are tapped straight from the cask. There is also a well weathered 'smoke room' plus a collection of model sailing ships.

Adnams now own the Butt & Oyster and I would plump for a pint of their Southwold Bitter, tangy and robust, an ideal foil for a plate of cod and chips (the menu features a selection of dishes making use of locally sourced produce). And then sit down and just watch the river make its journey to its rendezvous with the North Sea.

Opening hours: 11–11; 12–10.30 Sun

On a trip to Dublin, I once had a jar of stout in Davy Byrne's, though I should have plumped for a glass of Burgundy with a Gorgonzola sandwich just like Leopold Bloom did in James Joyce's epic novel *Ulysses*. At least the pub exists, which is more can than be said for the Sailors Arms, the Bull or the Rovers Return. If they did exist, in the Sailors you would be drinking in the village of Llareggub, Dylan Thomas' scurrilous re-imagination of a Welsh village and its appalling inhabitants in *Under Milkwood*. At the Bull you would be enjoying a pint of Shires and discussing both rural affairs and Ambridge gossip (*The Archers*), while the Rovers Return would see creamy ersatz pints of Newton & Ridley served to the *Coronation Street* crowd.

Pubs abound in the pages of literature and the world of soap, being the places where people meet and dramas occur. There's been many a cliffhanger ending seen at the Queen Vic (*Eastenders*). The Shakespearian clown Falstaff caroused with his drinking cronies in the Boar's Head, while Mr Pickwick went to the Magpie and Stump (for a nice glass of porter perhaps?). GK Chesteron went on the move with The Flying Inn and Graham Swift's characters met in the Coach & Horses in *Last Orders*. Imaginary pubs aside, you might want to create your own just as George Orwell did in his famous essay on the perfect pub, *The Moon under the Water*.

Canalhouse

48–52 Canal Street, Nottingham, NG1 7EH
0115 955 5060
www.canalhousebar.co.uk

🍺 **Castle Rock Harvest Pale; guest beers**

How many pubs have names that don't add up? The New Inn is invariably a couple of hundred years old, while I once visited a Friendship Inn and got a very cool reception. However, it's heartening to report that the Canalhouse completely lives up to its name as it houses a canal.

Walk into the roomy brick-built former canal wharf and you will normally see two narrow boats recumbent, moored in a stretch of Nottingham's canal basin (this is the only pub in the UK with such a thing within its walls). Winter sees two boats take up a permanent berth but during the summer a portcullis into the basin is raised and the boats come and go, their owners tying up for a pint before returning to go off on their slow, gentle way. A footbridge spans the water and revellers have been known to leap into the water. It's not something that's encouraged, as I'm told by someone behind the bar; 'The water's not that deep'. Carp and trout occasionally find a way in as well.

However, the attraction of the Canalhouse is more than the novelty of a couple of boats moored indoors. For a start the striking interior has a spartan, industrial chic feel with iron columns, girders crossing the ceiling and walls which are a mixture of red brick and distressed wood. A covered and heated outdoor terrace offers the chance of drinking al fresco.

Owned by the Tyne Mills pub chain, the Canalhouse's transformation follows a modern trend of turning work places into centres of leisure. There are plenty of nightclubs and bars with a similar theme throughout the British Isles, but normally you would expect them to major in outrageous cocktails or boutique spirits. Instead, this is very much a place where beer is king.

Beers from Castle Rock brewery take centre space (as you would expect given that this is Tyne Mill's brewery). Its champion golden ale, Harvest Pale, is a regular while the brewery's Hemlock and Screech Owl often make an appearance. There are also guest cask ales alongside beers from Belgium, Germany and North America. Regular 'meet the brewer' nights take place and SIBA (Society of Independent Brewers) hold their National Beer Championships in a function room upstairs, followed by a beer festival.

It's a popular place with drinkers of all ages, as well as those who enjoy the well-priced pub grub, which includes speciality pies, while during National Chip Week the pub serves several different styles of chips. Along with a couple of pints and a plate of such earthy fare, just make sure you don't decide to take a dip in the canal or you'll probably sink without trace.

Opening hours: 12–11 (midnight Thu; 1am Fri & Sat); 12–10.30 Sun

The best **riverside pubs**

Dove

19 Upper Mall, Hammersmith, London
020 8748 9474
www.fullers.co.uk

🍺 **Fuller's Discovery, London Pride, ESB, seasonal beers**

. . . .

Down a little alleyway, on the Thames path in Hammersmith, looking out over the river (an ideal place from where to watch the Boat Race no doubt), you will find the Dove. It's in an illustrious part of West London – William Morris lived nearby and a mile or so away is the Dove's brewing owner, Fuller's. Needless to say, it's an old and well-varnished place that has seen a lot of people come and go since it was built in the 18th century, starting life as a coffee house. The Georgian poet James Thomas was a regular, a very regular regular. Some say that he wrote the words to *Rule Britannia* somewhere on the premises. In the front bar there's a plaque on the wall with the names of dozens of past celebrities who sat and enjoyed some time in one of London's most celebrated riverside pubs: actors, poets, conductors, artists and of course George Orwell, the connoisseur of the pub.

Who goes there now? Locals, tourists, beer fans and maybe celebrities, though they don't raise their heads like they used to. Yet anyone who doesn't go here is missing a treat. From the hidden entrance step into the dark wood surrounds of the main bar with black beams, various engravings and black and white photos on the wall (plus an incongruous jar of Bonios on a shelf). The snug on the right of the entrance is reputedly one of the smallest bars in the kingdom, measuring just 33 square feet.

Then there is the group of stubby traditional hand pulls from another era: brass tipped, short and stocky, dark wood. 'People don't think they are real,' says the friendly barman as he pours me a glass of London Pride. The pint of Fuller's signature beer, brewed just up the river, certainly had a fresh and floral presence that denotes its reality.

The Dove is an eminently civilized place that could so easily have been spoilt through the rampages of pub 'improvements' in the past few decades. Now the famous might go elsewhere, but it remains home to couples, connoisseurs, sightseers, drinkers on a spree wetting the baby's head (when I was there) and those simply in love with civilized London pub life.

Opening hours: 11–11; 12– 10.30 Sun
Also great for: Sporting

The best **riverside pubs**

Mug House

12 Severnside North, Bewdley,
Worcestershire, DY12 2EE
01299 402543
www.mughousebewdley.co.uk
🍺 Bewdley Worcestershire Way; Taylor
Landlord; Wye Valley HPA; guest beers

In summer the Mug House paints a pretty picture with its multi-coloured hanging baskets offering a smiling and warm face to the world. The frontage of the Mug House is within an easy mug's throwing distance of the river, and in good weather the crowds spill out onto the pavement opposite, enjoying the peaceful waterside views. However, the Severn has had its moody moments as local residents would no doubt attest – the flooding of 2000 was one of the worst in the last couple of centuries. Improvements have now been carried out and it's hoped that the river will stay its course in the future.

Time now to think of more clement things such as pint of Wye Valley's crisp and enticing HPA or Bewdley's Worcestershire Way, a fresh and frisky golden session beer brewed in an old school in the town. Both are regularly on tap here, alongside Taylor Landlord and a guest beer. There's also an annual beer festival over a weekend in May.

Grub is good as well: good value crusty cobs filled with roast beef, and honey- or mustard-roast ham. For something more substantial the menu includes seafood linguini, or mushroom, cranberry, hazelnut and brie Wellington. There's also a restaurant called the Angry Chef, while those looking to stay the night are offered the choice of seven en suite rooms.

Mug House? You may wonder what the name means. At one stage Bewdley was the largest inland port in the West – the cargo boats that were used on the Severn were called trows and once were sailed up as far as Bewdley – here they would then have to be hauled by hand up to Bridgnorth and Shrewsbury by bow hauliers. These guys were said to congregate in the Mug House waiting for work and when they were offered some the contract was sealed with a mug of ale. So you won't be surprised to find a collection of mugs hanging from the ceiling in the snug, over 100 apparently. Though there was a darker side to this contract as landlord Drew Clifford explains: 'It is also said that once the mug of beer was accepted the penalty for not carrying out the contract was punishable by death.'

Maybe that's the the true meaning of being taken for a mug?

Opening hours: 12–11 (midnight Fri; 11.30 Sat)
Also great for: Bed & breakfast

Old Bridge Inn

Dalfaber Road, Aviemore,
Highland, PH22 1PU
01479 811137
www.oldbridgeinn.co.uk

🍺 **Caledonian Deuchars IPA; guest beers**

• •

The Old Bridge Inn looks like a trio of high-gabled bungalows knocked together, with one side made into a conservatory (which it is – this is where the highly regarded restaurant sits) and the other with designs on being an upmarket bus shelter. It has clean lines though and sits just across the road from the Spey, Scotland's fastest flowing river. There's an open riverside space with benches where you can take your beer, and the sandy beach area will often find people turning up in their kayaks eager to quench their thirst at the inn.

Given that some might feel that there is a dour functionality about the Old Bridge Inn as seen from the outside (Aviemore town is not the prettiest place in the Highlands), inside it works very well in terms of hospitality, food and drink.

Five cask beers entice and titillate those in the lounge bar area. Local brewery Cairngorm is only down the road so there's always something on tap from them. The award-winning Tradewinds is a particular favourite, as is the roasty, toasty stoutness of Black Gold. Other Scottish breweries represented might include Isle of Skye, Caledonian and Harviestoun – the latter's Schiehallion is often recommended to those whose favoured tipple is Bud or Miller Lite (two beers which are not sold here) but I'm told that bottled Schiehallion as a substitute goes down a treat. The back bar also has a superb selection of whiskies (with a special focus on Speyside's elegant examples of the dram); you drink well here. You also relax well here. The lounge is comfortable and studded with an array of comfortable sofas, booths and armchairs, while music sessions often raise the tempo.

Opposite is the conservatory where food is served and such is the reputation of the menu (contemporary with a traditional twist) that reservations are pretty obligatory. Here you might find local organic trout, wild duck in season and venison taken in Morayshire. Vegetarians will salivate over the leek and truffle risotto. The Old Bridge Inn makes a virtue of trying to source as much of its food as locally as possible.

If you've had a hard day out on the river, then stow your kayak, change into dry clothes and make for the Old Bridge Inn. You know it makes sense.

Opening hours: 11–midnight (1am Fri & Sat); 12.30–midnight Sun
Also great for: Food; Sporting

The best **riverside pubs**

The best
seaside pubs

Oh we do like to be beside the seaside and stroll upon the prom (though the brass bands that played to the crowds in the old music hall song are mainly confined to history now). And when we are beside the seaside, there's nothing more enjoyable than a glass of beer, whilst watching the moods of the waters that surround these islands.

Take your pick. Some of these pubs beside the seaside, like the Anchor Inn at Seatown on the Dorset Jurassic coast, sit so close to the shoreline that you half expect to see shoals of seabass swimming in through the front en route to the kitchen. The Turf sits imperious on a spit of land that reaches out to the Exe Estuary, a favourite spot for watching bird life, while the Tigh an Truish harks back to the days of the Jacobite Rebellion. Others are merely content to be part of the ambience of a town known for its seafaring traditions: the Seven Stars has been a haunt of Falmouth's seagoing community for centuries whilst the Lifeboat is a brand new alehouse already gaining a reputation for its beer in the quintessentially English seaside resort of Margate. Meanwhile the Victoria Hotel overlooks the wide sweep of Robin Hood's Bay, a place where cliffs have been known to crumble…

See also
Anchor, Walberswick (p194)
Applecross Inn, Applecross (p78)
Pigs Nose Inn, East Prawle (p247)
Steam Packet Inn, Isle of Whithorn (p236)
Valley Bar, Scarborough (p59)

◄ Seafood at **the** Lord Nelson, Southwold

Anchor Inn

Seatown, Dorset, DT6 6JU
01297 489215
www.theanchorinnseatown.co.uk
🍺 **Palmers Copper Ale, Best Bitter, 200**

If the Anchor were any closer to the sea, shoals of fish would be swimming in through the front door fresh and ready for the kitchen. The pub sits comfortably just above the pebbly beach, a honey-pot for every pub-goer who loves nothing better than to sink a pint with the sea in sight (it also attracts families, day-trippers and the sort of people who don't normally go to pubs).

You can watch the ever changing moods of the English Channel from the small front bar; with its low ceiling, weathered wood fittings and old pictures it has the feel of a man-o'-war's ward room. You half expect it to sway on windy days. When the sun shows itself the crowds flock to the outside tables and catch the gentle zephyrs of the sea ruffling through the hair or just chill out with a glass of beer produced in nearby Bridport by the pub's owners Palmers. The brewery's Copper Ale, Best Bitter and 200 are regulars at the bar, and very good they are too.

People arrive by a variety of ways. Perhaps the healthiest option is walking the South West Coastal Path (the path marches right in front of the pub). This is superb walking country after all: to ramble here is to pass through a potted geological history of the area.

Others bring their cars down the narrow lane from Chideock, which sits on the Bridport road (though the pub car park's charge of £4, with a refund if you spend £20 in the pub, militates against coming down for a swift pint); a bicycle would be preferable.

The front bar (there's also another side room off the corridor) has a selection of black and white photos of regulars and fishermen from the last few years, a poignant but also vital record of the people who called the Anchor their local. This is the pub acting as a repository of memory, though given the Anchor's current popularity with tourists eager for their own slice of Jurassic coastline, you do wonder if such a project could be undertaken now. Forget such musings though, go to the Anchor for the seaward ambience, to sit in the shadow of Golden Cap, enjoy a pint and grab a bite to eat. Fresh fish of course, and I can only echo the words of the man at the bar on the occasion of my last visit: 'Super crab sandwiches.'

Opening hours: 11–11; 11.30–close Sun

Lifeboat Ale & Cider House

1 Market Street, Margate, Kent, CT9 1EU
07837 024259
www.thelifeboat-margate.com

🍺 **Beer range varies**

Parents used to come with their kids to buy school uniforms at the Georgian-era shop where the Lifeboat now trades, but as was common with many a small business it was killed off when the supermarkets began selling uniforms at deleterious discounts. This scenario is a bit too close to the way pundits often regard the direction the pub is going – easy prey to cheap booze offered by out of town supermarkets. Yet, it's all too easy and lazy to make this comparison – you might be able to waltz down the aisle and pick up a slab of tins along with the school blazer, but the Lifeboat (and many other pubs) offer more than a quick fix of alcoholic sustenance.

Margate is one of those British towns indelibly linked with the seaside. TS Eliot recuperated here after a breakdown, while Mods and Rockers battled on its sands in the 1960s. Nowadays sun-seekers might flock to the Med in search of their fix, but Margate still retains an elegiac sense of British seaside life – and when you've had your fill of promenading then make for the Lifeboat.

Landlord (and local man) Julian Newick is steadfastly Kentish in his prejudices when it comes to beer. All the county's craft breweries are dealt with – there are up to nine cask beers on at any one time; this includes Gadds (No 7 is a big favourite), Hopdaemon, Westerham and Goachers. All of them are served from an especially built stillage that divides this one-room pub (think bare brickwork, sanded floorboards, old pictures on the wall, big ingle-nook fireplace). Occasional beer festivals offer a maximum of 14 beers, while there are also up to 24 Kentish ciders on (plus two local perries), and a Kentish lager. The food has an equally local theme: seafood (as you would expect), pies from Broadstairs and every cheese made under the Kentish sun.

Even though it only opened in 2010, the Lifeboat has made rapid progress as one of Margate's leading cask beer pubs. Awards have rocketed its way. And why not? This is the pub as a public house, a public home, where people can come and chat, read the newspaper or a book and enjoy the range of beers and ciders on display. There is occasionally music too, maybe something folky, while there's a C3 Hammond organ at the back of the pub, a Rolls-Royce of organs apparently. 'It takes up far too much space,' laughs Newick, 'it's completely mad to have it but people do come in to play it.'

Opening hours: 12–midnight

The best **seaside pubs**

Lord Nelson

East Street, Southwold, Suffolk, IP18 6EJ
01502 722079
www.thelordnelsonsouthwold.co.uk
Adnams Southwold Bitter, Broadside, Explorer, seasonal beers

• •

The Lord Nelson is the first Southwold pub that I ever visited. Over a couple of decades and many happy returns since, it still remains a place in which I like to commend myself to the beers of Adnams. There's no shortage of pubs selling Adnams in Southwold, and they all have their own merits (as I have discovered over the years). Yet to me the Lord Nelson is a special place in which to drink Adnams' pristine bitter, surely one of the greatest expressions of this English beer style.

Maybe it's the location. After all, the Lord Nelson is down a side-street just off the promenade beyond which the North Sea casts its bleak but beautiful spell. On wild blustery nights as the waves crash and then draw back from the beach below, the sound of the pub's sign creaking in the wind casts a spell on the imagination and the Admiral Benbow of *Treasure Island* fame springs to mind. This is the time when you hope that the pub has a cask of Adnams' rich barley wine, Tally Ho, on the go: a beer that is meant for a pub like the Lord Nelson and nights like that. In the summer, have a couple of pints of the light and airy blonde-coloured Regatta and then wander onto the beach and ponder at the price of the beach huts.

Or maybe it's the fact that this was my first Southwold pub love and I've not been able to let go ever since (it obviously helps that it still feels the same as my debut visit). Or maybe it's the fact that it's cosy and homely but also bustling, a popular place where both locals and blow-ins can mix and mingle. It's multi-roomed, nooked and crannied, and dotted with all manner of knick-knacks including antique brewery signs and old paintings. Sometimes you cannot help but exchange a few words with your neighbour.

During the day, visitors pass in an endless stream through the doors (fish and chips in Broadside batter here, Thai green curry there), but later in the day, it's as if the town reclaims it for its own. It's also friendly to dogs. I do recall my long-gone boxer and his tendency to sit next to the table and watch everything and everyone. You don't get that with terriers...

The Lord Nelson was known as Noah's Ark prior to 1805 and its namesake's victory (and death) at Trafalgar. So it's got a couple of centuries under its belt and will hopefully get a few more in the future. It is a pub with few pretensions beyond that of providing good cheer and beer, which it does magnificently. In a changing world the Lord Nelson is timeless.

Opening hours: 10.30–11; 12–10.30 Sun

Old Inn

Flowerdale Glen, Gairloch,
Highland, IV21 2BD
01445 712006
www.theoldinn.net

🍺 **An Teallach Ale; Greene King Abbot; Isle of Skye Red Cuillin; Old Inn The Erradale; guest beers**

. . . .

Spectacular is the word that springs immediately to mind on spotting the location of the Old Inn for the first time. The west Highland village of Gairloch tumbles down to the shore where there are sandy beaches to hand and inspirational views of Skye and the Outer Isles over the water; meanwhile further inland chances are you'll spot (and hear) red deer. During the summer regular whale-watching trips take off from the harbour. This is a magical place, where nature and landscape combine to offer plenty to do.

And when the day is done, down at the harbour is where you'll find the Old Inn, a cosy and comfortable former drovers' inn whose sense of gracious Highland hospitality offers a goodly complement to the beauty of the surrounding area. Cask beers are mainly sourced locally (winter sees regular appearances of the strong-willed Cuillin Beast), while 2011 saw the Inn set up its own brewery – the first beer to be produced was The Erradale, though there are plans for a summer beer and winter warmer. The local principle also applies to the food, which as you would expect for somewhere so close to the sea features fresh seafood and fish dishes. Meanwhile, carnivores can tuck into local beef or venison. Finally, there are regular musical nights featuring local musicians and those from further afield. Beer, food, music, location – the Old Inn has it all.

Opening hours: 11–1am (11.45 Sat); 12–11.15 Sun

Olde Ship Inn

7–9 Main Street, Seahouses,
Northumberland, NE68 7RD
01665 720200
www.seahouses.co.uk

🍺 **Black Sheep Best Bitter; Courage
Directors; Greene King Old Speckled Hen,
Ruddles County; Hadrian & Border Farne
Island; Theakston Best Bitter**

• •

Seahouses was once a thriving port. The herring
trade prospered, with the fish being landed and
processed and then sent on by rail. That part of
Seahouses' history is now long gone, though a
fair amount of boats remain, ready to ferry visitors
to the Farne Islands or on fishing trips. It's a lively,
down-to-earth resort crammed with chip shops
and gift shops, as well as a handful of pubs.

The Olde Ship Inn is one of these pubs. Situated
on a street that runs down to the quay, never has
a pub been so aptly named. Step into the main bar
and you're face to face with all manner of maritime
and nautical bric-a-brac, hanging from the ceiling or
on show on the wall. Here an old-fashioned diver's
helmet, there a ship's wheel and in between so
many items that say seafaring you might feel
yourself in a museum. The whole décor has the
dark woody feel of a ship, while an open fire gives
warmth and sustenance during the cold winters
that come in hard and direct off the North Sea.
It all makes for a homely ambience, the sort that
attracts both locals and visitors.

Round the corner from the bar there's a cosy
space named The Cabin. Get in early and grab
yourself a seat to watch the comings and goings
in the pub. There are usually five cask beers on
display, including Old Speckled Hen and Courage
Director's, but the local beer hero on regular
display is the delicious Hadrian & Border's Farne
Island Pale Ale. This is a moreish session bitter, a
seductive alliance of crisp biscuity maltiness and a
biting bitter finish. It's an ideal beer to set yourself
up with whilst waiting for a fresh crab salad. And
when the wind comes step briefly outside to hear
the sea slap against the harbour walls, before
returning safe to port at the Olde Ship Inn.

Opening hours: 11–11; 12–11 Sun

Seven Stars

The Moor, Falmouth, Cornwall, TR11 3QA
01326 312111
www.sevenstarsfalmouth.co.uk

🍺 **Draught Bass; Sharp's Special; Skinner's Betty Stogs; guest beer**

. . . .

If the Seven Stars was a piece of clothing then it would be an artfully distressed pair of denim jeans, faded and frayed, stylishly down at heel. If you sit in the room at the back of the bar you will know what I mean: the paint is cracked and fading, while the wallpaper peels from the walls. The décor is nicotine orange, the carpets threadbare but clean. There's a curious hatch in the ceiling – apparently this was used to bring coffins down whenever there was a death up above as the stairs were too narrow and winding for the undertakers to do their job. And yet, coffins notwithstanding, like a favourite pair of old jeans, there's a compulsive charisma about the Seven Stars that makes it one of the most individual and best-loved pubs of the southwest.

It sits in the middle of town, back a bit from the pavement, tucked away between two newer buildings and with an old four-columned fountain in front. The colour scheme is black and white, and the building itself is compact yet three-storeyed. It's the oldest pub in Falmouth, with a history going back to 1660 when Charles II was restored to the throne – it's been open ever since say its champions. Given the longstanding nautical history of Falmouth as a port, you can imagine the tales told in the front bar by mariners home from the high seas. This sense of continuity and history also extends to the current licensee, the Reverend Barrington Bennetts, who as his title suggests is also a man of the cloth. His family have been in charge of the Seven Stars for five generations.

Behind the front bar sit several casks of beer, usually sourced from Cornish breweries such as Sharp's and Skinner's. Another favourite is Draught Bass – the pub is famed for its quality of this much-neglected classic pale ale. The Draught Bass here is some of the best I have ever been served, alongside the one that enchanted me at the Coopers Tavern in Burton upon Trent (p153). Also keep an eye out for Grandma's Weapons Grade Ginger Beer, which at 5.5% is very much a ginger beer for grown-ups.

Yes, the Seven Stars is definitely a pub-goers' pub: food is restricted to crisps and the odd roll, while the use of mobile phones is discouraged. There's a dedicated local following and if you spend enough time here I suspect you'll find yourself taking root. Much used and over-indulged a phrase it may be, but they really don't make pubs like the Seven Stars anymore.

Opening hours: 11–3, 6–11; 12–3, 7–10.30 Sun
Also great for: Heritage

The best **seaside pubs**

Ship Inn

Red Wharf Bay, Pentraeth, Anglesey, LL75 8RJ
01248 852568
www.shipinnredwharfbay.co.uk
🍺 **Adnams Southwold Bitter; Brains SA; guest beers**

. . . .

Such is the tranquillity of the vision that greets the drinker as they sit with their pint on the quay overlooking Red Wharf Bay that it's hard to believe the place was once a hive of shipping industry. Yet it was, being a busy port with ships coming and going, taking out coal and other combustibles, though some of them stayed for good after being shipwrecked during calamitous weather. The last one was as recent as 1971, which provides a neat symmetry, as it is when the current owners came aboard this particular Ship. There's an extra contrast with today's peaceful situation if you travel back further in time. The Welsh name for the bay is Traeth Coch ('red sands'), which might possibly refer back to a battle between invading Vikings and Welshmen back in the 9th century when the place rang with the screams of the dying and the clash of swords. These days, visitors are welcome and times are more pacific.

Nowadays, people come to the Ship for the magnificent view of the Bay and the low hills in the distance rather than a punch up or a keel full of coal. They also turn up for the tasty grub and a pint or two. Fine weather commands you to take your pint into the beer garden that overlooks the water. Watch the small boats and yachts bobbing up and down, children running about on the sands and the sun slowly sinking in the west.

When the wind turns and rain skims in from the west, take shelter in one of the low-ceilinged, wooden beamed rooms that make the Ship such a comfortable place to be. The cosy clutter of bric-a-brac (ships' lanterns, nautical bits and bobs, brewery mirrors, stuffed birds) will add to the ambience, almost giving the interior the feel of a small but well-appointed museum of curios. Given its position, seafood and fish dishes feature well on the Ship's menu: catches of the day entice, while its fish pie is a big and creamy mouthful. Meat dishes feature locally-sourced produce: Welsh lamb, Anglesey pork for a start.

The Ship Inn is not a pub pub and some might find it a mite pricey. Food is undoubtedly important here, but it serves a good drop of cask beer, has the sort of interior untouched by gastro-style makeover madness and – most importantly of all – its stunning location makes you want to set up camp outside and drink in the landscape (and the beer).

Opening hours: 11–11; 11–10.30 Sun

Tigh an Truish

Clachan Seil, Oban, Argyll and Bute,
PA34 4QZ
01852 300242
www.tigh-an-truish.co.uk
🍺 **Beer range varies**

. . . .

Island life, or maybe not… The isle of Seil lies off the Scottish mainland, separated by a narrow stretch of sea over which a late 18th century bridge stretches – this is the Clachan Sound and part of the Atlantic even though it seems narrow enough at the crossing to boot a football over. In 1792 Thomas Telford turned up and oversaw the construction of what the locals called the 'Bridge over the Atlantic', as they still do. So does that make the Tigh an Truish an Atlantic inn?

There it is within sight of the bridge, a whitewashed inn also built in the 1700s, though older than the bridge – a place that must have offered plenty of comfort and solace to islanders waiting to take the ferry across before the bridge

builders came. Some things never change. The bridge continues to take traffic, while Tigh an Truish offers hospitality in the form of appetising bar food and a couple of cask beers from a variety of Scottish breweries (Fyne and Atlas are particular favourites). The bar has a rustic, hearty quality – wood fittings, old photos, a piano, and a take-me-as-you-find-me quality (note on the outside of the porch an old Alloa Ales 'Y' sign, breweriana for the faithful). Lunchtime sees the lighter side of eating with baguettes and soup, while the evening features more substantial dishes including several that use locally caught seafood. The inn is also a popular watering hole for sailors who pull up on the other side of the island at Puilladobhrain anchorage and then just walk over the hill.

And the name? In Gaelic it means 'house of the trousers' and harks back to the aftermath of the Jacobite rebellion – islanders wishing to cross the waters would change out of their kilts into trousers at the inn…

Opening hours: 11–11 (11–2.30, 5–10 winter);
12–10 Sun

The best **seaside pubs**

Turf

Exminster, Devon, EX6 8EE
01392 833128
www.turfpub.net

🍺 **Exeter Ferryman; O'Hanlon's Yellowhammer; Otter Bitter, Ale; guest beers**

. . . .

Some pubs are worth going that extra mile for. The Turf is one such place. For a start it is one of the few pubs in Britain to which you can't just drive up, park and wander in (though people can be dropped off and collected). Finding the place is an adventure in itself. If driving, you lurch down a winding pot-holed road through desolate wetlands until you hit water; then you have to pitch out and walk half a mile or so along the canal tow-path (or, during summer months, take a brief boat-ride from the bustling town of Topsham). The Turf then comes into sight like a galleon at sail, its solid Georgian frame ploughing doggedly into the Exe estuary where salt water greets the old Exeter Ship Canal. Surrounded by water on three sides, the Turf sits in a magical setting – wild and isolated yet just across the water from Topsham and a few miles down river from Exeter.

The Turf was first used to provide accommodation for the lock-keeper and the crews that used the canal, but it became a popular place for whitebait teas in the years before the Second World War. However, it fell into disrepair and was due for demolition in the 1970s until the Exeter Maritime Museum sailed to the rescue and had it listed.

Inside, the pub has the ambience of an old-fashioned seaside café: warm, friendly and deeply laid-back. You half expect a huddle of grizzled old seadogs to be propping up the bar but the clientele are a lively mix of generally outdoorsy types. Dogs also enjoy themselves here. On my visit a rotund Jack Russell terrier was chewing on a log next to the wood burner. 'I'll put you in next,' joked the landlord Clive Redfern as he brought in bowls of steaming soup for the bird-watchers on the next table (the area is a paradise for birders).

The small but simple menu hits the spot too. Three home-made soups with locally baked bread and a variety of rib-sticking toasties dominate with a couple of specials thrown in for good measure, including lamb korma and a spicy noodle and prawn soup. The pub is proud of its support for local suppliers, a fact that is very much reflected with the cask beers on display: Otter, O'Hanlon's and Exeter are all within 20 miles. There are usually five available.

This is a place for all seasons: on warm days, take your pint outside and contemplate the shifting tides of the Estuary (the barbecue is pressed into service on summer nights), while it is also bleakly lovely in autumn. Be warned though: the Turf takes a break during December and January.

Opening hours: 11–3 (5 Sat & Sun)
Also great for: Pub gardens

Victoria Hotel

Station Road, Robin Hood's Bay,
North Yorkshire, YO22 4RL
01947 880205
www.victoriarhb.com

🍺 **Camerons Best Bitter, Strongarm;
Daleside Old Leg Over; guest beers**

· ·

Once upon a time we would have said hotels are to stay at and pubs are to drink in, but the world has long been turned upside down and at the Victoria Hotel you can sit in the comfortable bar with its inglenook fireplace and log burner and soothing ambience, and enjoy a choice of five cask beers. As well as the regulars can I suggest a creamy glass of Black Sheep's luscious Bitter, or, if you fancy striking gold, how about Daleside's Blonde, whose sunny disposition would more than match the brightest and warmest of summer days. Which is when you just have to step outside around the back of the hotel and stand and admire the view (glass in hand of course). For this is when the Victoria really comes into its own.

It's an imposing Victorian hotel, large and garbed with gables. It's solid and brick built, half covered with red tiles. Did Queen Victoria ever drop in for a glass or was the name given more of a hope that she might? But look past the impressive frontage and step into the garden to find the Victoria Hotel's USP – it stands high on the cliffs overlooking the curve of Robin Hood's Bay. In its garden you can look over the ever-changing temperament of the North Sea and experience one of the most dramatic sea views you could ever hope for from the grounds of a pub. Not bad is it, you'll hear parents tell their kids. There's just one problem – sea erosion. Cliffs are crumbling in the vicinity of Robin Hood's Bay. The one below the hotel is safe for the moment though, and when weather closes in and the sea crashes against the rocks below, then the bar with its warm fire, choice of ales and pleasing menu has its own attractions.

Opening hours: 6–11; 12–11 Sat, Sun & summer

The best **near motorways**

A visit to a motorway café can be a soul-destroying event as well as being heavy on the wallet. So why not consider a stopover in a great British pub?

If you're not the driver then there's even more of a reason to swap the intensity of roadwork on our crowded network of motorways for a relaxing glass of beer and the sense of getting away from it all for a short while. In this section I've picked a handy selection of pubs that are but a short distance from the motorway – up to 10 minutes or so. Even though the Black Horse is probably a couple of miles away as the crow flies, the countryside ambience is as comforting as a shoulder massage.

The majority of them do food (you might need to be helped into the car after the two pie special at the Bay Horse though), while others are particularly useful if you've got kids bursting to run about a bit – the Bell at Wendens Ambo has an adventure playground that should help to release a bit of steam and stem the flow of 'Are we there yet?' questions.

Meanwhile, the Alma Inn off the M50 runs a well-regarded musical festival every June that you might want to camp over for.

See also
Coach & Horses, Weatheroak (p34)
Crown, Stockport (p263)
Culm Valley Inn, Culmstock (p212)
Old Spot, Dursley (p267)
Surtees Arms, Ferryhill (p187)

◀ Walter de Cantelupe, Kempsey

Alma Inn

Linton, Ross On Wye,
Herefordshire, HR9 7RY
01989 720355

🍺 **Butcombe Bitter; Malvern Hills Black Pear; Oakham JHB; guest beers**

• •

Just north of Tewksbury a short stretch of motorway branches west off the M5 and takes the traveller on their way to central Wales where the red kites dwell. But en route it might be worth making a detour to the small village of Linton – one church, pub and village hall – where the Alma Inn makes a perfect stop.

It's not your usual roadhouse stop: the Alma is resolutely traditional and doesn't sell food. There are three cask beers though and sometimes up to four guests at the bar with showings from the local breweries such as Wye Valley and Malvern Hills. It's not open at lunchtimes during the week and even with the nearness of the M50 it can

seem a bit isolated. Yet folk make their way here both for the warm-hearted ambience of the pub and its annual music festival, which is held in June in the natural amphitheatre that is the back garden (there's also a beer festival at the same time). Camping is available over this weekend – so it's the perfect time to venture out along the motorway, take a turning at Junction 3, pass through narrow country lanes and pitch your tent to enjoy what's on offer.

Small village, big heart. The music festival raises money for various local charities and only came about when some local blues fans realised it would be cheaper to hire their favourite band rather than travel en masse to Dorset to see it. This was back in 2001 and the event has spiralled since then. The pub also hosts teams for pool, crib and darts and has been known to stage the odd quiz night. There's a lot going on in this so-called 'back of beyond' and the Alma Inn has been recognised for its efforts with several CAMRA awards.

From the outside, the Alma Inn (named, as if you don't know, after a Crimean War battle) is cream-yellow in colour with its ground floor dominated by large window spaces. The origins of the site are 17th century, but its core is Victorian. The décor is traditional, plenty of wood, real fire in the winter and old photos and framed awards on the walls.

As there's no food, bring a picnic and perhaps have it in the shade of a tree in the old churchyard. Time passes a lot slower when you come off the motorway.

Opening hours: 6–11; 12–3, 6–11 Sat;
12–3, 7–10.30 Sun
Access: Jct 3, M50
Also great for: Entertainment

The best **near motorways**

Bay Horse

Scholes, nr Rotherham,
South Yorkshire, S61 2RQ
0114 246 8085
www.bayhorsescholes.co.uk
🍺 **Kelham Island Pale Rider;
Taylor Landlord; guest beers**

'We're famous for our pies,' says the Bay Horse's landlord Darren Ainslie, and to prove it you can go onto YouTube (if you so desire) and watch him eat two of the pub's scrumptious looking steak and ale pies complete with home cooked chips, vegetables and gravy. It takes all of 30 minutes but at the end he looks a happy man and you might start feeling peckish yourself.

The undertaking used to only involve one pie and if you completed the meal ('you would have to eat everything up,' states Ainslie firmly) then you got a certificate, a badge and your picture on the pub's website. 'We're famous for our pies and I thought I'd up the challenge,' says Ainslie, 'and add another pie.'

I think the pie bar has just been raised.

The Bay Horse is a traditional village inn and a short drive from Junction 35 on the M1 (roughly a mile). It's situated in the small village of Scholes, somewhere that's yet to be gobbled up by Rotherham. It started off three centuries ago as a farm, then became three cottages and finally found its niche as a purveyor of pints sometime in the 19th century (the pies came when Ainslie took over in 2004). Inside the pub the décor is the classic jumble of antiquated pub furnishings and bric-a-brac with a restaurant behind the horseshoe shaped bar. There are old maps of the area on the wall, framed photos of the pub through the ages and wooden beams traversing the ceiling.

The Bay Horse is a classic local pub and well worth making a detour off the motorway to get to (be aware that it only opens in the evening during the week). Not only is the food hearty and robust (the beef stew served in giant Yorkshire pudding isn't for the faint-hearted), but there's also a sextet of cask beers, meaning you'll want to make sure you're not the driver. Guest beers come from the likes of Thornbridge and Acorn, whose Barnsley Bitter is a wonderful example of this classic British beer style. A lot goes on as well. There are quizzes, a singalong on Thursday evenings, giant vegetable competitions and even a pork-pie-making one. As I said this is the place where the pie bar keeps getting raised higher and higher.

Opening hours: 5 (12 Sat & Sun)-11
Access: Jct 35, M1

The best **near motorways**

Bell

Royston Road, Wendens Ambo,
Saffron Walden, Essex, CB11 4JY
01799 540382
www.thebellatwenden.co.uk

🍺 **Adnams Southwold Bitter; Woodforde's
Wherry; guest beers**

• •

Are we there yet? That's the perpetual whine
that sends parents mad as they speed along
the motorway with their kids in the back totally
unimpressed with I-Spy or spotting Eddie
Stobart trucks. Are we there yet? Well, if you're
travelling along the M11, possibly motoring north
in the direction of Cambridge and having just
passed Audley End, then come off at Junction
9 and make for the Bell at Wendens Ambo. Yes,
we're here kids.

But before even thinking about relaxing with a
drink and some food, you'll be pleased to know
that this lively village pub has several acres
of garden with a woodland walk and – most
mercifully – a kids' adventure playground. When
it's raining there are board games within (and
if they misbehave tell them that the ghost of a
former landlady who reputedly stayed behind will
be looking out for them).

Yet the Bell is also a proper village pub. It
has its roots in Elizabethan times, when it was
a farmhouse, but it's been serving the local
community as a pub for a couple of centuries
now and looks like going on for many more. A
good local trade ensues that there's plenty going
on at the Bell: it fields a side for an annual match
with the local cricket team, while its August beer
and music festival weekend (the Bell Bash) brings

in the hordes – and also raises money for charity.
And then there's Pub Dog the deaf, er, pub dog,
who will be wandering around and saying hello.

Inside, the rooms are low browed but
comfortable, stitched with venerable, weathered
wooden beams on which are tattooed a variety of
horse brasses. There are usually five cask beers,
with the three guests coming from East Anglian
beer heroes such as Oakham, Wolf and Crouch
Vale. If the latter's Brewers Gold is on, then be
prepared for a giddy cocktail of tropical fruit, spicy
hoppiness and a sober-shirted grainy biscuitiness
before it descends into a lasting helter-skelter of
a dry finish. If you're eating then perhaps it might
work well with the fish and chips or the home-
made burger.

And then it's time to hit the road once more,
legs stretched, bellies full, steam run off, fully
refreshed and replenished.
Are we there yet?
Not until next time.

Opening hours: 11.30–3, 6–11; 11.30–12.30am Fri & Sat;
12–11.30 Sun
Access: Jct 9, M11
Also great for: Family pubs

Black Horse

Clevedon Lane, Clapton in Gordano,
Somerset, BS20 7RH
01275 842105
www.thekicker.co.uk

🍺 **Butcombe Bitter; Courage Best Bitter; Otter Ale; Wadworth 6X; guest beer**

· ·

It's only a couple of miles from Junction 19 on the M5 as it skirts west of Bristol, but take the time to visit the Black Horse and you'll find yourself deep in the countryside, taking a well-deserved break from the mayhem of the road. Hidden away down country lanes the Black Horse is a rural treasure of an inn that has developed its own patina of age down the years. Inside, its flagstone floors, massive wooden beams, wooden settles, stools and wobbly tables and muskets hanging over the massive fireplace speak volumes about the sort of place it's become over time – there's a genuine sense of it aging gracefully and growing comfortable in its skin.

The Black Horse is a popular place, not only with refugees from the M5, but locals, cyclists and walkers as well. Sunday afternoon sees it comfortably busy, a dozen conversations veering off in all sorts of directions. The hubbub of voices is joined by the regular sound of the click of the latch being lifted as someone enters. It's a place where you cannot help but smile at fellow drinkers and often join in – talk about the pubs in nearby Bristol or Nailsea or admire a fellow drinker's dog. There's also another room across the corridor with a dartboard and the garden calls in summer with the insistency of a siren luring sailors onto the rocks.

At the bar the beers are served directly from the cask. History determines the choice of Courage Best Bitter (it was once brewed in the old Georges building right in the centre of Bristol), which is joined by Butcombe Bitter, Otter Ale and Waddies 6X. A popular guest beer is Exmoor Gold, famously the first of the new generation of golden ales back in the 1980s. It maintains its popularity – a light, frisky beer with a slight orangey character and tantalising biscuity dryness. Thatchers make their ciders not far from here, so they're also well represented at the bar. Food is simple and filling – sandwiches and pot meals such as chilli served at lunch from Monday to Saturday.

Pubs like the Black Horse give us a front room experience that generations of drinkers have loved. It's an imagined front room, an idealised one that rarely exists, but where it does exist drinkers fall in love with it, which is why the Black Horse rightly thrives.

Opening hours: 11–11; 12–10.30 Sun
Access: Jct 19, M5
Also great for: Country

The best **near motorways**

Gwaelod-y-Garth Inn

Main Road, Gwaelod-y-Garth,
Cardiff, CF15 9HH
029 2081 0408
www.gwaelodinn.co.uk

🍺 **Wye Valley Bitter; guest beers**

· ·

Gwaelod-y-Garth is Welsh for 'at the foot of the Garth', the mountain that famously inspired the Hugh Grant film *The Englishman Who Went Up A Hill but Came Down a Mountain*, though it's not the actual hill and nobody lugged stones and soil up there to make it a mountain. Nice story though. Seen from the M4 approaching Cardiff, it's a long rounded outcrop, purple with heather in the summer. Junction 32 is where you need to exit and about 10 minutes later you'll be at the inn at the foot of the Garth.

Stone-built though not dour, hanging baskets enlivening the frontage in the summer, the Inn stands on the road through the village, offering views towards Taff's Well and the wooded slopes of Fforest Fawr. There used to be quarries in the area once upon a time but now the land is quieter, all the more attractive for the walkers, hikers and occasional hang-gliders who come this way. Locals make it their home and the city isn't too far away – Taff's Well, just across the river, is a short train journey from Cardiff. The village feels part of the countryside, as well as clinging onto the shirt-tails of the city.

Inside there's an L-shaped room with a neat caramel-brown wooden bar. On top, there's an array of handpumps (five at least) offering beers from the likes of Wye Valley, Purple Moose and Otley. Wye Valley's refreshing Bitter is the regulars' favourite, refreshing and clean on the palate with a shimmy of citrus fruit and a firm backbone of biscuity crispness. Those whose tastes veer towards the apple will be rewarded with a perry or cider from Gwynt y Ddraig. The 'Gwaelod' (as it's known locally) has rightly been handed several CAMRA awards. And of course you will need to eat – the Inn has a restaurant upstairs. Here, traditional South Walian cuisine gets a look-in with a laverbread and bacon starter, while more substantial dishes include steak and ale pie, grilled seabass fillets with braised fennel and Glamorgan sausages for those who want a meat-free option.

Gwaelod-y-Garth might lie at the foot of the mountain, but lose the translation and you'll find that it soars to the top when it comes to offering a rest from the rigours of the road.

Opening hours: 10–11
Access: Jct 32, M4
Also great for: Food

Plough Inn

Wreay, Carlisle, Cumbria, CA4 0RL
016974 75770
www.wreayplough.co.uk

🍺 **Cumberland Corby Ale; guest beers**

. . . .

Look at the map of Cumbria. There's Carlisle and several miles south there's the small village of Wreay, bordered to the east and west by the M6 and the railway line, leaving Wreay bypassed in between these two lines of communication.

But detour from the M6 and head down the leafy lanes of the village and you'll find the Plough: a farmhouse-style solid stone frontage offered to the world, in keeping with many of the houses in the village. An exterior that says 'one of us', which is how the pub should be. And yet it was nearly one of them – a few years ago the pub was sold and closed with what seemed the certainty that pints would never be pulled there again. Yet it was saved and now you can step inside and enjoy both good food and a relaxed pub ambience.

The front bar has been done up. The floor is granite, there's heating underneath, which is why the fireplace is filled with flowers instead of logs. The bar is newly built with bricks from an old mill, while a ploughshare decorates the front. It's a light and airy space with many tables given over to dining, though drinkers are not pushed out – there are sofas provided for their comfort.

Food is important here as is the concept of local sourcing. Dishes on the robust menu include slow-cooked lamb shanks, steak pie, duck breast on spiced red cabbage and that old local favourite, Cumberland sausage served with mash. There are usually two cask beers on with guests coming from the likes of Hawkshead, whose Lakeland Gold is a satisfying blend of luscious citrus fruit and an appetising bitterness.

The story of the Plough's survival is a heartening one. After all, it's been the centre in the village for centuries and seen all manner of local jollities, one of which still remains to this day. In the 1660s the Twelve Men of Wreay first met to discuss local matters and help the poor. Today they continue to meet at the Plough, a local custom deservedly kept.

Opening hours: 12–2.30 (not Tue), 6–11; closed Mon
Access: Jct 42, M6

Walter de Cantelupe

Main Road, Kempsey, Worcester, WR5 3NA
01905 820572
www.walterdecantelupe.co.uk

🍺 **Cannon Royall King's Shilling;
Taylor Landlord; guest beers**

The original Walter de Cantelupe was a 13th century bishop of nearby Worcester, famed for thundering against his parishioners' penchant for putting on Church Ales (basically a boozy version of the modern church fete). Doubtless his eternal rest would be much disturbed if he knew of the use of his name for a place of alcoholic refreshment.

With the M5 passing by only a couple of miles away, this compact inn is an ideal watering hole for travellers who want to avoid impersonal service stations (it also does accommodation). Partly dating from the 17th century, when a row of cottages was knocked into one, it's a friendly place that attracts both travellers and locals.

Landlord Martin Lloyd-Morris has been here since 1991 and as he trained as a chef in France good food is naturally a passion. The vast paella pan that hangs on the wall is a reminder of the popular paella parties that the pub puts on in its delightful walled garden at the back, while bar conversation might touch on the merits of various local tomato growers. A nice touch is also provided by a blackboard that gives the day's weather forecast and the occasional snippet of local news as well as highlighting upcoming events.

So after a long drive you can feel pretty secure in ordering lunch. Try a salad of grilled organic chicken breast and dry cured bacon, or if you have an appetite for offal you might consider the black pudding potato cakes, which are sweet and filling. Yet, the Walter de Cantelupe doesn't forget those who want to come in and order a pint. King's Shilling from local brewers Cannon Royall is a bittersweet and bracing session beer and is joined as a regular by Taylor's lush Yorkshire bitter Landlord; there are usually two guest beers that come from the likes of Wye Valley, Malvern Hills and Mayfields in Leominster. Perry and cider from Dunkerton are stocked in bottle. The pub has also carried out a bi-annual 'beer election' in which customers were invited to nominate the beer they would like as a regular on the bar. Brewers of both the regulars and challengers are invited to present their beers and then a vote is taken.

Maybe Walter de C might have experienced a change of heart were he to step into his namesake today. After all, the medieval clergy took a keen interest in the pleasures of the table and you could imagine the bishop settling into a quiet corner to enjoy a plate of Malvern Victorian sausages with gravy and mashed potato and giving the nod to anyone who wanted to set up a Church Ale.

Opening hours: 12–2, 6–11; 12–3, 7–10.30 Sun; closed Mon
Access: Jct 7, M5

White Lion

Fritwell Road, Fewcott,
Oxfordshire, OX27 7NZ
01869 346639

▌Beer range varies

• •

If you're travelling on the M40 and fancy a brief stop then come off at Junction 10 and make for Fewcott. It's not far away. However pick your times wisely… The White Lion is closed during the day in the week: there's no lunchtime trade – it sounds as if the whole village decamps to Birmingham to work (it's 45 minutes away by motorway). It doesn't do food either. 'We're a pub not a restaurant,' says landlord Paul King. So if you're in search of a genuine local free house where conversation and craft beer rule the roost then the White Lion roars defiance against the notion that pubs have to be more than pubs to survive. And in celebration of this stand, the White Lion serves up four cask beers at any one time. These are constantly being rotated: beers come from the likes of Salopian, Goddards, Blue Monkey and Wyre Piddle.

The White Lion was originally a trio of cottages, built in the year when the United States of America declared independence. The village pub was originally next door, but the demolition men came calling sometime in the 19th century; it was not very salubrious according to those in the know. Insalubrious isn't a word you could say about the White Lion; words like robust, honest and earthy come to mind instead.

Unpretentious as well. Walk into the White Lion (remember the opening times) and you enter one room (there might have been a snug and lounge here at one time) with an annex where the dartboard is. Nothing fancy on the walls: brewery mirrors, some long gone (Morrells, Morlands) and others still active (Marston's Pedigree). Old maps and pictures of the village provide further visual furniture for drinkers. Oh and outside the pub on the front wall there's an old plaque to remind passers-by of the White Lion's former owners: Halls of Oxford, though they eventually ended up being owned by Allied Brewers. There's also a beer garden and it's here on Wednesdays and Thursdays at certain times of the year that you will feel the electricity and passion of the Aunt Sally players. 'Thursday is the most serious night,' says King, 'the guys playing on that night are always desperate to win.'

In search of pub passion on a Thursday night? Turn off at Junction 10 and make your way to the White Lion.

Opening hours: 7 (5.30 Fri; 12 Sat)–11; 12–6.30 Sun
Access: Jct 10, M40
Also great for: Pub games

The best **near motorways**

sbury

transpennine express

MEALS
SNACKS
TEA/COFFEE

REAL ALE
TELEPHONE
TELEVISION

BLACK
SHEEP
BREWERY

NO SMOKING

WEST RIDING
Licensed Refreshment Rooms

BLACK
SHEEP
BREWERY

BREWED IN MASHAM

The best **railway pubs**

You'll have to forget about the train now waiting on Platform 1 as the splendid pubs in this section are either on the concourse of a railway station or close enough to repair to if you've got a few minutes grace. It's a simple fact: they are well worth delaying your journey for. The Centurion in Newcastle is a study in splendid pub architecture, a classy and democratic resurrection of a classic Victorian lounge for first class passengers.

Others re-imagine the (mythical?) golden era of railway travel with atmospheric recreations of the buffet room, that have the added attraction of cask beer: the refreshment room at Stalybridge is a place where good beer is served alongside the local delicacy of black peas from a cup; meanwhile the King & Castle at Kidderminster goes the whole hog for all our yesterdays with its succession of steam trains coming in and out. And the Rat Race Ale House in Hartlepool celebrates the 'small is beautiful' ethic and offers an ever-changing timetable of cask beers.

Meanwhile, do not forget the Euston Tap, which is a magnificent post-modernist use of a Victorian building that has been marooned outside the unlovely front of the eponymous station.

See also
Cricket Inn,
Totley (p210)
Crown,
Stockport (p263)
George Inn,
Borough (p155)
Signal Box Inn,
Cleethorpes (p169)

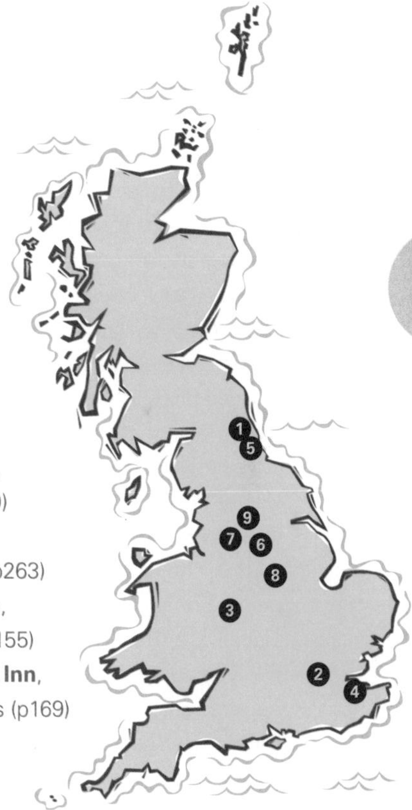

◀ West Riding Licensed
Refreshment Rooms, Dewsbury

Centurion

Central Station, Neville Street,
Newcastle upon Tyne, NE1 5DG
0191 261 6611
www.centurion-newcastle.co.uk/bar.asp

🍺 **Black Sheep Best Bitter; Jarrow Rivet
Catcher; Theakston Traditional Mild;
guest beers**

There are station bars and then there is the
Centurion at Newcastle's Grand Central Station.
Breathtaking might be one word to describe a
debut visit to this sumptuous space that was built
in 1893 as a lounge for first class passengers. Or
you might just want to keep quiet and stare about,
jaw clanging onto the floor, senses bombarded
by the richness of the surroundings. The ceiling
reaches to the heavens, celestial light pouring
through a large deep skylight. All around the room
a host of decorative touches overwhelm: art-deco
lights suspended from the ceiling, every inch of
wall space covered with patterned tiles of many
colours (estimated to be worth £3.8 million),
marble columns rock solid behind the spacious bar
counter, ornate carvings and at the opposite end
of the bar, across the room, a massive painting
depicting a rural scene – river, trees and mountains
in the background. An ironic touch given the
location of the Centurion: right in the hard urban
heart of the northeast's most iconic city.

It's not always been such a splendid sight
though. After its debut as a luxury waiting room
for the upper classes, times moved on and the
lounge lurched into disrepair and by the 1960s was
attracting a less salubrious sort of custom – local
transport police were using it as cells. British Rail
did their best to neglect it as well, but when the
current owners bought it in 2000 the restorative
work began. You don't need to be an architectural
genius to know that it's been a success.

In the wrong hands (or even the wrong city),
the Centurion would be a gaudy, self-satisfied
mausoleum. Drinkers would be urged to keep
their voices down, while anyone who showed the
slightest disrespect for the fixtures and fittings
would be shown the door. That's not happened
here. Straightaway, on first entrance, heading for
the bar, you will be struck by a buzzy, bright feel:
the voices of drinkers echo to the high heavens
and pints of local cask beers from the likes of
Wylam and Mordue join the regulars at the bar.

A lot goes on here, after all Newcastle's main
railway station is a busy place – the Centurion
mirrors this hive of activity. This is also a football
city and the Centurion has the largest screen in
Newcastle. But if you're in need of a quiet drink
there is a snug to the back of the main bar.

The Centurion has come a long way since
it first opened – and why not? This is a visual
experience that shouldn't be left to first class
passengers from the Victorian age.

Opening hours: 10–11 (midnight Fri & Sat)
Also great for: Pub design

Euston Tap

190 Euston Road, Euston, London, NW1 2EF
020 3137 8837
www.eustontap.com
🍺 **Beer range varies**

. . . .

New concept, old building. The Euston Tap is housed in a 19th century stone lodge once part of the entrance to the original station (this was demolished in the early 1960s amid much outcry, with Poet Laureate John Betjeman leading the charge). It's a few moments walk from the modern monstrosity of today's station from which you'll want to exit swiftly en route to the Tap; cross the lanes through which the buses pass and you'll see what looks like some sort of overblown crypt from one of the old Victorian cemeteries of London. An outdoor umbrella featuring the name of Czech brewery Bernard will offer up a clue as to its current use, while the neon-lit name of the bar above the door in the entrance brings it up to date in a slightly kitsch sort of way.

The Tap opened in 2010, hot on the heels of the successful debut of the Sheffield Tap (see p132), which is run by the same beer-friendly company; the two of them might be related but they're as different as chalk and cheese, apart of course from the devotion the both of them have to the cause of great beer. Step inside and you're in a compact space with a high ceiling; stools and standing room only. Yet what takes the breath away is behind the bar, something that has the feel of an old piece of brewing kit – a copper-faced front with taps sticking out while there's a narrow copper sink at the bottom (it all looks as if it were from the same piece of metal). For those who have never been to an old brewery, it's the sort of thing you would see being used for running off wort during the mash. At this wonderful, magical point there are normally eight cask beers alongside beers from all over the world. This is the dispensation of beer as theatre. Bottled beer is also well represented: both sides of the bar feature glass cabinets full of more bottles, with a great emphasis on US craft brewers.

A long spiral staircase takes the drinker away from the bar to the second floor, which is more casual and dotted with chairs and low tables. Here the quiet buzz of conversation, punctuated by the high notes of laughter, holds court. There's no food, though pizzas can be ordered from nearby. It's a magnificent concept, in an unlikely but welcome position offering a space where some of the world's greatest craft beers can be enjoyed. As beer continues to find new and exciting ways to engage with the drinking public, the Euston Tap is firmly in the vanguard of this wave.

The best **railway pubs**

Opening hours: 12–11; 12–10 Sun

King & Castle

Severn Valley Railway Station,
Comberton Hill, Kidderminster,
Worcestershire, DY10 1QN
01562 747505

🍺 **Batham Best Bitter; Hobsons Mild;
Wyre Piddle Royal Piddle; guest beers**

• •

The King & Castle feels like a time slip. Outside steam trains are shunting back and forwards. Inside an archetypal Edwardian railway bar takes shape around you. The walls are deep pink below the dado rail, and cream above. The art deco-esque fireplace has a period firescreen in front and an old London Pride poster framed above. Come winter, it roars into life, creating a cosy snug retreat from the modern world. The wood is suitably dark and shiny, the tables and chairs reminiscent of every pub one visited in one's youth. Yet all is not quite as it seems. The trains are attached to the restored Severn Valley Railway Station and the King & Castle is a recreation of an original GWR refreshment room. It's a fake.

They've carried it off really well though. This doesn't feel like a museum piece; it doesn't feel horribly self-conscious; nothing jars. The level of their success is shown by the fact that the bustling bar doesn't just attract visitors to the railway and its museum. Instead it hosts a merry crew of locals, often accompanied by their dogs. The atmosphere is welcoming and inclusive, though it can get very busy. But then, if it's too crowded inside, you can take your pint and stand outside, watching the world go by as trains move back and forth. Children will be fascinated – and are also made welcome.

There are six handpumps, with Batham's Best Bitter consistently rated as excellent. Wyre Piddle Royal Piddle is brewed especially for the pub and there are guests from local brewers such as Kinver and Bewdley. The owners venture further afield too, with beers coming from all points of the compass to keep their regulars' palates content.

Unlike modern train fare prices, the bill should come as a pleasant surprise – beer is markedly good value here. So much, in fact, visitors often feel they really have slipped back through time. Food won't scare the horses either. It's plain, simple, unpretentious and, once again, good solid value for money. Expect a plateful whether you plump for toasted sandwiches, soup, ploughman's, cottage pie, or fish and chips. They also offer up a rib-sticking breakfast (the refreshment room opens at 9am), a good selection of children's meals and, if you hit lucky, Sunday lunch.

Time really is fluid here in Kidderminster.

Opening hours: 11–11; 12–10.30 Sun

Railway Hotel

Preston Street, Faversham, Kent, ME13 8PE
01795 533173
www.railwayhotelfaversham.co.uk

Shepherd Neame Master Brew, seasonal beers

• •

I do love a confident hostelry; one that has no doubt whatsoever about what it is and what it does. The Railway Hotel is one such place – it's pleasantly certain of itself; opinionated even – but in the nicest possible way.

This 19th century redbrick building sits, unsurprisingly, right opposite Faversham railway station. Inside is a large airy bar with the original, deeply imposing, Victorian back bar dominating the room. The dividing screens have been reinstated and the pub hopes to bring back the snob screens too in the course of time. It's timeless and traditional, with a surround of encaustic tiles on the floor around the bar. Large windows mean the light pours through, yet the red ceiling and rich wood makes it feel snug and, like all good bars, protected from the world outside somehow. A boar's head peers snootily down from the half-panelled walls, presiding over the cheerful bustle. No 'reserved' notices on the tables here. The Railway has very firm ideas about bars being, well, bars. Conversation and chatting to your neighbour is positively encouraged here, hence no television screen, jukebox or background music. However, there is a bar billiards table that provides entertainment for both those playing and watching.

There is no food served and even certain drinks are out of bounds: shots or alcopops are not stocked. However, what they do stock is cask beer. The house special is Shepherd Neame's Master Brew joined by one of the same brewery's seasonal beers, such as Late Red (Sheps' brewery and visitor centre is only a short stroll away).

If you want to eat, that's fine – you just go to the attached Provenance Restaurant whose mission statement is 'ethical' food. Locally sourced, organic where possible, Fairtrade where necessary. Hmm, you might think, are we in the realms of the stodgy and worthy? Far from it. Think crab and prawn gratin; pigeon and chicken paté; tomato, basil and feta bruschetta for starters. And then there's Brogdale toad in the hole, game pie, or chilli glazed salmon for followers. They also serve a tapas menu on the terrace every evening from 6-8pm. And there are hotel rooms.

So, The Railway is, in effect, a curious mix. It's a very traditional – one might say old-fashioned – bar; a pretty on-trend restaurant, a perfectly serviceable hotel and a continental tapas bar to boot. But because it is all done with such ease and certainty, it works a perfect treat.

Opening hours: 12–11; 12–10 Sun

The best railway pubs

The majority of train stations either have no refreshments or offer up the usual selection of invidious near-beers that might have alcohol in their make-up but shy away from flavour like a cat does when confronted with a terrier. An hour on a platform without some comfort and cheer can seem double the time. Luckily, there is now a happy band of stations that has seen a post-modern attempt to create a fantasy land of a rail buffet where cask beer, the ambience of the pub and hearty snacks draw people in, even if they've no intention of going on a 15.20 to Woking or whatever.

It's a noble tradition – stations of a certain size would always refresh their travellers once upon a time, while the railway hotel can be still seen in many a town – even if many of them have long been converted into private homes. In the late 1940s, when Britain seemed perpetually wreathed in smoke and fog, the film industry latched onto the homely, den-like aspect of the railway buffet – witness the awkward meeting of equally awkward lovers Celia Johnson and Trevor Howard in *Brief Encounter* (with the resolutely proletarian Stanley Holloway chortling away in the background). This was a place for secrets and clandestine meetings. Nowadays, the modern railway buffet has a celebratory air, albeit with a different way of doing things, as the Sheffield Tap and the Rat Race Ale House in Hartlepool demonstrate in their divergent ways.

The Sheffield Tap – a refurbished Edwardian refreshment room on Platform 1 of Sheffield station

Rat Race Ale House

Station Approach, Hartlepool,
County Durham, TS24 7ED
07889 828648
www.ratracealehouse.co.uk

🍺 **Beer range varies**

· ·

Small really is beautiful at the Rat Race Ale House. This most micro of micro-pubs is squeezed into what was, until 2009, a newsagents on the platform at Hartlepool train station. It's tiny – just 20ft by 14ft – big enough for around 15-20 people to squeeze in. There's not even room for a bar so drinks are ordered off the board and poured from the cellar, a cramped room off the main room. It's a rough and ready, back-to-basics approach.

The range of drinks is equally narrow. The Rat Race sells just real ale and cider, along with soft drinks and wine. Food? Don't be daft. If they don't have room for a bar, how on earth would they fit in a kitchen? But you can nibble on crisps and some excellent pork scratchings.

The décor is equally stripped back and functional with pride of place going to the blackboard with the current range of ales chalked up. And this is the point at which the Rat Race stops being small and becomes distinctly capacious; expansive, gargantuan even. This tiniest of pubs is big, nay vast, on beer. The pub's tagline is 'It's all about the beer' and their website pays testament to their passion. It doesn't give their full address or telephone number but it has a counter showing how many different beers have been on sale since their opening at the end of 2009. At the time of writing it stood at 341. There's a customer forum where they list the beers and you can record your thoughts on their quality. The list features all manner of craft breweries from Otter to Thornbridge, and Daleside to Wharfedale.

Owner Peter Morgan is evangelical about real ale. On the eve of opening his micro-pub he was quoted as saying, 'What I'd like is for anybody who gets on or off the train in Hartlepool to try a proper real ale and go, "wow, that's good stuff", that's what the Campaign for Real Ale is all about – encouraging people to try it.'

Judging by the bodies crammed into the tiny space, he's achieved his aim. This tiniest of railway taverns is packed, not only with the serried ranks of the local CAMRA branch but by surprised and delighted commuters and passers-by. Small on space the Rat Race might be but it's very big on heart and taste.

Opening times: 12.02–2.15, 4.02–8.15; 12.02–8.15 Sat; closed Sun

The best **railway pubs**

Sheffield Tap

Platform 1, Sheffield Station, Sheaf Street,
Sheffield, South Yorkshire, S1 2BP
0114 273 7558
www.sheffieldtap.com

🍺 **Thornbridge Wild Swan, Kipling, Jaipur IPA, Seaforth; guest beers**

. . . .

There they sit, Celia Johnson and Trevor Howard in *Brief Encounter*, snatching a brief moment of love amidst the smoky and spartan surroundings of a postwar railway station buffet. In the background, Stanley Holloway's gruff but honest character chunters away oblivious to their misery, while closer scrutiny of the scene can also detect an advert for Bass. There has always been an inherent romanticism about such places in the past – maybe it was due to their transient nature. People came and went, their train drawing in, a quick gulp of tea (or beer) taken and off they rushed.

At the Sheffield Tap there's no need for such melancholic thoughts. This is the modern age after all. Slap-bang on Platform 1 at Sheffield station,

this refurbished former Edwardian refreshment room has swiftly become a magnet for beer- and pub-lovers after its 2009 debut. Its plush but understated makeover has been nothing short of a triumph. Talk to someone who remembers it in its previous incarnation and you'll get tales of a hollow shell of rotting timbers, broken windows and graffiti from the 1970s era of soccer hooligans.

Now it's the very picture of pub elegance. There's a long mahogany bar, polished to perfection, with an equally lengthy grand mirrored back-bar fitting topped by a carriage clock. You can sit down at comfortable leather chairs or stand and contemplate your beer at chest-high tables dotted about. Pop in on a Friday afternoon, and you will find the place heaving with all manner of folk settling down for a glass or two. Many, I suspect, aren't even travelling. At the bar, you can see why trade is good.

A plethora of handpumps and beer taps stand tall offering at least four ales from local brewery Thornbridge, plus six guests that might feature cutting edge breweries such as Dark Star, Roosters, BrewDog and Summer Wine. There is also a peerless selection from Czech brewery Bernard and other excellent world breweries. Plump for Thornbridge's crisp and fruity lightly coloured bitter Kipling, and you will get a beer to rouse and raise the most jaded of palates. Talking of which, if you're peckish this is sandwich and panini territory when it comes to food. But frankly, who cares – we're here for the beer.

Whether you're after a brief respite from changing trains or on a beer quest, the Sheffield Tap is a destination you must not miss.

Opening hours: 11–11; 10–midnight Fri & Sat
Also great for: Pub design

Stalybridge Station Refreshment Rooms

Platform 1, Rassbottom Street,
Stalybridge, Greater Manchester, SK15 1RF
0161 303 0007
www.buffetbar.org

🍺 **Boddingtons Bitter; Flowers IPA; guest beers**

The majority of the old-fashioned Victorian railway buffets were swept away years ago when the then British Rail decided that what travellers really wanted were cellophane-wrapped sarnies and Styrofoam cups of lacklustre coffee. Here, on Platform 1 of Stalybridge station, the buffet bar remains a rare survivor of a time when waiting for the train could be a pleasure.

Entered from the platform, first impressions of the front bar are of a narrow space, but also a railway enthusiast's delight. On the wall there are station nameplates, old style notices declaring what can and cannot be done in the vicinity of the station, locomotive names and tin plate ads for cigarettes. Newspaper cuttings from the 1990s tell the story of the bar's fight for survival. All this gives a sense of a slow but steady mania of collecting, a hoarding of bric-a-brac over the years, something that imbues the buffet bar with an identity as well as a warmth and character.

This is very much a place for lingering. After all, there's usually another train that can be caught after the one you missed. The attraction of five cask beers might have something to do with this sloth. Alongside the regulars, craft beers from the northwest usually celebrate the likes of Empire,

Brewhouse and Mancunian beer heroes Phoenix; there's a small but useful list of foreign beers as well. As for food, the bar counter features a glass case that is home for crisps and biscuits, while the short but decisive menu offers the likes of pie and mushy peas, sausage and mash, plus a local speciality: black peas from a cup.

A conservatory-style extension is fitted to the left of the bar, handily facing west, which makes it a delicious way of catching the last of the sun. Through a corridor to the right, there's another room, possibly a former waiting room, with more train artefacts and a shelf of books for those with a long wait. This is the pub as a beer palace, railway museum and waiting room, all in one. Your train awaits but you might wait a bit longer.

Opening hours: 10–11; 12–10.30 Sun

The best **railway pubs**

Victoria

85 Dovecote Lane, Beeston,
Nottingham, NG9 1JG
0115 925 4049
www.victoriabeeston.co.uk

🍺 **Castle Rock Harvest Pale; Everards
Tiger Best Bitter; guest beers**

The Victoria is history personified: a classic survivor of the great age of railway, a time when the travelling public expected and also received a measure of comfort on their journeys, especially when they were changing trains. The Victoria stands trackside, within yards of the trains that come into Beeston station. It's had its ups and downs, but has survived down through the years and is currently a much-favoured pub for drinkers in the East Midlands, especially given the ease with which it can be reached.

Before entering the Victoria it's worth taking some time to admire its redbrick frontage crowned with the twin curved gables and below these the legend 'Ind Coope & Co Burton Ales' picked out in whitewashed stone. A hotel was first built on this site in 1840, but the current building dates back to 1899 when its then owners Ind Coope opened it under the name of the Victoria Commercial Hotel. This was an age of expansion and growing affluence. 1914 was just a date in the future.

There are two bars. To the right is the Red Room, the public bar; to the left the bar is open-planned with arches leading to several other rooms. The walls are coated with all manner of beery memorabilia: hundreds of beer bottles stand on shelves, almost as if they are laying siege to the place like the man-eating triffids from the famous John Wyndham novel. Blackboards detail the food and drink available. It's a busy interior, but pleasing and informative. First timers to the Victoria will no doubt find themselves, glass in hand, wandering through the rooms, intrigued by the beery treasures on show. It's a veritable museum of beer. Even though there are regular jazz nights, there's a welcoming lack of piped music, with the muted tones of drinkers and the occasional rustle of a newspaper providing the background.

Beer is king here with up to 12 cask beers on at any one time. Guests come from the likes of Leeds brewery, Oldershaw and other regional craft breweries. Devotees of the dark brewing arts will be heartened to discover that there is usually a mild and stout on tap. The menu is chalked up in the main bar, a mouthwatering array of dishes including a platter of Spanish cured meats, seafood, and a cranberry, beetroot and orange risotto with goats cheese – it's an inclusive rather than exclusive menu.

You eat and drink well at the Victoria and given how easily it can be reached, it'd be a shame not to pay your respects to this great survivor.

Opening hours: 10.30–11; 12–11 Sun

West Riding Licensed Refreshment Rooms

Railway Station, Wellington Road,
Dewsbury, West Yorkshire, WF13 1HF
01924 459193
www.imissedthetrain.com

🍺 **Black Sheep Best Bitter; Taylor Dark Mild, Landlord; guest beers**

• •

Seeing your train receding into the distance as you stand there panting on the platform is a special kind of hell. When is the next one? Will it stop? What can you do as you wait? Where's the nearest pub? As the web address chosen by this drinking establishment makes clear, at Dewsbury Station it's almost obligatory to miss your train (unless of course you're off to a funeral or a job interview) – because there's a rather special pub that is an essential visit if you're travelling on this stretch of the Trans-Pennine line.

Platform 2 at Dewsbury Station is the place to be. It's here where the West Riding Refreshment Rooms has been refreshing and reviving beer lovers since it first opened for business in 1994.

In the same way as travellers on the train like something to look at as they trundle along, pub-goers also want their environment to be visually pleasing. And at the West Riding they will not be disappointed. Seen from the car park, the building itself is impressive – solid local stone with some nice architectural flourishes. Inside, archways connect the three rooms. The central bar is a symphony in wood, while the walls are covered in framed photos, old adverts, the odd clock and station plates. A shelf of beer bottles also runs round the room – offering bottle-collectors the chance to see if there are any they haven't got. The whole effect is of a visual harmony – you won't get bored here.

Then there's the beer. There are always eight cask beers on with guests coming from a variety of northern brewers including Thornbridge, local brewery Anglo-Dutch, Marble and Durham. Of course, that old Yorkshire favourite Landlord is always available – a bittersweet, dry, citrusy best bitter that was reputedly Madonna's favourite ale at one time. Food includes curries and Mexican dishes and the whole package is topped off by regular music events.

Missed your train? Head inside and hope that you miss the next one too. The West Riding manages to turn hell into heaven.

Opening hours: 11 (12 Mon)–11 (midnight Thu & Fri);
10–midnight Sat

The best **railway pubs**

The best
pub design

Pub design? Compared to the old and venerable buildings in which they have made their homes, these pubs are fairly recent – fresh-faced even – but there's nothing callow about the imaginative uses to which they have been put.

In the Cheshire countryside, Sutton Hall was once a manor house and home to the Earls of Lucan (of vanishing fame) but thanks to its diligent pub company (the last three words are not often seen together) owners Brunning & Price, it now offers a comfortable country house ambience along with a delicious range of beers. The Brewery Tap in Chester also has aristocratic pedigree plus a range of Spitting Feathers' beers and a robust, hearty menu. Stripped down modernistic minimalism is the hallmark of the Bristol member of the Zerodegrees chain, a beautifully austere space complete with the workings of its brewery on show. The Beer Hall also has its brewing kit on show while its clean Swedish-style interior is a stylish complement to Hawkshead's fabulously accomplished ales. Meanwhile, Brains' creative and original reordering of the Yard demonstrates that old breweries don't always have to become flashy flats or carpet warehouses when the mash tuns move on.

**See also
Butcher's Arms**, Herne (p166)
Centurion, Newcastle upon Tyne (p126)
Port Street Beer House, Manchester (p74)
Sheffield Tap, Sheffield (p132)

◀ Beer Hall, Staveley

Beer Hall

Mill Yard, Staveley, Cumbria, LA8 9LR
01539 825260
www.hawksheadbrewery.co.uk

🍺 **Hawkshead Bitter, Red, Lakeland Gold, Brodie's Prime, seasonal beers**

Sometimes it pays to switch careers: in 2002 former BBC journalist Alex Brodie swapped the microphone for the mash tun when he set up Hawkshead Brewery in the Lake District. It was a success and in 2006 as sales soared he moved the brewery from the 17th century barn site in Hawkshead to Staveley and opened up a larger outfit. The building had a dual purpose: Brodie's vision also incorporated the Beer Hall, which is very much an organic part of Hawkshead. The Beer Hall is a bar, visitor centre, beer shop and kitchen all rolled into one, a place to enjoy great beer and food, a place far removed from the traditional idea of what makes a pub – not that there's anything wrong with traditional pubs, as this book demonstrates, it's just heartening to see a brewery like Hawkshead try and redefine the space in which we drink beer. Such was the reception that greeted Brodie's idea that it became the first winner of SIBA's Local Brewing Business Awards in 2006.

First impressions: clean bleached wood fittings suggest a bar as designed by IKEA with a nod to the aesthetic of the American brewpub – clean lines, minimal clutter, a canteen feel even. At the bar there are usually seven of Hawkshead's beers – the stainless steel, tubular shaped handpumps offer a subtle yet another marked sense of the 'modern' to the beer drinker. Brodie's Prime is a particular personal favourite, an enticing dark beer that offers roast notes alongside a luscious flurry of fruitiness. More stainless steel is visible by the entrance in the form of a brace of tall fermenting vessels, while drinkers can also glance through glass into the brewhouse. 'The Beer Hall looks down into the brewery,' says Brodie, 'so that you can see the brewing process. It also gives us a considerable retail outlet and is a showcase for our beers. We have spent a lot of money on it to create a very modern environment with new wood, leather sofas and an environment that tells people "this is serious'." Seen from outside the building's visionary aspect is even more striking and imposing – it is glass fronted, there are no mysteries hidden behind high walls here.

As you might expect from the ideas at work within the Beer Hall, care and attention is given to the food, with a menu that is deliciously retro in its scope. Beer Tapas is the title and there is a selection of beer friendly mouthfuls including scotch eggs, pork pies, sausages, beer-battered plaice goujons and pea and ham soup. Beer's gastronomic abilities are justly lauded here.

Opening hours: 12–6 (5 Mon, 11 Fri & Sat); 12–7 Sun
Also great for: Brewery taps

Lake District pub walk

Start the walk at Ings, a small hamlet on the A91, and home to the Watermill Inn (p87). After that welcome start, cross the road from the Watermill and adjacent to the eastbound bus stop (from where you can catch the bus directly to Staveley if you've overindulged on your first stop) there is a lane running off to the north. Walk up this lane and in about 10 minutes you'll come across a bridleway leading off to the right. Navigation remains easy: ignore paths to right and left until you pass the buildings of Hugill Hall farm, and just after this, joining tarmac again, continue in more or less the same direction until you reach the heavily restored buildings of Heights Farm. Just after the bridleway bears left there's a step stile on your right (GR 451002), which you take.

Walk more or less in the direction of the signpost, staying quite close to the right-hand wall to find the next stile. You should be able to pick up a steadily improving track in the grass leading downhill through a gate, keeping the plantation on the far fellside straight ahead of you as you then join and follow the winding track down towards a quiet lane which you join via a gate. Simply continue downhill on this lane which turns sharply right near the valley foot (ignore the bridleway running off to the left) and follow the road for about a mile until you reach Scroggs Bridge. You're unlikely to meet traffic on this very quiet byway.

Cross the bridge and bear immediately right on a footpath and then turn uphill by the cottages and join a wider bridleway where you turn right. Continue through the farmyard at Scroggs Farm on the bridleway and join another very quiet lane down towards the outskirts of Staveley by the river bridge. Don't cross the bridge but rather continue along on the road on the left bank of the river for about a quarter of a mile, then take the signed footpath for Staveley on the riverside, as the road veers away. There is evidence of former industry here at the weir, and in fact the industrial yards across the road contain the remains of the site of Staveley Mill. These days the mill yard is home to the new site of Hawkshead Brewery and its justifiably-popular Beer Hall (opposite) where you can sample a wide range of Hawkshead's brews.

Nearby Staveley station has connections to Windermere and Kendal.

Adapted from *CAMRA's Lake District Pub Walks* with the kind permission of Bob Steel

Map used: OS Explorer OL7

Bow Bar

80 West Bow, Edinburgh, EH1 2HH
0131 226 7667

🍺 **Caledonian Deuchars IPA; Stewart 80/-;
Taylor Landlord; guest beers**

• •

You will always find Deuchars IPA on at the Bow
Bar – and with good reason. When this beer
was developed in the early 1990s, it was at the
Bow Bar that it was first trialled. It obviously
was a success given the beer's subsequent all-
conquering progress throughout the UK. The Bow
Bar also offers a neat symmetry with the then
infant brand: even though it looks like it's been
anchored on the Grassmarket for centuries, the
Bow Bar was just then starting out. It was once a
shop and only opened its doors in the early 1990s.
You wouldn't think so when looking around the airy
and well-lit single bar with its burnished dark wood

gantry behind the counter and various other fittings
such as brewery mirrors (refugees from city pubs
that dispensed with such 'traditional' accessories
as they sought to ditch the past in the 1980s).

As you contemplate your pint of Deuchars
IPA (alongside one of the hot pies available at
lunchtime), don't think that history lets the Bow
Bar escape its clutches that easily. Look at the bar
and note the tall founts – these are rare survivors
of the old Scottish Aitken system of dispensation,
in which cask beer is served using air pressure
driven by a water engine. The Bow Bar is one of
the few still to stick with this system and it doesn't
seem to affect the beers. The contemporary beer-
drinker's lust for choice is mirrored in the eight
cask beers available, with guest beers coming
from around both Scotland and the rest of the
UK; the whisky drinker is also well-served with a
humongous selection of 150 native single malts.

Opening hours: 12–11.30; 12.30–11 Sun

Brewery Tap

52 Lower Bridge Street, Chester,
Cheshire, CH1 1RU
01244 340999
www.the-tap.co.uk

🍺 **Spitting Feathers Thirstquencher, Old
Wavertonian, seasonal beers; guest beers**

. . . .

Not many pubs can claim that Charles I spent a
night beneath its roof but the Brewery Tap does –
during the English Civil War the doomed monarch
stayed here for a couple of nights, prior to a battle
which he then lost. Gamul House wasn't a pub
at the time, but the home of a local royalist (who
saw it forfeit when Cromwell came to power).

Over the centuries it underwent a variety of
uses, but in 2008 Cheshire brewery
Spitting Feathers came
on the scene and
opened it

up as its tap. It now stands, redbrick and
imposing, in a row of buildings from the same
period, a lucky survivor given the damage that
Chester endured during the Civil War.

Go in and make your way to the massive
Jacobean banqueting hall with its enormous
sandstone fireplace where the bar is placed. This
is a light room thanks to a high arched ceiling
and wide windows. Even though centuries have
passed it's still got that feel of an old aristocratic
hall, a place where you'd imagine royalist voices
discussing the urgent political issues of the day.
Yet there's also a sense of easy pleasure in the
hall – even though the building is Grade II listed,
which meant that Spitting Feathers had to be
very careful what they did, it's not a museum
piece. Sit in there with a glass of the brewery's
boisterous stout Old Wavertonian (or maybe you'd
like to refresh yourself with Thirstquencher, a
clean and crisp golden ale) – whatever the drink
you're completely at ease with your surroundings.

There are usually seven cask beers on, with
Spitting Feathers being joined by a variety of craft
breweries from the northwest and beyond. As for
food, alongside classic pub dishes such as beef
and stout pie and bangers and mash, there are
more eclectic dishes, perhaps produced with a
nod to the House's original owners: how does
braised pig's heart with celeriac mash or braised
pig's lungs, dumplings, potatoes and mushrooms
sound? All this makes for a glorious pub
experience, something that has been recognised
elsewhere – in 2009 the Tap won two awards in
the National Pub Design Awards which was jointly
organised by CAMRA and English Heritage.

Opening hours: 12–11 (midnight Sat); 12–10.30 Sun
Also great for: Brewery taps

The best **pub design**

Brewery Tap – Derby's Royal Standard

1 Derwent Street, Derby, DE1 2ED
01332 366283
www.derbybrewing.co.uk

🍺 **Derby Triple Hop, Business As Usual, Dashingly Dark, Double Mash, Old Intentional; guest beers**

· ·

The Brewery Tap is the latest name to be given to this fabulous pub that stands alone at a junction, its balustrade-topped front jutting out between the traffic like a ship's prow ploughing through the waves. It began life as a pub in 1862, but was rebuilt in 1890 and named the Royal Standard to celebrate a royal visit. Fast-forward to 2006 and redevelopment was on the cards and there was a chance this historic landmark could be lost. However, two years later, new owners the Derby Brewing Company had turned what was a dingy bikers' pub into a fantastically bright and breezy advertisement for modern craft beer.

Walk into one of its two bars now and you're in a roomy airy space. A bleached pinewood floor, exposed brickwork, gleaming handpumps and fonts, and a white ceiling lined with old beams all manage to maintain a sense of the pub's venerability. It's a thoroughly modern makeover, sympathetic to the pub's heritage, individualistic without being irritatingly quirky.

That's the design, but does it cut the mustard as a pub? Well the local CAMRA branch obviously thinks so as they gave it their Pub of the Year award in 2009. Given that Derby Brewing Company are the owners it's also no surprise to discover that beer is a major part of the Tap's offerings. There are up to 10 cask beers on tap, half of them produced by DBC. Classic European and North American beers are also available in bottle.

Like matching ale and food? Ask for the rack, a wooden palette drilled with holes that hold five 1/3rd pint glasses, which are filled with DBC's beers. A small bowl of locally sourced cheeses completes the offering. The aim is to encourage beer and food matching and promote the virtues of beers such as Copperhead Road, Dashingly Dark and Triple Hop. The menu also features hearty helpings of robust pub grub with a twist: pea and ham pie, sausages made with beer and home-cooked fish fingers lead the way.

The nature of the British pub is transitory. Names change, buildings get a makeover, the landscape moves on, people come and go, yet the essential nature of a good pub remains constant: a warm welcome, excellent food and drink drunk in pleasing surroundings, a home from home. The latest incarnation of the Royal Standard has it all.

Opening hours: 11–11 (midnight Thu; 1am Fri & Sat)
Also great for: Brewery taps

Sutton Hall

Bullocks Lane, Sutton, Macclesfield,
Cheshire, SK11 0HE
01260 253211
www.suttonhall.co.uk
🍺 **Thwaites Original; Weetwood Cheshire
Cat; guest beer**

. . . .

Down a tree lined driveway off a country lane,
hidden from the road when the trees are in leaf –
you'd hope that there's something special hidden
away up here, and quite a few people having
gone to Sutton Hall would say there is. Over 450
summers have passed since the Hall was built;
it was once home to the Earls of Lucan (family
of the vanished Lord). As well as being home to
the rich and infamous, it has been a hotel and a
convent. Now it's one of the stars of Brunning
& Price – a pub chain that has marvellous pubs
dotted about North Wales and Cheshire.

A pub in a manor house? Surely we're talking
a country house hotel or a restaurant where the
waiting staff come styled in suits of armour, but
Brunning & Price are adamant that the Hall is a
pub, a place where you can drink cask beer and/
or choose dishes off the hearty menu.

Weetwood Cheshire Cat is a regular at the
bartop, smooth and refreshing with a dry
bittersweet finish, while others that appear will
come from the likes of Three Tuns and Salopian.
Outside there's a shiny courtyard and gracefully
groomed gardens, while inside there is a warren
of rooms (somewhere for Lord Lucan to hide
perhaps), with the main bar area featuring a
decent amount of nooks and crannies. This is a
baronial pub experience: as well as the bar there
are several dining areas, a snug and a library. The
décor is resolutely aristocratic and country house
with a forest of old prints on the walls. And when
you're ready to eat the menu offers a selection of
substantial dishes – carnivores will plump for the
slow roasted pork belly while vegetarians might
like the mushroom burger in focaccia.

So it's a pub but it's also a joy to behold, an
historical gem that hasn't been tampered with to
its detriment. It might not be everyone's idea of
a place to have a few pints but to get a glimpse
of how the other half lived as well as appreciating
Brunning & Price's impeccable work you'd be
recommended to go to Sutton Hall. You never
know, you might see Lord Lucan…

Opening hours: 11.30–11; 12–10.30 Sun

The best **pub design**

Yard Bar & Kitchen

42-43 St Mary Street, Cardiff, CF10 1AD
029 20227577
www.yardbarkitchen.co.uk

🍺 **Brains Dark, Bitter, SA, Rev James, seasonal beers**

. . . .

Brains used to brew their beers in Cardiff city centre until 1999 when they upped sticks and moved half a mile south. Here they set up home at the old Bass brewery where another Cardiff favourite – Hancocks – was (and still is) produced. What to do though with the former plant, a place that was part of the city centre, regaling shoppers with the warm aromas of the mash on brewing day, and the brewery tap – the street face of Brains – the Albert, on the same site?

Many breweries, having made a similar relocation, would have been keen to sell to the highest bidder, move on and shield their eyes from perhaps a conversion to a block of flats or a host

of shops. Not Brains though. It's true, part of the old brewery is now a leisure area and piazza, part of the city centre's shopping experience, but since the Yard opened in 2003 it has seen the brilliant re-imagining of a former brewing space into a slick and comfortable venue; the modern world of design making use of yesteryear. There is more: at the Yard cask beer remains on the same terms as wine and food and the memories of yesteryear are warmly recalled, without descending into some sort of sickly pageant of nostalgia.

As people and cars whizz by on the street an open glass front – the old Albert – lets light in and gives passers-by a glint of stainless steel and gleaming beer fonts. At the bar, there's a serious Victorian-style wooden fixture, while on the wall next to the bar, footage of the old brewery runs on a continuous reel. Various bits of old brewing equipment – tubing, pipes, exposed brickwork, girders – are open to the world, while modern touches come in the shape of gleaming metallic surfaces and a flickering log fire playing on a plasma screen. Upstairs at another bar, reached by a wide spiral staircase, some intriguing touches: a row of former cinema seats bolted to a wall; wire mesh tables, sanded wooden floor and more bare brick walls. At the front, there's a space that has the feel of an ersatz gentlemen's club with comfortable leather bound chairs and shelves of books.

For those who hanker after spit and sawdust and the old world of brewing, the Yard is possibly heresy. On the other hand, we are in a post-industrial world and you could argue that Brains has designed a space just for that. The brand new world of beer starts here.

Opening hours: 10–11 (midnight Thu; 2am Fri & Sat)

Zerodegrees

53 Colston Street, Bristol, BS1 5BA
0117 925 2706
www.zerodegrees.co.uk

🍺 **Zerodegrees Wheat Ale, Pale Ale, Black Lager, Pilsner, seasonal and speciality beers**

• •

Pub or bar? Gastro? Brewpub? Post-modernist? Post-industrialist? A visit to Bristol's Zerodegrees could pose more questions than answers, which could be a bore if you're only in for a pint. Part of a brewpub chain with outposts in Cardiff, London and Reading, Bristol's version is a big open bar, high-ceilinged and light with windows looking out over the Colston district of the city. The semi-circular bar counter is devoid of frills, with five oblong metal discs identifying the beers, while the marble-like floor is dotted with chairs and tables that wouldn't be out of place in

a sixth form common room. The brewing kit is also on display, a naked animal of stainless steel pipes and tanks, high above the bar, the smell of brewing pervading the space at certain times.

The beers have a continental influence: the Wheat Ale owes its soul to Bavaria (bananas, cloves), the Black Lager looks to Bohemia for its brewing influence (creamy, smoky, gentle roastiness), while the Pilsner is exactly what it says on the tin, a Pilsner influenced by the brewing traditions of the Czech Republic. The Pale Ale is a light chestnut brown: aromatic on the nose with tropical fruit on the palate – it goes like a dream with an anchovy-topped margarita pizza. All these beers are unfiltered, stored in tanks beneath a bag of air with none of them experiencing exposure to air or extraneous gas. There is often a fruit beer on.

This promiscuity of brewing could all so easily disappear up its own self-conscious fundament, but Zerodegrees' serious approach to beer and hospitality means that this Bristol branch is a seriously good experience. The devotion to beer extends to samplers being offered to newcomers to the bar, while food and beer choices are also pushed forward. There's an irony that this very modernistic brewpub is in Colston, an area that was home to one of the earliest West Country micros in the 1970s – Smiles. Maybe the chain's owners deliberately decided on this position as both an homage to the past and a representation of the next move up for beer and breweries in the beer city of Bristol. This is a place where the past and future of Bristol's great beer heritage come face to face and move drinkers onto an entirely new plateau.

Opening hours: 12–midnight; 12–11 Sun

The best **pub design**

The best
heritage pubs

The barbarian hordes of pub improvers swept through the trade in the years after the Second World War – snugs, saloons and tap rooms were all overwhelmed and torn apart with a ferocity worthy of Attila the Hun. Tales are told of fixtures and fittings from the glorious age of Victorian pub elegance that had served generations of drinkers being thrown onto the scrapheap, an arrogant dismissal of history that was replicated by those brewers who thought drinkers would be happy with Watneys Red Barrel and its insipid like. As CAMRA has campaigned to protect our beer heritage, so its heritage arm has fought to protect and have recognised our important pub heritage.

So, many pubs managed to survive the onslaught, or at least were able to mitigate some of the more barbaric changes. In the Suffolk countryside the King's Head is a shining example of the rural pub of many rooms. In the city, the ornate flourishes of Victorian artistry lift the Bartons Arms into another galaxy and offer the drinker a rich understanding of what has been lost in so many other like-minded places. Meanwhile the Coopers Tavern in Burton upon Trent is a place that stands as a testimony to the magnificent brotherhood of beer.

See also
Boat Inn,
Ashleworth (p90)
Café Royal,
Edinburgh (p66)
Nursery,
Heaton Norris (p255)
Old Green Tree,
Bath (p73)
Olde Swan (Ma Pardoe's),
Netherton (p35)
Seven Stars,
Falmouth (p109)

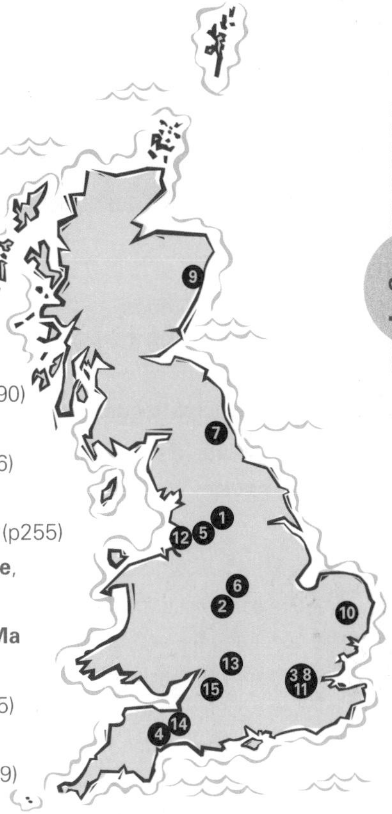

◄ George Inn, Borough

Adelphi

Hunslet Road, Leeds,
West Yorkshire, LS10 1JQ
0113 2456377
www.theadelphileeds.co.uk

🍺 **Leeds Pale, Best; Taylor Landlord;
guest beers**

• •

Despite some recent quirky café bar touches to the décor and the soft furnishings, the Adelphi remains a perfect example of a late Victorian drinking house – as true to its purpose now as when it was built in the late 19th century.

One thing has certainly changed. The pub's majestic curving frontage stands just a stone's throw from the Tetley Brewery gates, and it was for years considered the unofficial 'tap'. From just across the road, the brightly-lit crimson of the company name burned into the night sky. Generations of workers from across the sprawling site – once the world's biggest producer of cask beer – would end their shifts with a pint of the product at the Adelphi. The sad closure of the brewery in June 2011 not only robbed Leeds of a major commercial icon but removed a significant part of this famous pub's natural constituency.

Yet it continues to thrive. And just as Leeds brewery has become the biggest brewer in the city, so their products now dominate on the Adelphi bar, a potent symbol of how this confident stripling has stolen into the Tetley heartland. Handpulls dispensing sharp and refreshing Leeds Pale and the more rounded Leeds Best stand alongside lovely firm Timothy Taylor Landlord and at least one guest ale. Fruli, Leffe, Sierra Nevada and a cosmopolitan host of bottled beers add extra interest. The Adelphi's menu of up-market modern pub food changes daily.

As in a number of pubs of this vintage, the bar fronts onto a corridor. In only one of the four drinking spaces can you be served directly from the counter. Big curved windows, tiling and intricate wooden carving each speak of a golden age of pub architecture. Etched screens – some original, some tasteful later additions – divide the space effectively, affording intimacy and privacy, though many drinkers choose to linger in the busy corridor. A Tuesday quiz, a monthly comedy club, occasional live music and DJ nights, and private parties in the upstairs function room will also keep the punters coming through the door, long after the last man stripping the kit from the famous old brewery has switched off the Tetley lights for good.

Opening hours: 12–11 (midnight Thu, 1am Fri & Sat)
National Inventory part 1; Grade II listed

Written by Simon Jenkins, Beer Writer of the Year 2010

Bartons Arms

144 High Street, Aston, Birmingham,
West Midlands, B6 4UP
0121 333 5988
www.oakhamales.com

🍺 **Oakham JHB, Bishops Farewell,
seasonal beers; guest beers**

· ·

Past and present (and future too) come together
in the best possible way at the Bartons Arms. The
past: this is one of the most stunning examples
of late Victorian pub architecture, a magnificent

building in its own right – dominated by a clock
tower below which the pub's name is picked
out, Tudor style chimneys, gables and etched
windows. Terraces surrounded the place when it
was built, but the area was cleared in the 1960s
and the Bartons Arms now stands like a splendid
island of haughty isolation, hemmed in by roads
and looking for all the world like a town hall rather
than a pub. In through the doors and you are in
an overwhelming world of classic pub fittings:
stained glass windows, snob screens, the original
tiling and a massive wrought iron staircase.

And the present? The pub was closed in 2002
but Oakham Ales bought it and brought in an army
of craftsmen to bring it back to life. This award-
winning Peterborough brewery was always noted
for its love of well-hopped golden beers and a
modern approach to the world, and you could
argue that their relationship with the Bartons Arms
was like that of an old millionaire with a young
pretty woman (a touch of Hugh Hefner perhaps?).
Yet, this has been a marriage that has worked.
The pub still maintains its wealth of period fittings,
whilst managing to offer a selection of both
Oakham's cask beers and guests from around the
country. JHB remains an old favourite here, with
its lime and citrus nose and a light bubblegum-
like fruitiness before its bitter and citrusy finish.
There is also an intelligent bottled beer selection
featuring some of the classics of the beer world.
As if that wasn't enough, the food is a zesty, spicy
selection of Thai dishes (following the tradition set
by Oakham's Brewery Tap in Peterborough, p42).

As for the future? If you haven't been here then
that's your future.

The best **heritage pubs**

Opening hours: 12–11; 12–10.30 Sun
National Inventory part 2; Grade II* listed

Black Friar

174 Queen Victoria Street, City of London,
London, EC4V 4EG
020 7236 5474
www.nicholsonspubs.co.uk

🍺 **Fuller's London Pride; Sharp's Doom Bar;
Taylor Landlord; guest beer**

. . . .

Distinctive in its design, the Black Friar is triangular, tall and narrow, its front jutting out into the street. The contrastingly benevolent figure of a pot-bellied Dominican friar – whose order had a friary here in the Middle Ages – stands over the entrance, beckoning passers-by to enter.

As if the startling exterior is not enough, enter the Black Friar and you will be immediately overtaken by the abundance of art nouveau fittings inside. The pub dates from 1875, but it was redone in 1903 (some might say overdone), complete with the ornate flourishes on show today.

Marble is everywhere, whether in the form of pillars or panels. Meanwhile, look out for the friezes of monks in varying stages of rest and recreation that figure all over the place, and the slogans that are engraved on the walls. Phrases of the order of 'Silence is golden' and 'A good thing is soon snatched up' suggest that the designer had his tongue firmly in cheek. At the front end of the pub (the jutting part), you will find a semi-circular bar, from which four cask beers are dispensed; food is robust and hearty as exemplified by the ham hock and pea suet pie (no doubt the carousing friars would have approved). The mullioned windows make the space light and expansive.

Beyond the bar there's an open lounge with an inglenook fireplace surrounded on each side by banquette-style seating and through a couple of marbled arches is the back room with its myriad of mirrors. The whole effect is of art installation as much as a unique pub – no wonder John Betjeman lent his name to save it from demolition in the modernising wave of the 1960s.

Naturally, being close to many offices, the Black Friar is busy during lunch and early evening, so to get a feel for its amazing décor and contemplate on the connection that medieval religious orders had with beer and good living, mid-afternoon might be an ideal time to visit. Don't forget your camera.

Opening hours: 10.30–11; 12–10.30 Sun
National Inventory part 2; Grade II* listed

Bridge Inn

Bridge Hill, Topsham, Devon, EX3 0QQ
01392 873862
www.cheffers.co.uk
🍺 **Branscombe Vale Branoc; guest beers**

• •

In 1998 the Queen chose the Bridge for her first ever pub visit. As is usually the case with Buckingham Palace, little emerged afterwards to indicate what Her Majesty thought of her pub debut, but a case of specially brewed beer was sent to Prince Philip to celebrate the day. As landlady Caroline Cheffers-Heard (whose family have owned the pub since the 19th century) was later invited to the Palace, the chances are that the Queen viewed her visit as a good one.

The Bridge Inn is a venerable time machine with history permeating its bricks and mortar. Its origins are in the middle ages and it has also done time as a brewhouse and malthouse (you can see the old brewery behind the pub). Inside you're faced with a warren of small old-fashioned rooms, parlour-like in their ambience and packed with memorabilia. One hosts ancient bunting that was hoisted for the coronation of George VI in 1937, while the other is notable for a long wooden table that apparently served in the 19th century as a counting table for local farmers on market day. Service is either in the corridor or from a serving hatch into the royal room. There is also a parlour behind the bar that is strictly by invitation only – asking to sit there stymies your chances for good, I'm told. Ale can also be taken outside, where the bird life on the sludgy mudflats of the Exe can be watched. As if that's not enough the old Maltings often doubles up as an overspill bar and concert venue.

As for beer you can enjoy a massive selection of cask beers, mainly served from the barrel. There are normally six available with an emphasis on West Country ales coming from the likes of Otter and Branscombe Vale (it was they who produced the commemorative beer for Her Majesty). Local cider comes from a mile away and local country wines are also served.

Food is solely served at lunch: accompany your pint with a sturdy and honest ploughman's served with local cheese or a round of home-cooked ham sandwiches brought to vibrant life with lashings of elderflower and gooseberry chutney from nearby Budleigh Salterton. This is the sort of pub where time stands still and before you know where you are it is closing time (note the Bridge operates an old-fashioned regime). Not being a beer drinker, the Queen didn't know what she was missing.

Opening hours: 12–2, 6–10.30 (11 Fri & Sat);
12–2, 7–10.30 Sun
National Inventory part 1; Grade II listed
Also great for: Riverside

The best **heritage pubs**

Britons Protection

50 Great Bridgewater Street, Castlefield,
Manchester, M1 5LE
0161 236 5895
www.britonsprotection.co.uk

🍺 **Jennings Cumberland Ale; Robinson's
Unicorn; Tetley Bitter; guest beers**

- -

The Britons Protection celebrated its 200th
birthday over a June weekend in 2011 – two
centuries spent serving beer and hospitality to
the folk of Manchester through thick and thin
(over these two days the first 200 customers
were able to buy their first pint for 10p).
Men signed up for the army here during the
Napoleonic Wars (hence the name), while several
years after Waterloo the shameful episode of
Peterloo happened right on the pub's doorstep.
Chances are that some of the same men who
took the King's shilling might have been in the
crowd that day agitating for basic rights. The
event is commemorated within the pub with a
mural; strangely enough this is the only pub that
commemorates the Peterloo Massacre.

Even though the Britons Protection wears
its Georgian look on the outside with pride,
inside is where the décor really takes the breath
away. It is thought that the pub was remodelled
sometime in the 1930s – luckily it's hardly been
touched since. The pub's rambling selection of
rooms feature a wealth of gorgeous moulded
plasterwork on the ceiling, tiling (both floor and
wall), a wooden bar counter as unyielding as the
Thin Red Line, an arched gantry above the bar,
leaded windows and banquette seating with bell
pushes still in place. There are two rooms off the

bar where you can even get beer served through
a hatch. It is no wonder that the pub is a popular
destination for all manner of folk.

Musicians for instance. Bridgewater Hall
is opposite so you might find yourself sitting
next to an oboe player taking a break between
movements and slaking their thirst on a pint of
Jennings Cumberland Ale (one of the regulars)
or a guest beer from Coachhouse. Beers from
Robinson's, Arran and Allgates are also amongst
the guest ales tipping their hats at those that
come through the door (there's a massive
selection of whiskies as well). Food is served
lunchtime and features a robust selection of pies.
In the spirit of what the protestors at Peterloo
demanded, this is really a place for all.

Opening hours: 11 (11.30 Sat)–midnight;
12–midnight Sun
National Inventory part 1; Grade II listed

The best **heritage pubs**

Coopers Tavern

43 Cross Street, Burton upon Trent,
Staffordshire, DE14 1EG
01283 532551
www.cooperstavern.co.uk
🍺 **Castle Rock Harvest Pale; Draught
Bass; guest beers**

. . . .

A visit to Burton upon Trent is a visit to the
historical heart of the British brewing industry.
Stand on the railway bridge next to the station and
look towards the town centre – great monolithic
blocks of red brick mark the passing of formerly
great names like Allsopps, Bass and Worthington.

The Coopers Tavern also claims an historical
pedigree. This small square Victorian pub was
once a sampling house for Bass and went on to
become the brewery tap. Here, brewers came to
check that the beers they brewed were ready to
be sent out throughout the country. For the retired
head brewer of Bass, Arthur Seddon, this place
was where he was first introduced to the magic of
beer: 'My father was a brewer with Worthington's

and took me in one Saturday morning. After he had
walked me round the brewery checking all was
well, we went to the Coopers Tavern. I remember
him getting permission to smuggle me into that
little snug, and I was given what I think was a
brewery sampling glass with about an inch of cask
Worthington E; the rest of the glass was filled with
a tight foam. I think I was 10 years old.'

Nowadays, the Coopers Tavern is part of a
small estate of pubs owned by Joule's brewery
and stands as a testimony to the magnificent
brotherhood of beer. A snug off to the left offers
quiet and contemplation, while the front room is
a hotchpotch of brewery mirrors and old faded
portraits of Burton worthies. The floor is tiled and
the furniture distressed wood; comfortable leather-
coated settles line the walls. Further inside another
snug adjoins the open bar, which offers up to eight
cask beers (as well as a handful of ciders and
perries). The ambience is traditional and orientated
towards the celebration of beer – the background
music is the murmur of chat, while no food is
served apart from Sunday lunchtime. However,
those in the know happily bring their own grub in.

A pint of Draught Bass (now brewed by
Marston's), served straight from the cask, can
be a sprightly little number, with the trademark
sulphury, struck match 'Burton snatch' on the
nose. Beers from across the country are available
with Thornbridge's Jaipur being another favourite.
Burton upon Trent may have lost its role as the
brewing engine of the nation, but a visit to the
Coopers Tavern is to experience what was and
what is good about beer in this historic town.

The best **heritage pubs**

Opening hours: 12–2.30 (not Mon & Tue), 5–11;
12–midnight Fri & Sat; 12–11 Sun
National Inventory part 2

Crown Posada

31 Side, Newcastle upon Tyne,
Tyne and Wear, NE1 3JE
0191 232 1269

🍺 **Hadrian Border Gladiator; Jarrow Bitter; Mordue Workie Ticket; guest beers**

• •

Conviviality marks out Newcastle's city centre. This is a place where, at the drop of a hat and a glass of brown ale (still called Newcastle but now brewed in Yorkshire…) men of all ages will regale newcomers with tales of past football geniuses. People are not shy in coming forward either. As I sat in the Crown Posada, notebook in hand, taking in this glorious survivor of Victorian pub architecture, I was even asked if I was a poet. If I were then this magnificent city centre treasure would be first in line for a rhyme or three.

As the crowds parade up and down the Quayside, the Crown Posada offers a port in the storm, a more leisurely and traditional sense of geniality and hospitality. As one of the oldest pubs in the city, this Grade II listed building has been greeting drinkers since the late 18th century, when its first clientele were the clerks who worked in the shipping industry. The name of the pub boasts a nautical connection as well – legend has it that a married Spanish captain once bought it for his locally based mistress (*posada* is Spanish for inn or resting place). Whatever the truth, what really makes it stand out is the magnificence of its fixtures and fittings, dating as they do back to the 19th century. From the outside, the frontage features elaborate stone work. There's attractive wrought iron work over the entrance, while the two windows feature a brace of pre-Raphaelite figures. One is of a man raising his glass high in salutation, while the other is of rather glum-looking woman filling a glass. Make of that what you will.

Inside, on a sunny day the light shines through this coloured glass, giving the long, narrow bar more than a hint of the sanctity of a cathedral. Inside there are reddish-mahogany wood surfaces, brass foot rails, Victorian-style banquette seating lining the wall and moulded ceilings. There's a snug at the front of the bar that locals gravitate to. Framed photos and mirrors dot the walls. The effect is of considered and classical design for that most humble of places: the pub. A quirky touch is added by the use of a vinyl playing record player. From this you will hear a selection of artists, from Nat King Cole to Neil Young to Blondie. On the beer front, half a dozen cask beers feature, usually from local breweries such as Hadrian, Jarrow and Wylam. Meanwhile food is confined to lunchtime sandwiches and why not – there's enough here to sate the greediest of pub appetites.

Opening hours: 12–11 (1am Fri & Sat); 7–10.30 Sun
National Inventory part 1; Grade II listed
Also great for: City

George Inn

George Inn Yard, 77 Borough High Street,
Borough, London, SE1 1NH
020 7407 2056
www.nationaltrust.org.uk/main/w-georgeinn

🍺 **Greene King IPA, Abbot; guest beers**

Of all London's galleried inns that serviced the coaches that once came and went, the George Inn is the sole survivor – and even then, it's not complete. Two wings were pulled down to make room for engine sheds in the 19th century as London Bridge's importance as a railway terminus grew (neighbouring inns the White Hart and the Tabard, of Chaucerian fame, were not so lucky and only plaques remain to remind us of their existence). To ensure the George's survival it passed into the care of the National Trust in 1937.

The single wing that still stands offers a time capsule of what the coaching inn stood for: a time when the pace of travel was dictated by horses and a far from comfortable ride in a vehicle with inadequate suspension. It was also a period when inns like the George offered travellers a welcome respite from the trials of their journey: thanks to Charles Dickens, whose *Pickwick Papers* is a veritable trawl through the world of the coaching inn and its delights, we can imagine tired travellers arriving to the appetising aroma of roast beef and a lively jug of porter. No doubt though the reality was far starker in many places.

Take a moment to look at the outside of the George. Two galleries tower over the cobbled courtyard, in which it is claimed – by virtue of the Globe being a few minutes walk away – that Shakespeare acted here in his plays. By the

time Dickens came to set the George within the pages of *Little Dorrit*, it was a replica of Will Shakespeare's (possible) local – it had been rebuilt in the 1670s after being badly damaged by fire.

The inside of the George is a ramble of rooms, furnished with dark wood, wooden floorboards, settles and benches. Those in the know make for the snug, which is also home to an ancient beer engine – a corridor links this with a bigger more spacious bar. Upstairs, along a rather splendid staircase, is a series of rooms that are used for dining. Also look out for the 18th century parliamentary clock, an ironic horological comment on an Act of Parliament that aimed to tax clocks.

Naturally, this living slice of pub history gets very busy, as it lies on the London tourist trail. You don't come here to look for the latest craft beer (the Rake p22 is near enough for that), while the menu features a host of solid pub favourites such as bangers and mash, and ham, egg and chips. However, for the serious pub lover it's an essential stop on any crawl around London.

Opening hours: 11–11
National Inventory part 2; Grade I listed
Also great for: Railway

The best **heritage pubs**

City streets, especially in historic places like London, can provide just as stimulating a stroll as a walk in the country – with the added bonus of regular pub stops. This ramble visits some of my favourite London pubs and (if it's later in the week) allows the perambulator the chance to go shopping in the gastronomic paradise of Borough Market.

Borough was once the hub of London brewing with the gigantic Barclay Perkins sitting next to the river, while five minutes from Southwark the Hop Exchange thrummed and thrived with the produce of Kent's fine hop fields. Now, there's a different kind of beery ambience in the air.

Emerge from the Borough High Street exit of London Bridge underground station and walk in a southerly direction down the busy High Street and after about 100 yards you will come to an alley that leads to the George (p155) – London's sole surviving galleried coaching inn. After a glass of Greene King Abbot, return back onto Borough High Street and continue south until you come to the St George the Martyr church (here members of the Young family of Wandsworth fame lie). Turn left down Tabard Street and a few minutes walk will bring you to the Royal Oak (p75). This is Harveys' only London pub and the ideal place to contemplate the brewery's wondrous Sussex Best Bitter.

Retrace your steps back down Borough High Street to the George and arrive at the busy junction with Southwark Street. Cross the road for Borough Market and after pausing to admire the Hop Exchange proceed into Stoney Street. Halfway down you will find the Market Porter, which offers 12 cask beers, many of which come from all over the country. After this, it's but a short trip around the corner to the Rake (p22), where an Imperial Stout might lurk to finish off the walk. It's then five minutes through Southwark Cathedral back to London Bridge.

The Market Porter, a haven of cask ale next door to Borough Market

Grill

213 Union Street, Aberdeen, AB11 6BA
01224 573530
www.thegrillaberdeen.co.uk

🍺 **Caledonian 80/-; Deeside Talorcan;
Harviestoun Bitter & Twisted; Shepherd
Neame Spitfire; guest beer**

. . . .

The Grill. Sounds like a 1970s eating place. Mixed grill, London grill, sausages, steaks, kidneys, a male kind of eating place (you wouldn't have been far wrong in the past). The Grill is actually a pub, serves five cask beers and is noted for its selection of whisky. Noted too is the unchanged décor, with many of its fittings from 1926 when the Grill went from being a restaurant to a pub. Sitting on the ground floor of a rough-hewn granite faced terraced property from the 1830s, its frontage a mix of glass and panelled wood, the Grill has the air of yesteryear when you couldn't see into a pub.

Once inside take time to have a look about – and admire the plasterwork ceiling, the mahogany panelled walls and the hand carved gantry and clock. It's a long narrow bar with banquettes fitted to the opposing wall, but otherwise it's a place where people stand for their pint or dram (or both even). With all this period pub architecture on display, it's hard to concentrate on the matter in hand (the beer) as you take it all in.

There are five cask beers available including regulars Caledonian 80/-, Bitter & Twisted, Spitfire and the rich and creamy Talorcan stout. Guest beers come from Scottish breweries including Fyne, Orkney and local (well, Fraserburgh) bad boys BrewDog. Space is an issue hence food is limited to snacks. Despite the pristine fittings on display there's a sense of inclusivity about the Grill, though this wasn't always so. When the pub opened in the 1920s women were banned from coming in. This ban wasn't rescinded until 1975, despite an invasion of female Scottish Trades Union delegates in 1973. The ladies of 1975 may not have felt truly welcome even then – it was another 23 years before a ladies loo was built.

Opening hours: 10–midnight (1am Fri & Sat);
12.30–midnight Sun
National Inventory part 1; Grade B listed

The best **heritage pubs**

King's Head (Low House)

Gorams Mill Lane, Laxfield, Suffolk, IP13 8DW
01986 798395
www.laxfieldkingshead.co.uk

🍺 **Adnams Southwold Bitter, Broadside, seasonal beers; guest beer**

· ·

Laxfield is slap-bang in the midst of the glorious Suffolk countryside, a few miles inland from the coast. This is a landscape of wide skies and handsome villages, whose distant church spires and towers stand up like ships' masts.

The King's Head is a similarly pleasing prospect, ancient, thatched and untouched by the passing of time. Also known as the Low House (a reference to its low-lying position as opposed to any slight on the clientele), it was built in the 1500s and named after Henry VIII. It sits in the centre of the village, opposite the old church, a remainder of the long and loyal link between pub and pulpit.

Once inside, passing through the solid oak door into the low-ceilinged front room, note that time has not altered the traditional layout: first-timers tend to ramble through the warren of rooms, pub-going explorers in search of hidden treasure. A snug here, a snug there, nooks and crannies all branching off a central corridor. The tiled floor is uneven and gently sloping, worn smooth by countless drinkers, with the latest generation gathering around the massive fireplace in the front of the pub. The walls are the colour of parchment, cracked and smoke-stained, adorned with a variety of old photos, some of long-ago football teams, many of whose players now take their rest in the churchyard opposite.

There's no bar. Just make your way to the rear of the pub, passing the 'crisps cupboard' and wait to be served in the back cool room where racked casks of Adnams magnificent beers await.

What will we choose? Will it be Adnams pristine Southwold Bitter with its backbone of English malt and spicy, pithy citrus Kentish hop character; or the stronger and more robust Broadside? Or maybe a glass of one of the Southwold brewery's specials such as Oyster Stout or, come winter, the brewery's mighty barley wine, Tally Ho. The pub also organises two beer festivals every year, coming complete with music and all manner of fun and frolics – when the weather's clement a large green garden at the back offers the chance of al fresco drinking. And when hungry, try the home-cooked, locally sourced, fresh and filling food: ham, egg and chips; steak and ale pie or maybe a curry.

Rooted in the heart of the village with the permanence of a stout oak tree, this is a place that could stand as surety for the timeless and venerable appeal of the country pub.

Opening hours: 12–3, 6–midnight; 11–midnight Fri & Sat summer; 12–4, 7–11 Sun
National Inventory part 1; Grade II listed
Also great for: Country

The best **heritage pubs**

Old Brewery

The Pepys Building, Old Royal Naval
College, Greenwich, London, SE10 9LW
020 3327 1280
www.oldbrewerygreenwich.com

🍺 **Beer range varies**

Look about the compact bar at the Old Brewery and you'll see a visual love letter to the remarkable talents of the 'beerhunter' Michael Jackson. Up against the exposed brickwork of one wall, standing on shelves behind a protective wall of glass, there are dozens of beer bottles from all around the world – just a small selection of the mammoth collection of the late and sorely missed Jackson. What better way to pay tribute to a writer who opened up the fascinating world of beer to so many – and in the process encouraged the likes of Meantime, whose dream the Old Brewery is.

The Old Brewery is the creation of Alastair Hook, founder of Meantime, a brewery that has become famous for producing beers inspired by the great beer styles of Europe: Helles, Pilsner, London Porter, India Pale Ale. The bar is equally inventive, boasting a thoroughly modern aesthetic: it is light and airy, making good use of its space with clean lines and unfussy fixtures and fittings. It has the air of an exclusive upmarket cocktail bar, but it's devoted to that most democratic of drinks: beer.

Four cask beers feature, from breweries such as Adnams and Dark Star, while the beer menu also includes a battalion of classic bottled beers from all over the world, plus Meantime's own beers, one of which is brewed in the small brewery that stands at the head of the adjoining restaurant. Also make time for Meantime's rich and heady College Porter, brewing with a nod to the 18th century.

Even if you are not eating (highly recommended – the shoulder of mutton braised in Meantime Pale Ale is a succulent dream), pop your head round the corner and see the magnificent three-storeyed display of copper vessels, reaching high into the glass lit ceiling. On brewing days the rich aroma of the brew reaches out its tantalising arms. Glance around the wall and note the brewing history timeline etched on its surface. This is a place where beer neophytes can be taken and gradually introduced to the delights of John Barleycorn.

The Old Brewery is situated in UNESCO-listed maritime Greenwich on the site of the Christopher Wren-designed Old Royal Naval College, a place that throbs with the beating heart of history. The Old Brewhouse naturally has a brewery, but more than this: Meantime have managed to bring about a magical fusion of past and present.

Opening hours: 11–11; 11–10.30 Sun
Also great for: Brewpubs

The best **heritage pubs**

The Philharmonic

36 Hope Street, Liverpool,
Merseyside, L1 9BX
0151 707 2837
www.nicholsonspubs.co.uk

🍺 Caledonian Deuchars IPA; Jennings
Cumberland Ale; guest beers

· ·

Tell anyone in the know that you're visiting
the Philharmonic and chances are you'll be
commanded to visit the gents even before
ordering a pint. Marble urinals and wash-tops,
copper taps and glazed tiled walls turn what should
be a mere place of convenience into a brief but
grand tour of ornate décor. And once out of the
loo everywhere you look your eyes will land on
some of the finest Victorian pub architecture in the
land. The pub was built in 1898 for the Robert Cain
Brewery – perhaps an indication that its owners
wanted to attract a classier type of customer than
was prevalent in most of the city's boozers.

The magnificence starts with the exterior. The
pub is sited on a corner, opposite the Philharmonic
Hall. Stand across the road to take in the
flamboyant display of stepped gables, balconies,
turrets and balconies. Even the entrance makes a
flourish with a colourful pair of wrought iron gates.

If you've never been in before, be prepared
to have your breath taken away with the sheer
extravagance of design. A large island bar acts as
the hub – the public bar is around the back, while
off the lobby there are a couple of rooms (cheekily
called Brahms and Liszt) while a corridor leads
to the Grande Lounge. The latter was once used
for billiards, but is now a comfortable dining area
(note the two massive skylights of coloured glass).

Elsewhere, there are snob screens, mahogany
wood fittings, embossed glass, decorative
plasterwork on the ceiling, stone carvings and tiled
flooring. This is a pub as a piece of art.

All this splendour gives the place a reverence
not usually found in a pub, something akin to
a quiet movement in a symphony perhaps (an
apt comparison given that the Philharmonic
is a popular watering hole for concert-goers
and musicians) rather than intimidation; voices
murmur rather than shout.

Sitting on a battered leather sofa in the public
bar I enjoyed a glass of Cairngorm Trade Winds
whilst contemplating my surroundings, finding
new fittings to admire. The well-chosen selection
of cask beers is also something to appreciate, as
is the menu: hearty, robust and belt stretching.
Beef and Fuller's Vintage pie was a rich and juicy
plateful that demanded another beer. Once you're
in the Philharmonic you might be some time.

Opening hours: 10–11 (midnight Fri & Sat)
National Inventory part 1; Grade II* listed
Also great for: City

The best **heritage pubs**

Red Lion

Ampney St Peter, Cirencester,
Gloucestershire, GL7 5SL
01285 851596

Taylor Golden Best, Landlord

. . . .

Choose carefully the timings of your visit to this glorious piece of living pub history. Opening hours are limited to evenings – last orders are called at 8.30pm during the week; but there's a bit more time plus Sunday lunchtime during the weekend (sadly the last bus back to Cirencester leaves at 6.15pm, which doesn't even give you a moment for a mouthful). But by hook or by crook (or with a driving friend who doesn't drink) get there as it's worth it. The Red Lion is a living and breathing architectural survivor of a simpler pub style and the Taylor Landlord you'll drink here will be as good as anywhere in the north. 'There's not many pubs left like this anymore,' says the landlord John Barnard. And he's right.

Find it first. It's several miles to the east of Cirencester, at a fork on the A417, a honey-coloured Cotswold stone building with an 18th century core and later extensions. It looks like a farmhouse with a couple of stables built to the side. However, it's when you go inside that the magic takes place. Off a narrow corridor there are two rooms; the one on the right is the designated bar – though there's no bar counter – this is one of only 15 pubs left in the whole of the UK without one. Two handpumps lurk in the corner, dispensing Landlord and the light mild Golden Best (though Hooky Bitter occasionally makes an appearance), the landlord's narrow space defined by a bench in front. Elsewhere in the room the ambience is rural simplicity: there is wooden dado panelling and the flooring is quarry tiled while the tiled fireplace looks a bit modern. Postwar perhaps... Back into the corridor and opposite is the lounge with prints on the walls, stools and a spartan yet comfortable feel to things.

In the past the pub was owned by the Stroud Brewery (not the current one), which was then bought up by Whitbread and amalgamated with a couple of other breweries under the title of West Country Breweries – you can see the ceramic plaque to the side of the entrance. It's now a free house with John Barnard only being the fourth landlord since 1851. There's no food and it's the sort of pub where conversation forms part of the soundtrack while the ancient rooms keep mute their memories of those that have come and gone before them. And I hope that many more will continue to come.

Opening hours: 6–8.30 (10.30 Fri & Sat); 12–2.30 Sun
National Inventory part 1; Grade II listed

The best **heritage pubs**

Rose & Crown (Eli's)

Wincanton Road, Huish Episcopi,
Somerset, TA10 9QT
01458 250494

🍺 **Teignworthy Reel Ale; guest beers**

• •

My first visit to the Rose & Crown (or Eli's as it's locally known) was about 20 years ago. There it stood on the road, thatched roof, the body of the building a cottage from the early 19th century with several add-ons built about it. In the main bar, beneath a ceiling traced with black beams, there was no counter, just a trio of handpumps emerging from what looked like a shelf and nobody to serve me. A farmer (well I thought he was a farmer – he was jolly and red-faced and, well, looked like a farmer should look), who obviously had been drawing deep on the pub's cider that afternoon, cheerfully invited me to help myself. He wasn't the landlord, just a satisfied local. I turned down his advice and waited for someone to come and serve me, which they did with a smile a few moments later. I recently told this story to one of the bar staff and they were completely unruffled: 'Some of the locals, if there's no one about, still serve themselves and put the correct money down.'

On its own such a sense of trust would mark out Eli's as an utterly unique establishment. But there's more to it than a barless bar. For a start it's been in the same family for over a century and a half – Eli was the name of the grandfather of the current family members in charge (his great-grandson also helps out in the pub). Inside there's a real sense of time having kept still with uneven stone floors, rustically inclined rooms radiating off the central bar and the thatched top outside. The style is halfway between the austerity of an old non-conformist chapel and the warmth of a country farmhouse. The rooms have names as well: the Trivia Room and the Piano Room, which yes, does have a piano in it, but I'm told that it might need a bit of fine tuning, so be aware of this if you fancy a go.

Three cask beers are available: Teignworthy's Reel Ale (so called because the brewer is a keen fisherman) is the regular chap, while guests come from West Country breweries such as Hop Back, Cottage and Otter. The food is traditional pub grub such as cottage pie, steak and ale pie, and pork and cider cobbler. There's a sense of community about the Rose & Crown as well. The field to the back hosts cricket games and car boot sales, while there's a food cooperative in the pub every Friday afternoon with local produce up for sale.

Opening hours: 11.30–3, 5.30–11; 11.30–11 Fri & Sat; 11.30–10.30 Sun
National Inventory part 2; Grade II listed

Star

23 The Vineyards, Bath, Somerset, BA1 5NA
01225 425072
www.star-inn-bath.co.uk

🍺 **Abbey Ales Heritage, Bellringer, seasonal beers; Draught Bass; guest beers**

• •

Not many pubs can do this, but the Star is the sort of place that might make you think about how British social life has changed in the last century. On the left of the main entrance there's a lounge as evidenced by the word on the small, letterbox-sized plaque on the door. Inside is a compact space that immediately whispers front parlour, but – and here's where the debate starts – does it whisper this to everyone? Do you have to be of a certain age? Some will see ornaments that might have featured in their grandmother's cramped front parlour plus seats for Aunty Eileen and Uncle Bob, where they could have sipped their tea out of china cups after a family funeral. On the other hand, others might see a compact space, 'old fashioned', comfortable though –

maybe our heritage of cave-dwelling has had a lasting impact…

You might just want to enjoy the warren of rooms that constitute the Star, rooms full of crimson-chestnut coloured wood panelling, each room with its own character and sense of seclusion. The Glass Room is near the bar, a small room, while next door the bar has a space of its own. It's here where five solid, old fashioned handpumps dominate the bar top, four of them devoted to cask beer, three of which come from the local brewery that runs the pub, Abbey Ales. Bellringer is a sprightly golden beer, with light orange pastille notes on the nose and a bitter dry finish, while the strong bitter Maximus is rich and leathery, fulsome and vinous. You will also find Abbey's Heritage, a guest beer from the likes of Hop Back or Braydon, plus Draught Bass. This is famously served from a cask behind the bar, being poured into a jug before being dispensed into your glass.

Go during a quiet time as there is plenty to look at and admire. By the side of the bar is an old telephone, while winter sees a fire being lit in the Glass Room. 'It's an old building and there are plenty of draughts,' I'm told by the friendly barman, 'it can get positively Baltic in here.'

As befits such a deliciously austere place, food is minimal with rolls being offered at lunchtime. Truth to be told, you come to the Star to drink beer, talk to friends or indulge in contemplation and marvel at the survival of its sense of pub antiquity. Whatever you believe a front parlour is.

Opening hours: 12–2.30, 5.30–midnight (1am Fri); 12–1am Sat; 12–midnight Sun
National Inventory part 1; Grade II listed
Also great for: City

The best **heritage pubs**

The best **record breakers**

The Nutshell in Bury St Edmunds is the smallest pub in Britain – or is it? Contenders crop up with the regularity of mushrooms after an overnight rain shower. The Olde Trip to Jerusalem claims to be the oldest, but then so do a couple of others elsewhere on these isles. No such worries in Yorkshire for the Tan Hill though. Until the café atop Snowdon becomes a pub, or someone has the bright idea of building a Munro Arms on one of the eponymous Scottish mountains, then it looks like this regularly snowed in Inn on the Yorkshire Moors is set to keep its position as the highest pub in the UK.

In this section the featured pubs all lay claim to one element of record breaking, but it's not always easy to get to the bottom of the claim. So take the records with a pinch of salt and just enjoy the likes of the Butcher's Arms (it might have been the smallest at one stage – supplanting the Nutshell – but then along comes the Signal Box Inn, which seems Hornby like in size, if we're talking in railway metaphors) and the Witchball (tucked away on the Lizard peninsular, making it the most southerly pub on the British mainland): all these are pubs first and record breakers second.

The best **record breakers**

See also Kelham Island Tavern, Sheffield (p266)

Butcher's Arms

294 Herne Street, Herne, Kent, CT6 7HL
01227 371000
www.micropub.co.uk

🍺 **Dark Star HopHead; Fuller's ESB;
Old Dairy Copper Top; guest beers**

Is this the smallest pub in the country? At 14x12 feet it might or might not be (see the Nutshell and the Signal Box Inn), but visit it on a busy session and you will certainly feel as if you're in a record-breaking establishment. You won't be able to avoid talking with your neighbours either, so don't take a paper and look for a quiet corner. 'I offer the pub in its most basic sense,' says landlord Martyn Hillier, 'Conversation is the appeal. If I didn't have any banter here then it wouldn't work.' There is no music, and very little food apart from some snacks and pork pies brought in on a Saturday by a regular; 'You should see the size of them,' says Hillier, 'they're like a dinner plate'. There's a glorious sense of pub stubbornness about the Butcher's Arms, a Cnut-like stance against the waves of change. Yet, unlike Cnut, Hillier is winning his battle.

The Butcher's Arms, as the name might just suggest, was once a butcher's and you can see the old rails and butcher's block; there are also some cleavers on display. A multitude of beer towels cover large parts of the walls, plus other beery ephemera. The front window, in which once lay trays of meat, helps to make this 'micro-pub', as it's been dubbed, a light and airy space.

There's no doubting Hillier's devotion to John Barleycorn. There are up to six cask beers available with Dark Star's HopHead and Old Dairy Copper Top on regularly. Gale's HSD or

Adnams Broadside plus Fuller's ESB take up a couple more pumps. Guests come from all over the country, both old school and new wave: Thornbridge, Gadds' and Marble for instance. Occasionally if you're lucky you might be able to contemplate a glass of cask JW Lees' Harvest Ale – Hillier has several casks ageing in the cellar. This is just the ideal beer for a cold night.

The Butcher's had a varied career between selling sausages and becoming an award-winning pub. Hillier initially set up shop here with a florist's at the front and an off-licence selling draught beer at the back. The florist's ended and the pub started back in 2005 after Hillier had spoken with his off-licence regulars who thought it a great idea. With the success of the Butcher's Arms 'micro-pub' Hillier has gone out and offered advice to others who want to do the same. Yet as he insists, 'I don't want to make it a chain. I want people to go away and put their own spin on it.'

Opening hours: 12–1.30, 6–9 (or later); 12– 2 Sun; closed Mon
Also great for:
Pub design

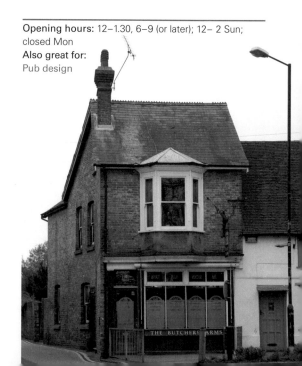

Nutshell

The Traverse, Bury St Edmunds,
Suffolk, IP33 1BJ
01284 764867
www.thenutshellpub.co.uk
🍺 **Greene King IPA, Abbot**

- -

From the outside the Nutshell has the appearance of a corner shop from the Victorian era. Perhaps a hardware store or maybe an old fashioned grocer's where the sweaty aroma of cheese hangs in the air while the sound of the bacon cutter adds its own metallic soundtrack to that of the customers' chatter.

But the Nutshell is a pub, a tourist hotspot in Bury St Edmunds and a place to go because it is famously one of the smallest pubs in the United Kingdom. It was once the smallest until the Signal Box Inn made a claim for rail ale fame and fortune. Yet if you sit within its confines the question of who's smaller than whom doesn't really matter – the Nutshell is undoubtedly a compact space to take a glass of Abbot, the divine Greene King ale that is brewed a stone's throw away by the pub's owners.

Get 12 people in and it starts to feel cosy, more and you will start making new friends whether you like it or not. It's a good idea to take some time during a quiet moment to have a look around – for such a confined space there's a lot of visual furniture. A mummified cat hangs from the ceiling. It was apparently found walled up (a common practice in more superstitious times). The ceiling is covered with banknotes from all over the world, brought in by those customers eager to share in the claustrophobia. There are other bits and pieces of bric-a-brac: old bottles, military plaques, pictures, stuffed animals' heads and collector's cabinets. This all adds to the Nutshell's unique and compact air, though you do wonder how they manage to get it all in.

Fancy a sit down? There's a table and a couple of benches, while there's also a bar to lean against. In the summer, tables are put outside, and the big shop front windows let in plenty of light. It could all be one big gimmick, but there's a sense that this is a pub that has been left to its own devices over the years, which is a good thing. It's not been prettified, and turned into an example of Ye Old Beer Shop for example. No food either, though anyone after a small chicken dinner might be content with a pickled egg...

Opening hours: 11–11; 12–10.30 Sun

The best **record breakers**

Olde Trip to Jerusalem

Brewhouse Yard, Nottingham, NG1 6AD

0115 947 3171

www.triptojerusalem.com

 **Greene King IPA, H&H Olde Trip, Old Speckled Hen, Abbot; Nottingham Rock Ale Mild Beer, Extra Pale Ale; guest beers**

• •

This venerable inn, bolted onto the side of the rock which Nottingham's castle stands upon, claims to be the oldest in England, going all the way back to 1189 (before this it served time as a brewhouse for the castle). Legend has it that Crusaders on the way to the Holy Land stopped in for a pint, though like many legends of the sort it should probably be taken with a large pinch of salt.

It's not backwards in coming forwards – its whitewashed frontage bears the bold statement 'The oldest inn in England', not just once but twice (although the statement is contested – a couple of other pubs claim to be older). Looking at it, you feel that it has the influence of several eras of architecture with a smaller cottage-like dwelling abutting the cliff behind (from the 18th century or perhaps earlier) and a thinner, longer addition at the front (almost in the shape of a watchtower). Even if there's little left from the time of the Crusaders, the effect still is of age.

Inside is where it the Olde Trip really puts on the style. Some of the ceilings have been carved out of the rock as the pub burrowed its way into the hillside, the ancient old brickwork on the walls is painted black, while the stone floors are uneven and undulating. Hidden alcoves, a haunted snug, passages, cellars, more rooms upstairs and a small museum add to the extra-ordinary feel of what should be just an ancient city inn. Old pictures, a list of former landlords from the past three centuries, various artefacts, a (modern) suit of armour and a blackened model ship hanging from the ceiling all add to the spectacle. Beer was even brewed on the premises until just after the Second World War – in old black and white photos you can see the legend 'Home brewed ales'.

Now owned by Greene King, who bought out previous owners Hardys & Hansons, there is a decent spread of cask beer, while the food is pubby and hearty: a ham hock and broad bean pie is a warming dish on a cold winter's day. The Olde Trip might be touristy but it has a real patina of age; it is a pub that you should visit once and then make up your own mind if you want to return. I know I will.

Opening hours: 11–11 (midnight Fri & Sat)

Signal Box Inn

Lakeside Station, Kings Road, Cleethorpes,
Lincolnshire, DN35 0AG
01472 604657
www.cleethorpescoastlightrailway.co.uk
🍺 **Beer range varies**

. . . .

Lilliput visited. The Signal Box Inn is the smallest pub in the world – measuring 64 square feet (though no doubt someone will come along and start a pub in a matchbox). This makes other contenders for the crown of the most compact boozer around seem like a Wetherspoons in comparison. Half a dozen drinkers can sit down and the rest crowd around the bar. Despite this, there are plans for a pool table and a small stage for music. Did anyone mention the Tardis?

The Signal Box has been open for five years now and is an integral part of the Cleethorpes Coast Light Railway, a small gauge line that is a major tourist attraction in this part of the world. It's a genuine Victorian signal box that started life in a Scunthorpe steelworks, but as the industrial climate changed it followed a lot of the workers into a file marked redundant. 'Anyone want a signal box?' was the query and the railway said yes. At first it did time as a shed but then the lightbulb moment arrived – its use as a pub was suggested and once more the railway said yes.

Other than the thrills and spills of railway life, cask beer is the attraction of the Signal Box Inn. There are usually three and they come from all over the country. One week you might be imbibing the creamy Black Sheep Bitter, the next it might be Batemans XXXB, robust, bittersweet, nutty and dry in its finish. 'It's all guest beers,' says licensee Alan Cowood, 'that is what my regulars like.'

Inside there's a relatively high ceiling and the walls are covered with pumpclips, a history of the Signal Box's ale affiliations. Get too many people in and it becomes cramped, but there is a beer garden outside. The Signal Box Inn could so easily be a miniaturist gimmick but it has a sense of a real pub with conversation, smiles and good beer. There's just one snag: winter sees the opening hours being limited to weekends.

Opening hours: 11–11 (not Mon–Thu mid Oct–Christmas); closed Christmas–Easter
Also great for: Railway

*The best **record breakers***

Tan Hill Inn

Tan Hill, Keld, Richmond,
North Yorkshire, DL11 6ED
01833 628246
www.tanhillinn.com

🍺 **Black Sheep Best Bitter; Dent Tan Hill Ewe Juice; Theakston Best Bitter, Old Peculier; guest beers**

• •

Remote? The Tan Hill Inn, high up on the Yorkshire moors, far from the maddening crowd, offers remoteness taken to the max. There are no other buildings around for miles (12 miles to the nearest village), just bleak but beautiful moorland. Yet, its remoteness is not a bar to those who make their way to what is generally recognised as England's highest pub (1,752 feet for those with an interest in figures).

It's an inn in the best of traditions offering accommodation and food (steak and ale pie, hunters chicken with BBQ sauce, various steaks) as well as a pint or two of Theakston's Old Peculier, one of its bar top regulars. An inn was recorded here in the 16th century, while the current establishment dates back to 100 years later. Miners dug for coal in the vicinity for several centuries and they even lived up here, but when the last of the mines shut down at the end of the 1920s, it would have been easy for the inn to go the same way. It didn't, even though tales are told of winter isolation and one landlord wishing a shepherd happy new year at the start of April – he was the first person in through the doors since the turn of the year...

It's still here offering shelter to walkers – it sits on the Pennine Way, Britain's first long-distance footpath – tourists, bikers and anyone else that looks forward to enjoying ale within these thick stone walls. Theakston and Black Sheep are popular up here and the Tan Hill Ewe Juice is produced by Dent. The interior is as hardy as the Yorkshire character: flagstoned floors, roaring fire (often as not lit during the summer) and lots of old photos detailing the history of the area. Across the beams sit dozens of postcards from all over the world, sent in by those who can't forget the good times they have had here.

As mentioned above, come the winter and the Inn is often snowed in – a couple of years ago the media had a field day when a group were marooned at the pub for three days. Yet the Tan Hill is not just about splendid isolation – it puts on plenty of music and then there's an annual sheep fair. Talking of sheep, there's a pet lamb and various cats and dogs. There's also the odd ghost hunt – the Inn is supposedly haunted by a former landlady who obviously doesn't let go of somewhere she had such a good time at in her life.

Opening hours: 10–late

Witchball

Lighthouse Road, Lizard, Helston,
Cornwall, TR12 7NJ
01326 290662
www.witchball.co.uk

🍺 **St Austell Tribute; guest beers**

. . . .

A witch ball is a hollow sphere of glass, traditionally hung in windows to ward off evil spirits – apparently the spirits would be attracted by the pretty coloured strands (usually blue or green) and become trapped inside. It doesn't take much to find oneself caught in the spell of this most southerly pub in mainland Britain. Set right in the heart of Lizard village, it's a low-slung squat building whose origins reach back to the 1400s when it started life as a traditional Cornish longhouse farm. It was built of fieldstone (stones found lying around in the fields) and cob (a mix of mud, straw and animal dung). Inside it's equally earthy and unpretentious with thick walls, tiny windows and very low-slung ceilings. Walls are whitewashed and the furniture is a carefree mix of traditional dark wood tables, chairs and banquettes.

Beers tend to stay loyally Cornish. St Austell's Tribute is on all the time, a bittersweet golden ale with lashings of tropical fruit, a beer that has taken the brewery's name and reputation far beyond the borders of Cornwall. Meanwhile guests might also come from St Austell or near-neighbour Chough (formerly the Organic Brewhouse), whose Kynance Blonde has a grassy nose and an appetising bitter finish.

Food, unsurprisingly for this coastal location, majors on seafood and fish, and the owners like to see how quickly they can get it from boat to table – one of the pub's favourite boasts is that lobster landed just that morning at nearby Cadgwith Cove will be sitting on your plate by lunchtime. Crab and shell-on prawns also feature frequently alongside steaks, scampi, pizza and burgers.

Inevitably, in such an old building, ghost stories abound. The Witchball has two for sure – George and Ferdinand – plus a further cast of wandering spirits; all apparently friendly, just like the staff and locals at this welcoming little place.

The pub's own witch ball hangs in the restaurant window. It dates from 1721 and has initials on it. Superstition states that if your reflection can't be seen in the ball you're probably possessed by evil spirits. To be honest, many a visitor to the Witchball will leave possessed by spirits – but they will most likely be good ones.

Opening hours: 12–11.30 (midnight Fri & Sat)

The best **record breakers**

THE BAT & BALL

The best **sporting pubs**

Once upon a time sportsmen were wont to hang up their football boots/rugby boots/cricket pads and go and run a pub. In the 1960s, the likes of Bobby Moore and Martin Peters appeared in TV adverts promoting the pub (imagine Joey Barton doing something similar nowadays – actually don't!). Times change and sportsmen become property magnates, TV pundits or clothing manufacturers, but the pub still remains a place to where sports fans repair to watch the big game or to celebrate (or commiserate) after. And then there are the pub's sporting associations that come from history, or just a closeness to a temple of sport.

The Tom Cribb celebrates the famous 19th century pugilist, while the City Arms in Cardiff stands in the shadow of the Millennium Stadium and is just to place to enjoy a jar before repairing to see the Welsh team. Football gained its rules at the Freemasons Arms in Covent Garden (though it would take another century or so before it lost its soul), while cricket entered the modern age at the Bat & Ball in the middle of the Hampshire countryside. And if you want a flutter on the Cheltenham Gold Cup, then visit the Royal Oak first – you might just pick up a tip.

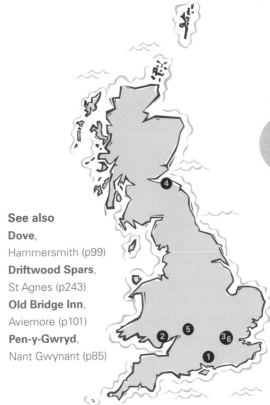

See also
Dove, Hammersmith (p99)
Driftwood Spars, St Agnes (p243)
Old Bridge Inn, Aviemore (p101)
Pen-y-Gwryd, Nant Gwynant (p85)

Bat & Ball

Hyden Farm Lane, Clanfield, Waterlooville,
Hampshire, PO8 0UB
02392 632692
www.fullers.co.uk

🍺 **Fuller's London Pride; Gale's HSD,
Seafarer's Ale**

· ·

As the name might suggest, cricket is the game most associated with this cosy country pub. Not just any old cricket – the Bat & Ball sits opposite Broadhalfpenny Down where the game that defines the English summer really got going in the 18th century. On this green swathe of land a mile or so from the village of Hambledon, the local team would play matches against an all-England XI in front of hundreds of people – and they famously won once. Afterwards, refreshment no doubt would be dispensed at the Bat & Ball, whose name was changed from the Broadhalfpenny Hut (or just the Hutt according to some sources) during those thrilling times. The pub would also function as the match's pavilion. Richard Nyren was the landlord from 1762–72 and captain of the local side; he helped to formulate many of the rules that now govern the modern game. The focus of cricket moved to London towards the end of the 1700s, but Hambledon has always had a special place in the heart of cricketers – along with the pub.

Nowadays, Fuller's is the owner of this brick and flint building, and the interior is choc-a-bloc with all sorts of cricketing mementoes (though the bats used by the early players have long resided at the MCC). However, this devotional side of the pub wasn't always so. At one stage, Allied Brewers ran the place and dispensed with all the cricketing memorabilia. Thankfully, the locals held onto these precious relics and when Gale's brewery bought the pub and changed it back they were able to return them to their rightful home.

Even if you're usually left cold by cricket, the Bat & Ball will momentarily spark your interest. Try it when there's a match on the Down opposite. With a glass of Gale's bittersweet HSD to hand and the sun shining, you would have to have a hard heart not to be moved by the thwack of leather on willow (and maybe that distant figure standing on the boundary is Richard Nyren returned for old time's sake).

Opening hours: 11.30–11.30 (11 Fri & Sat);
11.30–10.30 Sun

City Arms

10–12 Quay Street, Cardiff, CF10 1EA
029 2022 5258
www.thecityarmscardiff.com

🍺 **Brains Dark, Bitter, SA, Rev James; guest beers**

. . . .

Sit in the correct window of this famous Cardiff pub and you can gaze at the magnificence of the Millennium Stadium just across the road as you sip your pint. Just out of sight, to the right, is Cardiff Arms Park, home of Cardiff Blues. This is the very stuff of rugby heaven.

The City Arms has long been a destination for rugby fans and a famous place where tales of derring-do on the pitch have been told and retold alongside the odd reminiscence of the great Welsh actors who used to forgo Hollywood whenever an international was on. On my visit, I could not help but overhear a drinker recounting the tale of how, when he was walking to see a match at the Arms Park, he'd banged into a visibly refreshed Stanley Baker. 'I wished I'd taken a picture,' said the man with a wistful air, 'he died a couple of years later'.

Yet this is not a pub that trades on its memories, even though it has been on this street corner since the 19th century. In 2010, brewery owners Brains took the decision to transform it into a craft beer bar celebrating the ongoing renaissance of British and world beer. The full range of Brains' beers remains available but this is also joined by a large selection of ales from smaller breweries, four of which are served straight from the cask at the back of the bar. With the beer sourced from all over the country, you are just as likely to enjoy Marble Brewery's Best (grapefruit crossed with tangerine and a mouth-catching bitterness) or Otley's big-hitter of a golden ale O8 – there is a beer for every mood of the moment. And if that isn't enough there is also a comprehensive selection of world beers, both in bottle and on tap.

The interior is honeyed distressed wood, with sepia-toned prints of yesteryear: old gents, old teams, old towns, rugby and beer. There's a warmth and easy comfort about the pub's furnishings with this memorabilia, though the wooden flooring and high stools create a more modern impression, placing the City Arms halfway between old and new and stopping it from being some antiquated nostalgia festival. Two bars and a back room offer plenty of space with an open and airy feel. Brains should be proud of their conversion and the City Arms already feels like it's going to be a classic pub for years to come.

Opening hours: 11–11.30 (2.30am Fri & Sat); 12–10.30 Sun

Freemasons Arms

81–82 Long Acre, Covent Garden,
London, WC2E 9NG
020 7836 3115
www.freemasonsarmscoventgarden.co.uk

🍺 **Shepherd Neame Master Brew,
Kent's Best, Spitfire, Bishops Finger,
seasonal beers**

• •

If you can't get to the ground, then watching a big match in a pub can often be the next best thing. There's a sense of communalism, especially if it's an international. With a glass of beer in hand, commiseration or triumph feel that little bit better with a group of likeminded souls around.

Big matches are regularly shown at the Freemasons Arms, but the history of this Covent Garden pub should add an extra sense of frisson to watching a game. Back in 1863, it was the venue for half a dozen meetings where the rules for what became known as football were discussed and agreed on. It's a long way from there to today's multi-million pound entertainment industry.

Standing in Long Acre, within apron throwing distance of the imposing looking Freemasons' Hall, this Shepherd Neame-owned pub is a grand example of late Victorian pub design. Four storeys high, it has the look of a Flemish merchant's house, with a few ornate flourishes – it's one of those solid-looking buildings that central London remains full of.

As you might imagine, the world-changing series of meetings is celebrated inside the Freemasons with a cabinet display of old photos and sporting artefacts, including an ancient leather football that could probably cause serious injuries if headed during a particularly wet match. However, football is not the only thing that the Freemasons Arms has been used for. The founders of the Geological Society met here and are commemorated with a plaque, while the London Irish Rifles also first gathered at the Freemasons Arms during the Napoleonic Wars (albeit actually in a pub of that name that stood where the Freemasons' Hall now stands) – and are also commemorated.

This lively city pub could so easily be a sterile theme bar, but under the careful tutelage of owners Shepherd Neame it manages to maintain a pubby feel that attracts those who work in Covent Garden's many businesses, tourists in search of sporting history and local residents. Whatever their background, the enjoyment of a pint of Spitfire or the stronger Bishops Finger is a bonus, while the menu unashamedly looks to traditional pub grub for its inspiration. Cumberland sausage and mash, or gammon, egg and chips might just do the trick. And after this, if there's a match on, get your scarf and just enjoy taking in a bit of sporting history.

Opening hours: 12–11 (11.30 Fri & Sat); 12–10.30 Sun

The best **sporting pubs**

Old Clubhouse

East Links Road, Gullane,
East Lothian, EH31 2AF
01620 842008
www.oldclubhouse.com
🍺 **Caledonian Deuchars IPA; Taylor Landlord; guest beers**

. . . .

This single-storey half-timbered sprawl of a place was built in 1890 to cater for the members of the original Gullane Golf Club, whose perfectly manicured greens it overlooks (in the distance the Lammermuir Hills offer a different sort of exercise). Gullane itself is east of Edinburgh, on the so-called Scottish Golf Coast, the area that is known as the birthplace of golf. The golf club outgrew its premises and moved, and in 1989 Guy and Brenda Campanile took over the restaurant and bar, set about a spot of refurbishing and the Old Clubhouse has gone from strength to strength.

There's a quaint, old-fashioned, deliciously raffish air about the place – step inside and note that the porch is papered with sheet music from the '20s and '30s. You almost half expect to hear the dulcet tones of someone tinkling an ivory somewhere or other within its confines. *Everything Stops For Tea* suggests one piece of music; substitute the word beer for tea and you've got the perfect suggestion…

Venture further inwards and you're in classic clubhouse territory – leather chairs, plush banquettes and wood paneling all served up with a helping of shuttered blinds. Bric-a-brac and memorabilia crowd the walls, alongside a curious menagerie of stuffed animals. It all feels pleasantly well-heeled and contented with a side

order of friskiness stopping it from veering into the world of clubhouse stuffiness.

The food policy is 'back to basics with the occasional twist'. Tapas-style starters include olives, various bread and roasted peppers, but beware of nibbling too much as the main courses come in hale and hearty – pie of the day, fish and chips, ribeye or sirloin steak and that old favourite: haggis, neeps and tatties. Beers include Taylor Landlord and what has almost become the Scottish national ale in recent years: Deuchars IPA. There are usually four beers on, all served from distinctive traditional Scottish fonts while guest beers can come from large breweries such as Belhaven or smaller microbreweries such as Hadrian Border down near Newcastle.

The Old Clubhouse is an ideal place for armchair sportsmen who can watch the golfers teeing off from the comfort of the bar. On the other hand, if you should feel the sudden urge to flex your arm, the Clubhouse can arrange tee-times.

Opening hours: 11–11 (midnight Thu–Sat); 12.30–11 Sun
Also great for: Pub gardens

The best **sporting pubs**

Royal Oak

43 The Burgage, Prestbury, Cheltenham,
Gloucestershire, GL52 3DL
01242 522344
www.royal-oak-prestbury.co.uk
🍺 **Taylor Landlord; guest beers**

• •

It's a short gallop to Cheltenham racecourse from the Royal Oak in Prestbury, a pretty village on the northern outskirts of Cheltenham. However, the only riding that goes on in the vicinity of the Oak is the ghostly Civil War-era horseman that trots down The Burgage, the quintessentially English street on which the pub resides, and reputedly one of the most haunted streets in England.

However, any ghosts expecting a quiet life in this 19th century honey-coloured Cotswold stone pub will soon search for other mortals to haunt come race day. Not surprisingly, the Royal Oak positively hums with activity then, while during the annual Cheltenham Festival, jockeys, trainers, punters and locals mix and mingle, swapping stories and enjoying pints of Taylor's Landlord and other ales at the bar. In fact, the influence of the sport of kings runs deep through the veins of the Royal Oak – the legendary Victorian jockey Fred Archer was born in Prestbury while the 1954 winner of The Gold Cup, Four Ten, was trained at the back of the pub.

Rest assured, though, there is a lot more to the Royal Oak than putting money into the pockets of bookies. This is a comfortable and welcoming pub in its own right. From the outside, it has the air of a true pub haven. There are two bars; the one to the left can be seen as the locals' area, a place where glasses of cask beer encourage pub chat (and no doubt the exchange of racing tips). It's a comfortable and welcoming space, with buttermilk-coloured walls, an open fire, wooden beams on which horse brasses hang plus a couple of old framed prints advertising the glories of the long-gone Whitbread brewery that used to exist in town: in its quiet and unfussy way this bar bears the patina of use that all good pubs should have.

The dining room next door is equally welcoming. A corridor connects the two rooms, suggesting that although there is a divide it is not divisive and diners and drinkers meet on equal terms. Four cask beers are sold, with Landlord being joined by beers from surrounding counties. The Royal Oak is keen on supporting local breweries and the same goes for the food. The menu ranges from filled baguettes to robust and hearty dishes such as belly pork with chorizo and sweet chilli relish or the seasonally inclined roast wood pigeon crown on a bed of local game. The pub also has a lively social life: Whitsun Bank Holiday sees a sausage and beer festival, while August bank holiday witnesses a weekend-long celebration of cider and cheese. This is a pub for all seasons.

Opening hours: 11–3, 5.30–11; 11–11 Fri & Sat

Tom Cribb

6 Panton Street, Piccadilly Circus,
London, SW1Y 4EA
020 7839 3801
www.tomcribblondon.co.uk
🍺 **Shepherd Neame Canterbury Jack,
Master Brew, Spitfire, Bishops Finger,
seasonal beers**

• •

Cast your mind back to the 1950s, a time of
flickering TVs and pubs that fill up quickly. In the
boxing ring, Harry Edwards is taking on Eddie West
at the Rink Market in Smethwick. It's a probability
that no one still living will know the result of the
bout, but these guys' names (and others) still live
on in the posters that are displayed around the
walls of the Tom Cribb. Even without knowing
who Tom Cribb is, chances are that these posters
will help to direct strangers to the pub's theme:
boxing. Tom Cribb? He was a champion pugilist of
the early 19th century who kept a pub in the area
on his retirement, though not this one.

Mementoes of the noble art dot the walls of this
compact but comforting corner boozer that lies in
a quiet street between the madness of Haymarket
and the air-kissing gala nights of West End
theatreland. There's the late Our 'Enry on one wall,
while Lennox Lewis poses elsewhere. And let's
not forget Cribb whose portrait adorns a laminated
colour poster. It's entirely appropriate that the
sporting theme continues with the conversations
that swirl about me as I sit with a pint of Shepherd
Neame's Master Brew. At the table by the door, a
couple of blokes sit, intense and engrossed – one
is teaching the other the rudiments of poker. On a
table nearer the bar, a couple of businessmen in
blue exchange snippets about football and golf.

The one-room bar of the Tom Cribb carries the
echoes of old school West End pubs. Its décor
for a start could be called a study in brown, while
banquettes line the walls. I suspect it was two
rooms once but the pub 'improvement' men of
the postwar years had their say. The photos and
frames are not all boxing or sport though. Several
brewery mirrors refer to the pub's Kentish owners
Shepherd Neame. Master Brew is a chestnut
coloured session beer of theirs I have always
enjoyed: citrus orange peel, dry crisp grain and a
long dry bitter finish. For a 3.7% session beer I've
always felt that it punches far above its alchoholic
strength and is a refreshing lunchtime drink.
Bishops Finger, a heavier and weightier sort of
chap at 5%, also crooks his finger like a bishop's
crozier calling its flock but I resist as time presses.

Despite being named after a boxer who plied
his trade with bare fists, the Tom Cribb is a soft-
shoe shuffle of a pub rather than a destroyer –
and all the better for it.

Opening hours: 11–11; 12–9 Sun

The best community pubs

What defines a community pub? Maybe it's something about the pub being at the hub of a community: a pub that is more than just a drinking den but a place that has its own cast of regulars who are as much a part of the pub furniture as the stools on which they sit. Perhaps a community pub is a place where the locals sometimes go that extra mile to raise money for a charity, to help out a local child, or put money towards a hospice and maybe have a little fun in the process (though whether pushing a full 9-gallon beer cask up the Wrekin can be considered fun is another matter).

Then there is the village pub that is threatened with closure, a pub that has an atmosphere all of its own, friendly, chatty and convivial, but is seemingly doomed. At the Yarcombe Inn in Somerset the locals decided not to take the closure sitting down and they bought the pub; the same happened with the Old Crown in Hesket Newmarket. On the other hand, the likes of the Royal Oak and the Bell have an ineffable sense of community – the pub is almost like a family into which strangers are always welcome. The Triangle Tavern remembers former locals with a display of their shoes. Community spirit is at the heart of the British pub.

See also
Bhurtpore Inn,
Aston (p14)
The Grove,
Huddersfield (p19)
Lewes Arms,
Lewes (p253)
Roscoe Head,
Liverpool (p277)

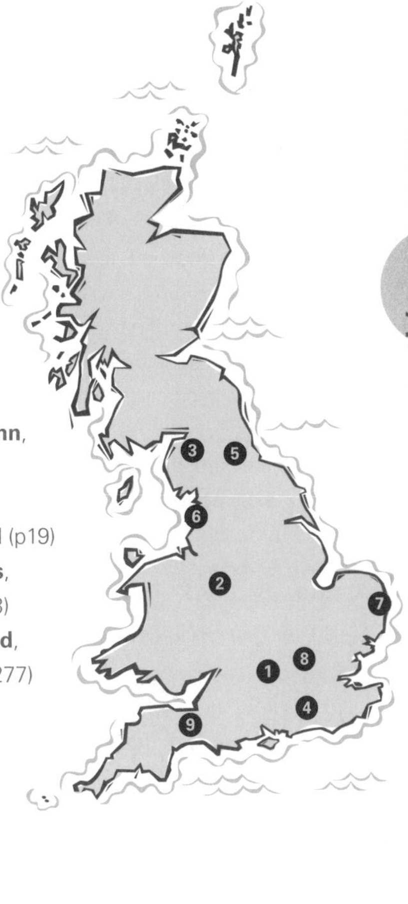

Bell

Bell Lane, Aldworth, Berkshire, RG8 9SE
01635 578272

🍺 **Arkell's 3B, Kingsdown Ale;
West Berkshire Maggs Magnificent Mild,
Good Old Boy, seasonal beers**

• •

Mobile phones are banned in the Bell. If you want to call a friend and tell them that you're in the pub or tweet about whatever has just entered your head then you'll have to go outside. Hardship? For some perhaps, but on the other hand you could put your phone down and enjoy the pub's wilful disconnect from the ways of the modern world. It's good for the soul to switch off now and again and what better place to do it than in the Bell. Oh and there's no piped music either, or games machine flashing in the corner as if auditioning for the role of a *Dr Who* baddie. While if you're hungry rolls and soup provide sustenance.

There's this thing called community in the Bell – people go there because they want to, not because they feel they have to. The cricket team play close by, while morris men and mummers drop in throughout the year. The parliament of the pub is very much alive here with gossip, tall tales, sporting endeavours and the general chaff of conversation filling the air. If it's your first time (you might have come for the beer or just traipsed across the Ridgeway) then you can either sit in a corner or join in with the chat.

Farmhouse style is how you might regard the Bell, though there might have been an inn on this site for centuries. Aldworth is an old settlement, the 'gateway to the Downs', a place where the Saxons came, and some have

speculated that the Romans passed this way too. There's a sense of permanence here: the Bell has been in the same family for over 200 years, which is why once you walk inside it's almost as if the years have unfolded and you're back in the 1930s. The tiled floor is uneven, the walls are part panelled and covered with all manner of plaques and framed photos while a one-armed clock keeps a sort of time. There's no bar as such, rather a serving hatch with glass panes on three sides – the idea of the 'theatre of the pour' might just get short shrift here. From this zone up to five cask beers are served, including Arkell's Kingsdown – dark amber in colour with a big mouthful of smooth silky maltiness balanced by a big hit of citrus fruit leading to a bittersweet finish. It's the sort of beer to sit down with at one of the weathered wooden benches and contemplate the agelessness of the Bell's interior.

Opening hours: 11–3, 6–11; 12–3, 7–10.30 Sun; closed Mon

Cock Hotel

148 Holyhead Road, Wellington, Telford,
Shropshire, TF1 2NH
01952 244954
www.cockhotel.co.uk

🍺 **Hobsons Mild, Best Bitter; guest beers**

• •

Pubs have long been fundraisers. Back in the 1950s and 1960s, piles of pennies were popular ways of raising money, with local celebrities sometimes being brought in to knock down the heap. I have seen a photo of the then captain of Exeter City FC wearing football boots with his suit as he kicks over a pile in a Norman & Pring pub. The Cock Hotel continues in this noble tradition and has raised money for a variety of charities, including one that is helping the sick son of an ex-employee. Whenever someone dismisses pubs as worthless, it's vital to remember the work that the likes of the Cock do.

Its sense of community stretches beyond its warm-hearted fund-raising. Every year there is an annual beer barrel race that goes up the Wrekin. The hotel organises it and it features teams of four pushing a full nine-gallon cask up the prominent Shropshire landmark. 'This has been going on for 10 years,' says landlord Peter Arden, 'one of our locals came in and said how about a barrel race up the Wrekin so we did it. We do it every April or May and it raises money for charities. In 2011 was for a young boy in a hospice. The Cock's team won it for first eight years but lost it in 2011.'

The Cock can trace its origins back to the 1740s when it was originally built as a hunting lodge. Various breweries have owned it, including Bass, but it is now a free house. It's Georgian style from the outside with a portico entrance. There's an original oak floor inside the entrance hall, while the main bar features hop vines all over the place. Have a look at the walls and you'll see framed certificates of all the awards the pub has won. The former smoking bar has been turned into a Belgian bar, Brasserie de Haan, and features a comprehensive selection of bottled beers and draught European beers, while there's also another room to enjoy your drink.

No food is served apart from local pork pies, while as the awards might suggest, cask beer plays a prominent part in proceedings. There are normally eight on, with guests divided between local brews from the likes of Salopian, Woods and Ludlow and ones from further afield such as Cotleigh and York

There are a couple of guest rooms, which Arden hopes to increase to five. 'We're a real ale pub with rooms,' says Arden. He's being modest: the Cock Hotel is much more.

Opening hours: 4 (12 Thu)–11.30; 12–midnight Fri & Sat; 12–4, 7–11 Sun
Also great for: Beer range

Old Crown

Main Street, Hesket Newmarket,
Cumbria, CA7 8JG
01697 478288
www.theoldcrownpub.co.uk

🍺 **Hesket Newmarket Great Cockup Porter, Blencathra Bitter, Skiddaw Special Bitter, Hellvellyn Gold, Doris's 90th Birthday Ale, Old Carrock Strong Ale**

. . . .

What's a community pub? A place where people gather and enjoy good company and good beer? Or maybe it's a pub that offers other services to the community – post office, doctor's surgery, even occasional chapel? Then there's another definition of a community pub: one actually owned by the community. That's the situation with the Old Crown in the beautiful fellside village of Hesket Newmarket. Instead of one owner or pub chain or brewery, around 150 local people have a share in both the Old Crown and the Hesket Newmarket brewery at the back of the pub.

The people bought the brewery first, back in 1999, when its owner looked to sell. A cooperative of 58 locals and their supporters combined to buy; a couple of years later the pub was on the market and the same thing happened. Now, the Old Crown and the brewery are a model of what a community can do when it puts its mind to it. Such has been the success that Prince Charles has popped in a couple of times for a pint and a quick game of darts.

What's the appeal? The bar at the Old Crown is traditional; in fact the pub itself is traditional – wedged in a terrace of stone-built houses in the middle of the village opposite the green. The bar is comfortably cluttered: real fire, bar stools, old fashioned red patterned carpet, framed pictures of the fells on the wall, wooden beams from which hang mugs and jugs. The pub is not trying to be anything else but a pub – and you will find locals, farmers, fell runners, cyclists, walkers and tourists all looking for a touch of community spirit. Walk in on your own and conversation will be served along with a glass of the beer brewed around the back.

Ah the beer. Some like Skiddaw Special Bitter with its biscuity bite and dry bitter finish; others will plump for Doris' 90th Birthday Ale, a robustly fruity best bitter that was brewed in honour of a previous licensee's birthday. Incidentally, this is the beer that mountaineer and shareholder Chris Bonnington rates as one of his favourite beers ever. There's food as well, with a tradition of good curries as well as pub grub favourites such as pies and Cumberland sausages.

So, the Old Crown is the ideal community pub, a pub run by the people for the people. That's something that doesn't always work, but it does in this case.

Opening hours: 12–3 (not Mon–Thu), 5.30–11 (10.30 Sun)
Also great for: Brewery taps

Royal Oak

Friday Street, Rusper,
West Sussex, RH12 4QA
01293 871393
www.theroyaloakrusper.co.uk
🍺 **Surrey Hills Ranmore; guest beers**

• •

The Royal Oak used to be a King & Barnes pub and during the 1990s you could drop in and ask for an Ale Trail Passport – the brewery had 57 pubs and if you visited them all you would be entitled to a prize. A lot of effort for something so small, you might think, but on the other hand it was a good way to discover pubs that you might not encounter in the normal course of the day. Given that the Royal Oak is a bit off the beaten track, there's a fair bet that passport holders would have sought out the pub for the first time then. There's a reminder of the long closed Horsham-based family brewery on the wall of the Royal Oak, an old sign with the brewery's stylised K&B logo in the centre. What would have been the pub's bestselling tipple? Sussex or the more full-flavoured Festive?

Badger bought up King & Barnes and closed the brewery in 2001. The Royal Oak would have been part of the deal but now it's a free house, garlanded with CAMRA awards and sought out by those in search of what others might call a 'genuine' pub experience. There is a question here: what is genuine when it comes to the pub? Does it mean old fashioned? Or is it the nature of the welcome you get, especially if you're on your own contemporary version of the Ale Trail Passport? Or is it something indefinable, something that you only know instinctively when you pass through the door?

It's probably a mixture of all three, but genuine in the case of the Royal Oak brings forth descriptions of its rambling set of rooms with a colour scheme that matches crimson red and digestive biscuit brownness. It's warm and evocative of some imagined past, but there's an honesty and solidity about its character. The bar counter is as solid as a rock and there are battered buttoned sofas which convey a sense of casual, almost bohemian luxury. There's a woodburner, old prints on the walls and pump clips. Ah, pump clips. Cask beer is taken very seriously here with seven handpumps usually on display, while another five dispense cider and perry. Surrey Hills' Ranmore (a light bittersweet ale with an appetisingly bitter finish) is a popular choice and it's not unknown for the brewery's head brewer to be found here holding court. To complete the circle of genuine, the pub is also home to a local tug-of-war team. But don't take my word for all of this, find out for yourself.

Opening hours: 12–3, 5–11 (9 Mon & Tue);
12–11 Sat; 12–7 Sun
Also great for: Country

The best **community pubs**

The pub is the hub of village life, a community meeting place quite different to anything you find in the city. It's a home from home, the place where friendships are made and often saved (there's nothing like a chat over a glass of beer to mend fences or put things right). It's also a place where plans are made: if the village green (or some other essential amenity) seems under threat, the concerned meet and plans are made, all at the pub. If there's a need to raise money – for a hospice, a sick child, a local good cause – good folk at the pub band together and start collecting. The barmaid takes a bike to Boulogne with the good wishes and coins of the locals; the landlord dresses up as a clown and gets soaked and pounded with sponges on a fun day, all in a good cause. And when their pub is threatened then sometimes the community decides that it's time to come together: just like Robin Hood and his Merrie Men banding together against the tyrant King John, the locals join forces, call in celebrity supporters, and save their much loved institution. The British pub is part of the community, and all too often is the community. Let those who would downplay the pub's role and those who suggest its responsibility for many of society's ills remember that.

HRH Prince Charles with mountaineer and pub part-owner Chris Bonnington at the Old Crown, Hesket Newmarket (p184)

Surtees Arms

Chilton Lane, Ferryhill, Durham, DL17 0DH
01740 655724
www.thesurteesarms.co.uk

🍺 **Yard of Ale Black as Owt Stout,
One Foot in the Yard; guest beers**

• •

A street corner pub. A village pub. It's the easiest thing in the world to say such a pub is the hub. But there should be more. The Surtees Arms is a pub at the hub of its local life. Radiating good cheer and beer from its corner of the County Durham town of Ferryhill, this lively and bustling award-winning pub offers a home from home for locals, as well as attracting beer lovers from further afield. Clubs and societies also troop through its doors – darts, pool and dominoes teams use it as a base, while local Scout groups and Ferryhill's brass band hold meetings here. Not to mention the Surtees Arms Leek Club.

So what's the attraction? Could it be the pub's own craft brewery – the Yard of Ale – which is based at the back of the pub? Or could it be that licensees Alan and Susan Hogg have worked very hard to establish themselves after buying the pub in 2007. 'We have expanded the pub's appeal through the real ale scene, Sunday lunches, good-

cause events and our own microbrewery,' says Alan Hogg. 'All of these activities involve the locals and newcomers – leading to a great mix of people.'

Ah people. Build a pub and they will come (to paraphrase *Field of Dreams*). The Surtees Arms was originally built in 1872 by local brewery Forsters – at the time Ferryhill was home to a thriving community of miners and quarrymen. They liked a drop. Surtees? This was the name of a prominent local family, with the hunting chronicler RS Surtees perhaps being the most famous of the branch. Times have changed along with what people do for a living, though the pub still manages to cater to the locals.

It sits on a street corner, a white stone building with bar, lounge and dining room. In the bar there are four cask beers, two from those brewed at the back of the pub, and two from all over the place. The beer mats from the 1980s in the bar are the landlord's own collection. Meanwhile take the kids into the lounge, where a log burner adds a warm glow to winter days. Sunday lunches are popular, freshly cooked – no frozen Yorkshire puddings I'm told – while for the rest of the week toasties are as substantial as it gets.

And the essence of a good community pub? People can't stop coming back, especially those who no longer walk the earth. 'A ghost walk suggested three ghosts,' says Alan Hogg, 'and everyone who has worked here has experienced strange shadows, noises and things being moved around. One is believed to be a slightly cantankerous old man with a liking for dropping things off shelves!'

Now that's not a community spirit...

Opening hours: 4–11; 12–midnight Sat; 12–11 Sun
Also great for: Motorway

*The best **community pubs***

Taps

Henry Street, Lytham, Lancashire, FY8 5LE
01253 736226
www.thetaps.net

🍺 **Titanic Taps Bitter; guest beers**

· ·

Taps stands at the back of Lytham's historic Clifton Arms Hotel. Two centuries ago the building provided accommodation for the hotel's ostlers and then it became the preferred drinking place for the servants and workers at the hotel, under the name of Clifton Arms Vaults and Tap. When it was owned by Boddington's it was known as the Taps and then Whitbread changed its name to the Captain's Cabin, which must have provoked a spot of head scratching. It was back to Taps when current landlord Ian Riggs took over in the early part of the 1990s, a man with a proven track record. He'd won awards for his previous pub in Blackpool and has continued to do so here.

Riggs' kingdom is an unpretentious one-room pub that usually features eight cask beers, including the regular Taps Bitter, brewed by Titanic Brewery. Riggs was in on the first brew of this beer, collaborating with Titanic's Keith Bott at the historic Shugborough Hall brewery, where the boil was wood-fired. 'It was an attempt to get back to Boddington's as it was before Whitbread got hold of it,' he says. 'Did we succeed? I think so.' Guest beers come from both near and far – as we talk he mentions that he has beers from Dark Star and Thornbridge on. Such is the popularity of Taps that all its beers come in 18-gallon kilderkins, while the house beer is served from that rarest of containers, a 36 gallon barrel. 'Meet the brewer' nights add to the appeal.

So you wouldn't be surprised to discover that the ambience of Taps is of an ale house – bare floorboards plus a lot of wood, the cellar can be seen and on the walls plenty of photos reflect Riggs' other passion: rugby (Brian Ashton and Bill Beaumont have been known to pop in here for a jar). On the ceiling there are also loads of rugby union club ties. The lifeboat corner is where the local lifeboatmen take their pints and sit surrounded by memorabilia of their trade (I recall a similar corner in the Snowdon in Llandudno during the 1980s). Food is served at lunchtimes, simple and homemade pub grub such as sandwiches and soup.

Riggs is a passionate licensee and down through the years has also been noted for his charity fundraising. An annual bike ride is held to raise money for local charities, while the summer of 2011 saw staff and regulars being sponsored to climb the 10 highest British peaks over the space of a week. No doubt their return will see a few barrels tapped.

Opening hours: 11–11 (midnight Fri & Sat); 12–11 Sun

Triangle Tavern

29 St Peters Street, Lowestoft,
Suffolk, NR32 1QA
01502 582711
www.thetriangletavern.co.uk

🍺 **Green Jack Canary Pale Ale, Orange
Wheat Beer, Trawlerboys Best Bitter,
Mahseer IPA, seasonal beers; guest beers**

. . . .

There are community pubs where everyone knows
your name but the Triangle Tavern goes one step
further. As you walk into the front bar you can't
help but notice three worn out shoes standing on
the windowsill, visible to all who pass outside.
These battered boots belonged to deceased
locals and were donated to the Tavern by their
families in memory of good times spent. Far from
being morbid curiosities, these dead men's shoes
palpably demonstrate how important a good
community pub can be in someone's life.

The Triangle Tavern originally consisted of
two pubs. The one at the front was called the
Oddfellows and laid claim to 300 years of history,
while the Triangle at the back was a mere stripling
at 100 years. Now they're as one and act as a tap
for local brewery Green Jack.

The front bar with its shoes, distressed wooden
floor and dried hops hanging from above the
bar, has the feel of a front parlour with benches
alongside the wall and a framed multitude of
Green Jack's awards on the wall. This is very much
the locals' bar with plenty of maritime chat, jokes
and pub bonhomie. There's an immediate sense
of comfort when you go in; you could argue that
this sort of bar is on a direct linear line from the
warm and safe cave where people once gathered
to communicate. In the back bar, the walls are
covered with all manner of beer memorabilia
including framed brewery posters, brewery mirrors
and a vast collection of beer bottles.

On my last visit, Green Jack's owner Tim
Dunford was helping out at the bar, pulling pints
and greeting locals – I ask him about the pub's
community spirit. 'If someone needs a fridge
moving, especially if they're elderly,' he says
as he pulls a pint of the smooth and succulent
Trawlerboys bitter, 'then they usually come in here
and there will be someone who'll do it for a pint.'

Lowestoft is not a town on the radar of many
people. It's the end of the railway line and the
collapse of the fishing industry has hit it hard.
When the wind turns to the east, it comes in off
the North Sea bringing with it cold and snow.
However, the Triangle Tavern is well worth the
journey – you might end up wanting to leave one
of your shoes in the window.

Opening hours: 11–11 (midnight Thu; 1am Fri & Sat);
12–10.30 Sun
Also great for: Brewery taps

Woodman

45 Wildhill Road, Wildhill,
Hertfordshire, AL9 6EA
01707 642618

🍺 **Greene King IPA, Abbot; McMullen AK; guest beers**

. . . .

'It's in the middle of nowhere, but close to everywhere.' It sounds like the sort of riddle you have to solve before crossing a bridge guarded by a giant. But these are the words of Graham Craig about the Woodman, the pub he used to run but is now looked after by his son Tom. Looking at the map, you can see what he means. The Woodman is down a country lane, in a hamlet with just over a dozen houses. Yet the M25 and M1 aren't too far away, neither are Hatfield and Potters Bar. According to Craig, 'people drop in after going past and tell us that they never knew we were here'.

The Woodman was built in the 1860s when the previous pub was knocked down – it stood where the Woodman's car park now is. It looks like a house, apart from the fact that there's a board bearing the pub's name over the wide front porch. Victorian is the style, unpretentious, solid, respectable, though according to Craig, who grew up locally, it was far from respectable when it closed in 1961. Thanks to the efforts of some well-connected locals it reopened a couple of years later. Craig took over in 1990 and since then the awards have whizzed in. The latest is South Herts CAMRA's Pub of the Year for 2011.

It's a one bar pub, though in the old days there was a saloon and public bar. It's a rather comfortable place, perhaps comparable to the front room of a largish terraced house. There are framed old maps of Hertfordshire on the wall and a few agricultural bits and bobs. It's a décor at ease with itself, not trying to prove anything. There's also a back room where rugby matches and Formula 1 are shown on terrestrial TV (no satellite here). The garden at the back opens out onto fields and offers a picture of rural calm.

Despite its relative isolation the Woodman has a strong following both local and further afield – as a result food is limited to rolls and jacket potatoes at lunchtime. 'We can't afford to have tables taken up by diners,' says Craig, which is the first time I've ever heard a landlord say this. Alongside the three regular beers, there are four guests featuring the likes of White Horse, Crouch Vale and many others. It's a generous pub as well. A lot of money is raised for charity. In 2011 one of the pub's barmaids cycled to Paris in order to raise money for a local hospice. The response from the regulars and local breweries was phenomenal. This is the British pub and its customers at their best.

Opening hours: 11.30–2.30, 5.30–11; 12–2.30, 7–10.30 Sun
Also great for: Country

Yarcombe Inn

Yarcombe, Honiton, Devon, EX14 9BD
01404 861142
www.yarcombeinn.com

🍺 **Branscombe Vale Branoc; Otter Amber, guest beers**

• •

A village pub closes. Villagers shrug their shoulders and drink at home or drive to the next village where two-for-one dishes keep things ticking over. The closed pub becomes a private home: the Old Inn, the Old Bell, the Old Rose & Crown. In rural England the closed pub is a familiar tale.

Yet the story has a different ending in Yarcombe, an ancient village that sits on the southerly slopes of the Blackdown Hills. When its old coaching inn closed in 2010, the locals decided to call time on the familiar story. With the aid of a TV programme dedicated to reviving ailing English pubs, the community stepped in and the Yarcombe Inn is now a thriving establishment that also won its local CAMRA branch's Pub of the Year Award in 2011.

The Yarcombe Inn sits on the road that cuts through the village, the church tower rising up behind. A jovial Falstaffian-style barman smiles a welcome as I enter. The phone behind the bar rings and it's handed to a regular on a stool who is enjoying his dimpled glass of Otter Amber.

'I'll be home immediately,' he says trying to keep a straight face. There are three cask beers, with the Amber joined by Branscombe Vale Branoc and Milton Nero. I grab a glass of Amber, light, floral, bittersweet and mouth-watering.

Inside, the pub is a mash-up of flagstones and black wooden beams, a big old fireplace with a brick built surround, the odd ancient agricultural implement, as if left behind by an absent-minded farm worker, and old photographs. The back bar has the look of an old farmhouse dresser, albeit decorated with bottles and optics instead of cups and plates, while the front of the bar counter itself features carved oak panels that wouldn't be out of place at the end of church pews. There's a restaurant of sorts at the back of the large open bar (the menu offers good value pub food such as pie and chips), while elsewhere there is a skittle alley and beer garden.

It's Friday evening and there's a steady trickle of people into the pub. Most seem to know each other, lending the area around the bar the feel of a family gathering. The phone rings again. The man with the glass decides its time to go home, but he now knows that he can come back the next day and the day after that – thanks to the efforts of villagers like him.

Opening hours: 12–3 (Wed–Fri in summer), 6–11; 12–11 Sat; 12–3 Sun

The best **community pubs**

The best **bed & breakfasts**

The best **bed & breakfasts**

The monasteries did it first, offering a bed for the night alongside a plate of food and jug of whatever they brewed on the premises. These establishments came to be called inns, and the tradition of hospitality for the tired pilgrim is maintained by many a British pub today.

The guarantee of a glass of good beer remains, and of a restful night in comfortable surroundings, though you might catch a glimpse of a friendly ghost or two in the odd historical hostel, after your evening meal with the kitchen presenting their labour with a flourish. Up with the lark for a breakfast of locally-sourced food. Not forgetting the beer, which might even be brewed on the premises, with the warming spicy aroma of the boil adding to the delight of the dawn chorus.

The pubs in this section offer bed and breakfast but they present something more for the traveller: the promise of a home from home, a place where even for one night the cares of daily life can be put aside. Whether it's the Anchor at Walberswick beside the bracing air of the North Sea or the bookish pleasures that enliven a stay in Kilverts in Hay-on-Wye, these are pubs where beer, bed and breakfast reflect the best in our island's long tradition of bibulous hospitality.

See also
The Anderson,
Fortrose (p206)
Castle Inn,
West Lulworth (p221)
Fisherman's Tavern,
Broughty Ferry (p273)
George Hotel,
Lower Brailes (p214)
Mug House,
Bewdley (p100)

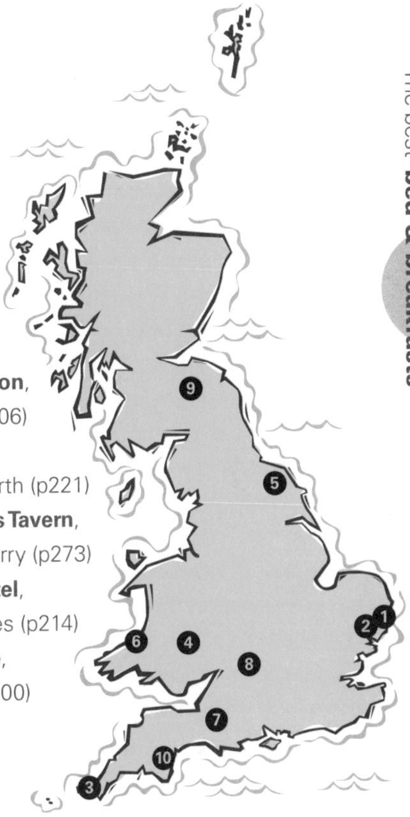

◀ Queens Arms, Corton Denham

Anchor

Main Street, Walberswick,
Suffolk, IP18 6UA
01502 722112
www.anchoratwalberswick.com
**Adnams Southwold Bitter,
Broadside, seasonal beers**

. . . .

The best **bed & breakfasts**

What would you like for breakfast? Some pubs offer the classic full English with a side helping of disappointment (watery bacon, sawdust sausages) but order this at the Anchor and you'll delight in its deliciousness: juicy, plump sausages, locally cured bacon and fresh eggs. But you could also order a haddock, smoked in nearby Lowestoft, topped with a poached egg, or – the speciality of head chef Sophie Dorber – a jalapeno omelette (see p208 for the recipe). Bread (from simple baguettes to herby focaccia) is baked on the premises. Oh and did I mention the coffee? The Anchor's triple shot cappuccino is an electric start to the day that wires you to the National Grid. With four bedrooms in the Anchor, and six garden rooms these breakfast choices will be yours, as well as the chance to discover many other reasons to love this place.

The Anchor was built in the 1920s and is a classic example of Brewers' Tudor – a mock Tudor finish beloved of pub architects: steep gables and Elizabethan chimneys bolted onto what is essentially a suburban house. At the time it would have been seen as modern, before being dismissed in the postwar years. Now enough time has passed to give it a patina of retro cool.

The open front bar is bright and comfortable: oak flooring, wood panels and a smattering of local scenes on the walls. It's gastro-smart, but also possesses an earthiness that halts any slide into suburban sterility. The pub is run by Mark and Sophie Dorber. Given that Mark famously made the White Horse in Parsons Green (p25) into a shrine of great beer, it comes as no surprise that the beer selection is a comprehensive and mouth-watering collection. The Adnams ales are perfect, while there's a generous selection of global bottled beers from the USA, Germany and Belgium. This is beer nirvana for the upmarket ale aficionado.

Walberswick sits beside the North Sea, a vista of grey stretching into the distance. Only the hardiest, even in summer, take themselves down to the pebbled beach and bathe in its cold but reinvigorating waters. However, you don't have to punish yourself to enjoy Walberswick's gorgeous location – an easier way is to repair to the Anchor. Good food (breakfast, lunch and dinner), great beer and a magical location – the Anchor is a trinity house of pleasure.

Opening hours: 11–4, 6–11; 11–11 Sat; 12–11 Sun
Accommodation: Ten bedrooms are available starting at £110 per night with breakfast available. Dogs are welcome in the dog-friendly rooms for an extra £5.
Also great for: Beer range; Seaside

Cherry Tree Inn

73 Cumberland Street, Woodbridge,
Suffolk, IP12 4AG
01394 384627
www.thecherrytreepub.co.uk

🍺 **Adnams Southwold Bitter, Explorer,
Broadside, seasonal beers; guest beers**

· ·

I highly recommend taking time to explore the beautiful town of Woodbridge with its miscellany of Tudor, Georgian and Victorian buildings. Woodbridge also sits on the River Deben and makes a great base for visiting the fabulous Anglo-Saxon cemeteries of Sutton Hoo on the opposing bank.

After your perambulation through history you might want to repair to the Cherry Tree Inn – there's no need to rush since it's open all day. This idyllic 17th century pub is cosy, comfortable and packed with character – think log fires and old beams. Meanwhile, its open-plan bar gives a sense of spaciousness, encouraging relaxation. It offers great food (the home-made pies and curries garner especial praise) and there's even a gaggle of friendly ghosts (supposedly heavy-drinking Cavaliers). Presumably they would approve of the Cherry Tree's reputation for fine cask ales. There are usually eight available, including three residents from Adnams: the fabulous Southwold Bitter plus Explorer and Broadside; there are also guest beers from breweries such as Mill Green, Elgoods and Batemans. The pub's two annual beer festivals strengthen this beery offering.

Given that Woodbridge is the sort of place you'd want as your base for exploring the countryside, then the Cherry Tree Inn is an ideal spot to lay down roots. You'll find a trio of spacious airy rooms housed in the converted barn in the large garden behind the pub (they are named after Adnams beers: Explorer, Broadside and Regatta). So you're guaranteed a peaceful night's slumber – and no ghostly revellers.

Opening hours: 10.30–11
Accommodation: Three rooms available, starting at £90 per night including breakfast

The best **bed & breakfasts**

Gurnard's Head

Treen, nr Zennor, St Ives, Cornwall, TR26 3DE
01736 796928
www.gurnardshead.co.uk

🍺 **St Austell Tribute; Skinner's Betty Stogs, Heligan Honey**

. . . .

The Gurnard's Head is one of those get-away-from-it-all places where the promise of escape from everyday life is faithfully kept. Even the first sight on approach marks it out as different: the name of the inn is picked out on the roof tiles, visible from afar, while a few hundred metres away the sea stretches off into the blue yonder. All around here is prime walking country, and the nearby rocky headland of Gurnard's Head, which gave its name to this inn, points out into the sea. On a rough day the sight of the sea crashing against the rocks and the sound of seabirds wheeling in the air makes for an invigorating symphony for the senses.

All this creates a splendid environment in which to enjoy the Gurnard's Head. This is a place with a winning reputation for its food. Locally sourced, simple ingredients are cooked with imagination: home-made pork pies, smoked haddock fishcakes, beef and ale pies, scallop risotto. Yet, even though this is a destination pub for those who love good food, the bar is also home to locals contemplating the day over a glass of St Austell's Tribute or Skinner's Betty Stogs. The interior is striking, featuring bold colour schemes such as terracotta and bright blue, while the furnishings are solid and seasoned, as well-weathered as the rocks that face the sea. Folk evenings occur monthly, and to complete the sense of comfort, the inn has a series of rooms, some overlooking the sea and others with a vista of the moor stretching inland. In the morning you might see a local farmer leading his cattle past the inn on their way to be milked. Get away from it all indeed.

Opening hours: 10am–11.30pm
Accommodation: Seven rooms from £95 per night including breakfast
Also great for: Entertainment

Kilverts

The Bull Ring, Hay-on-Wye,
Powys, HR3 5AG
01497 821042
www.kilverts.co.uk

🍺 **Breconshire Kilverts Gold;
Marston's Pedigree;
Wye Valley Butty Bach; guest beers**

. . . .

Books are to the Welsh border town of Hay-on-Wye what beer and brewing are to Burton upon Trent, and you cannot walk very far without encountering a bookshop offering a plethora of second-hand titles. Kilverts is the ideal place for a beery bibliophile to lay their weary head, and you can also taking delight in delicious great dollops of home-cooked food and lashings of superb beer.

It's an imposing building situated in the middle of town, dating from the Edwardian era. It became a hotel in the 1980s and was renovated by the

Davies family in 2006. For the bookish traveller, the inn offers 12 comfortable and recently refurbished rooms named after writers ranging from Shakespeare to Roald Dahl (one has a Jacuzzi, while another suite opens up onto the garden).

This same attention to detail comes with the food served in both the restaurant and bar: for vegetarians the imaginative menu might include wild mushroom risotto while carnivores will want to lavish some attention on the belt-straining steak and kidney pudding. All the meat is sourced locally, and the organic breakfast features both homemade yoghurt and bread.

Yet there can be no real satisfaction in an inn unless the bar is stocked with a super selection of cask beers – Kilverts gets this right as well. The bar is open and comfortable, a place through which drinkers can move easily. Tables and chairs are comfortably spaced, while the area around the bar is where you will encounter the locals: a raffish, friendly crowd on my visit.

Up to eight handpumps dispense cask beer, with local heroes Wye Valley and Otley turning up frequently – Wye Valley's HPA is a brisk and frisky golden ale, light and tantalising on the tongue, seductive with a dry, bitter finish. Cider-lovers can enjoy one of Gwynt y Ddraig's award-winning blends.

This bar is a magnet for bookish folk and celebrities during Hay-on-Wye's many literary gatherings. If you stand long enough at the bar you may pick up the name of a TV bookworm whose bibulous stay at the hotel necessitated a restorative breakfast Bloody Mary one morning.

Opening hours: 11–11 (midnight Fri & Sat)
Accommodation: 12 rooms from £60 per night including breakfast

The best **bed & breakfasts**

New Inn

Woolcroft, Cropton, nr Pickering,
North Yorkshire, YO18 8HH
01751 417330
www.newinncropton.co.uk

🍺 **Cropton seasonal beers; guest beers**

Like a lot of New Inns, this solid, stone-built village pub has been around for centuries. It sits alongside the road that cuts through Cropton, a village on the southern edge of the North York Moors, and an essential stopping point for those eager to tramp across the National Park.

Age does not wither the appeal of the New Inn. In the main bar, horse brasses glitter and shine beneath the ancient beams – on cold days the log fire crackles away like a wheezy old man. This is the perfect port in a storm, and summer days offer a different but similarly rewarding kind of berth, a place where you can sit outside and breath deeply of the fresh moorland air (you might also inhale the familiar smell of brewing but more of that in a moment). Meanwhile the modern world is brought into sharp perspective in the bright adjacent restaurant, where local artists' paintings on the wall are for sale.

Two Pints is the name of one of the beers that the Cropton brewery produces in a purpose-built building to the rear of the pub. It started off its brewing life in 1984 in a cellar beneath the bar, resurrecting the village's brewing traditions that apparently date back to 1613. The beer was named because it was said that drinkers couldn't make do with just one pint, they always wanted more – it has a firm, biscuit-like centre, dotted with delicate berry notes and a bitter finish.

Two Pints, two reasons to visit the New Inn. First of all there's its location. The North York Moors starts a couple of miles away and offers a stunning selection of country walks; secondly, the New Inn is home to the Cropton brewery whose products can be sampled and celebrated in the homely front bar (beneath the glitter of those horse brasses).

Maybe there should be a beer with three in its name, as a third reason to visit the New Inn is that it has accommodation. A weekend here is an ideal way to take the time to study the home-brewed beers – from Two Pints to Monkman's Slaughter to Yorkshire Moors Bitter and beyond. You can eat heartily as well. Food includes steak and mushroom pie cooked in the brewery's own stout and Whitby cod in pale ale batter with hand cut chips. These are exactly the kind of meals you really look forward to after a day in the hills. Beer and bed and plate of decent grub; what more can the weary walker ask for?

Opening hours: 11–11; 11.30–10.30 Sun
Accommodation: Nine en suite rooms available, from £85 per night, including breakfast. Dogs welcome in the cottage suites only for a surcharge of £10.
Also great for: Brewpubs

Pentre Arms

Llangrannog, Ceredigion, SA44 6SP
01239 654345
www.pentrearms.co.uk
🍺 **Evan Evans Cwrw; Gale's Seafarers Ale;**
St Austell Tribute

• •

Llangrannog is a handsome village on the west
Welsh coast, south of Aberystwyth, a gem of a
place framed on both sides by headlands reaching
out into the sea. This is excellent walking country,
while for those of a watery bent the waves offer
excellent surfing opportunities; it might not be
Bondi Beach or even Newquay, but there's every
chance of experiencing the odd rip curl or two.

For those with a more metaphysical bent, on
some evenings it is said that down on the beach
the shadowy figure of Huw Pugh can be seen
staring out at the water; Huw is supposedly the
ghost of a sailor who died in the 18th century.

The sea has always been part of Llangrannog's
life and nowhere does it impose its imperious self
more than down on the front where the Pentre
Arms sits. The pub has a list on its wall of the
ships that were once built here, recalling the days
when most of the men worked on or with the
sea. On some days you can stand outside this old
stone and slate-built pub and feel the spray on
your face, and on very stormy days, the hatches
have to be battened down as the waves come
crashing over. Yet, during calmer times, the sea's
immediacy adds an extra element of pleasure as
you sup your pint.

Small, cosy, neatly painted in yellow on the
outside with pine green fringes around the
windows plus a Welsh dragon picked out in red
next to one of the bedrooms, there's a soothing
tranquillity about the Pentre Arms. Inside, there's
an affable bar in which both locals and tourists
mix, with a babble of Welsh and English in the
background. Food inevitably features a selection
of freshly landed fish, while there are three cask
beers available during busy times of the year (the
Gale's might be dropped during the quieter weeks
of deep winter). As for accommodation there are
eight good value rooms, some of which overlook
the ever-changing moods of the sea. You never
know, you might catch a glimpse of Huw Pugh
from the comfort of your own room.

Opening hours: 12–midnight (1am Fri & Sat)
Accommodation: Eight rooms from £55 per night
including breakfast

Queens Arms

Corton Denham, Somerset, DT9 4LR
01963 220317
www.thequeensarms.com

🍺 **Moor Queens Revival, seasonal beers;
guest beers**

. . . .

The village of Corton Denham stands in splendid
seclusion, in a fold of deep-sided but gently
rounded hills on the edge of Somerset. This is
superb walking country and footsore travellers
will find the Queens Arms' charms hard to resist.

It stands on a quiet road, a square, sandy
coloured building from the Georgian era. It's an
unassuming looking place, lacking any hint of
gaudy frontage that would blare out its name –
the only indication of its purpose is a rather faded-
looking inn sign. However, it's been dispensing
hospitality and beer since opening its doors in
1760. It was originally built by the Portman family,
of cement fame, and the village has several
examples of their unique cement houses.

Inside the décor is calm, classic and collected,
with flagstones and wooden boards, clean cream
coloured walls and an imposing marble fireplace.
The sense of style also extends to the elegant
bedrooms – and if you need a romantic surprise
the pub can arrange flowers and chocolates to be
left in your room. It's little touches like this that
add an extra element of welcome to a stay.

The staff is young and friendly, and – unlike
many a country pub with gastro leanings – it's
also a place that is exceedingly knowledgeable
about beer. At the bar beers from Somerset's
trend-setting Moor can be studied in the tranquil
atmosphere. Try a glass of their Queens Revival,
a bittersweet session beer with a bracing bite
on the palate, or maybe a nip of the powerful
imperial IPA JJJ. The brewery's seasonal beers
also appear. Guest beers come from the likes of
Marble and Purity, while there is also a dizzying
selection of global beers as Trappist ales jostle for
space next to San Francisco steam beers.

Then there's the food. For a snack, try the
superlative pork pies at the bar, proffered with
homemade chutney. Naturally local sourcing is
a given and the pub picks up a lot of produce
from growers in the village; they also have their
own pigs and chickens. Maybe you'll go for the
basil crusted pork loin or the steak and haggis
sandwich with hand-cut chips.

The Queens Arms transcends mere gastro-
pub pretension: it's a pub that just happens to
serve great food and great drink in comfortable
surroundings with excellent company.

Opening hours: 10–11; 12–10.30 Sun
Accommodation: Five en suite rooms are available,
from £85 per night, including breakfast. There is a free
pickup service at Sherborne station for guests.
Also great for: Food

Red Lion

74 High Street, Cricklade, Wiltshire, SN6 6DD
01793 750776
www.theredlioncricklade.co.uk
🍺 **Moles Best; Ramsbury Gold; Sharp's Doom Bar; Wadworth 6X; guest beers**

• •

Beer is done well at the Red Lion – up to nine cask beers are on offer plus a thorough selection of some of the world's great bottled beers. A nice touch is a small shot glass of each individual beer in front of the handpump, allowing drinkers to see the colour of their tipple of choice before ordering. As if that's not enough, the menu offers up beer suggestions with the dishes.

This rambling town inn, which dates back to the start of the 17th century, also has a set of comfortable and expansive bedrooms – so it's a no-brainer for the serious beer lover who wants to spend some time swotting up on their chosen subject. You can bring Rover as well – two of the rooms are dog-friendly.

Yet there's more to the Red Lion than just the beer. For a start, it's located in the middle of a pretty market town that sits on the southern edge of the Cotswolds – it's almost halfway between Swindon and Cirencester as an old road sign on a wall in the bar proclaims. The upper reaches of the Thames pass through the town, the beginning of the journey that will end in the North Sea (Cricklade styles itself as the first town on the Thames). It's a gorgeous rural area with plenty of walks as well as the town's famous nature reserve the North Meadow; those with a penchant for water will make for the Cotswold Water Park several miles to the north.

Back to the pub, which has the look of several cottages that have been knocked together, with hanging baskets adding colour. The main bar is a comfortable space in which to drink beer – here a stuffed trout on the wall, there some old stone bottles gathered on a shelf; the traditional comforting bric-a-brac of the English pub. In the winter a log fire offers warmth, while summer days can be spent out in the garden. There's a restaurant at the back, where sturdy dishes such as creamed smoked haddock (chosen beer match: Odell's IPA) and rib-eye steak (Dogfish Head Palo Santo Marron) are served.

The stone-built pubs of the nearby Cotswolds might get all the attention in this part of the world, attracting tourists with romance on their minds, but the Red Lion deserves an equal amount of love. Beer and breakfast anyone?

Opening hours: 12–11; 12–10.30 Sun
Accommodation: Five en suite rooms available, from £75 per night, including breakfast. Two dog-friendly rooms.

Traquair Arms

Innerleithen, nr Peebles,
Scottish Borders, EH44 6PD
01896 830229
www.traquairarmshotel.co.uk

🍺 **Caledonian Deuchars IPA;
Taylor Landlord; Traquair Bear Ale**

. . . .

The historic Traquair House stands a mile or so along the road from this comfortable, stone-built 18th century hotel and bar that quietly but competently offers hospitality at the edge of the small village of Innerleithen. The House is a venerable place, rough-edged and beaten by the rigours of the centuries, but it also has a lived in feel (it is a family home as well as tourist attraction), which is remarkable for something whose origins go back to the 12th century. The English once took it during the wars of independence but it was returned to the Scots when Robert the Bruce ascended the throne. Bonnie Prince Charlie visited in 1745, the year of his doomed insurrection, and his descendants (and current owners) the Maxwell-Stuarts have kept the House's outer gates closed ever since – it is said that they won't be opened until a Stuart once again sits on the throne.

However, for those who like their beer, Traquair House has a more notable place in history – it is home to one of the pioneers of modern country house brewing. Even though the brewery only produces four beers, most of which are bottled and sent to the USA, plus the odd special, its 18th century brewhouse is a place of pilgrimage for beer fans throughout the world. The late Laird (and father of the current Lady Catherine)

famously rediscovered it in the 1960s. With the help of the legendary Belhaven brewer Sandy Hunter, the brewhouse was brought back to life and the beers are still fermented in oak vessels. With the majority of beers being bottled, places to sample the House's beers on draught are rare and far between, but the Traquair Arms, being just a stone's throw away, is one of those places.

Enjoy a pint of the rich, roasty Bear Ale in the comfortable bar, where a fire crackles in the colder months; meanwhile summer days can be savoured in the sunny garden at the back. It goes without saying that Innerleithen is in the midst of beautiful country so the hotel makes for a handy stopping point and base. There are 14 rooms, while the hotel's former stables have been converted into six self-catering cottages. There is also a restaurant, specialising in Italian dishes, though the menu also features local produce such as venison. Contemplate your pint and wonder if Bonnie Prince Charlie will no come back again.

Opening hours: 11–11 (midnight Fri & Sat); 12–11.30 Sun
Accommodation: 14 rooms, from £50 per night including breakfast, and six self-catering cottages

Waterman's Arms

Bow Bridge, Ashprington, Totnes,
Devon, TQ9 7EG
01803 732214
www.thewatermansarms.net

🍺 **Palmers Copper Ale, Best Bitter,
seasonal beer**

· ·

You'd be hard pushed to find a more idyllic setting for a pint than this spot. This whitewashed 17th century inn is perched right next to the Bow Creek at the bottom of a steep valley, several miles from Totnes. Even though it's relatively close to the intriguing South Hams town of Totnes, there's a sense of isolation and tranquillity about the location – a hideaway from the hurly-burly of life.

In summer the inn is swathed in greenery, and you can take your place on the shaded decking area out front and enjoy your pint while watching the slow waters of the creek. Yet, for all this seclusion, the pub has led a chequered past, serving time as a brewhouse, prison, petrol station and smithy; there's even a ghost called Emily, but no one knows why she elected to choose the Waterman's as her link with life. Perhaps it's the hospitality that it offers?

Food is all locally sourced with a menu that changes daily, according to what's fresh and in season. The kitchen bakes its own bread, makes its own pasta and ice cream, and the eggs come from the pub's own free-range hens. Palmers Best Bitter and Copper Ale are on regularly with either the brewery's 200 or Dorset Gold taking up the third handpump, depending on the time of year. Best of all, you can stay in one of the comfortable en suite rooms with (if you really must stay online) free Wi-Fi throughout. But really you'd be mad to do anything other than park yourself at a table by the river, sup a pint of BB and let the stress simply wash away.

Opening hours: 11–11
Accommodation: 15 en suite rooms available, from £30 per person per night, including breakfast
Also great for: Riverside

The best
food pubs

Good grub here. The pubs in this section endeavour to raise the gastronomic possibilities of pub food without turning themselves into sterile restaurants where the first greeting to a customer passing through the doors could just be 'Are you eating?'

Up on the high moors of Northumberland, Tony Binks at the Barrasford Arms buys a whole pig from a local farmer once a week and makes his own sausages from it. You will also find that his canny purchase brings forth such delights as a tantalisingly crispy roast rack of pork and juicy plump legs for Sunday lunch. Is it any wonder that local vegetable growers congregate at the pub?

The Highland town of Fortrose is exceedingly fortune in that they have The Anderson, where American beer writer Bill Anderson and New Orleans-trained chef and wife Anne produce a staggeringly magnificent menu – the pub has its own smokery and all meat is home butchered.

Meanwhile at both the the Stagg Inn and Bunch of Grapes you can take their homemade sausages and black puddings home (the Bunch of Grapes even features cookery courses) – and let's not forget that all these pubs also major in great beer. Eat, drink and be merry indeed.

See also
Café Royal, Edinburgh (p66)
Gwaelod-y-Garth Inn, Gwaelod-y-Garth (p120)
Marble Arch, Manchester (p47)
Old Bridge Inn, Aviemore (p101)
Queens Arms, Corton Denham (p200)
Ship Inn, Low Newton (p36)

◀ Beef with steak and kidney pudding at the Stagg Inn, Titley

The Anderson

Union Street, Fortrose, Highland, IV10 8TD
01381 620 236
www.theanderson.co.uk
🍺 **Beer range varies**

• •

Beer writers write about beer. They even lend a hand in a brewery sometimes, behaving like kids let loose in a sweetshop (or should that be hop store?). However, a beer writer behind the bar is a seldom seen sight, unless you find your way to The Anderson in the Highlands town of Fortrose. Here, at a former coaching inn and station hotel, American beer writer Bill Anderson and wife Anne (who trained as a chef back home) have established an essential stop for any beer-loving and foodie visitor to the Highlands.

Where do I start? From the outside, The Anderson has the air of yet another high street hotel, but step inside and the décor has the word eclectic stamped across its forehead: stag heads, wine paraphernalia, original art, candles stuck in bottles from unknown Dutch breweries – there is no shortage of things to look at. This sense of variety then extends to the beer range. Three cask beers are served, though never the same beer twice in a row. 'Our customers like real ale that is blond, bland and weak, which is why I try to disappoint them at every opportunity!' laughs Bill Anderson. Breweries that have featured include Atlas, BrewDog, Fyne Ales and Williams Brothers. Having done a fair bit of work with Belgian beers back in the US, Anderson has also built up a menu of over 100 Belgian beers in bottle plus 15 beers from Danish 'gypsy brewers' Mikkeller.

Then there's the food. Chef Anne Anderson trained in New Orleans, where you need to be fluent in several ethnic cuisines to get by. This might be the Highlands, but she's not afraid to challenge people's conceptions of what a good meal should be. Good quality local produce such as beef, pork and venison are made use of. Their meat is home butchered, all sauces and stocks are made in-house, meat and fish are salt- and air-cured and there is a smoking shed out at the back. As Bill Anderson says: 'Anne came out swinging from day one, making very few adjustments to her approach, feeling that for every customer we'd lose because they found her food "strange", there were two more customers out there who could imagine how delicious a vanilla beurre blanc might taste with halibut.' At the table you will find anything from a New Orleans-style seafood gumbo to guinea fowl stuffed with white pudding.

It is a formula that could have failed but to the Andersons' credit they've become a byword for greatness, with visitors begging them to set up in other parts of the UK. No chance of that. 'We like it here,' says Bill, 'frustrations and all. After all, if there's a hard way of doing things we'll find it!'

Opening hours: 4–11.30; 12.30–11.30 Sun
Food times: 6 (1 Sun)–9.30
Also great for: Bed & breakfast; CAMRA award-winners

Barrasford Arms

Barrasford, Northumberland, NE48 4AA
01434 681237
www.barrasfordarms.co.uk.

🍺 **Beer range varies**

• •

Food glorious food. Sitting down to eat at the Barrasford Arms is a life-affirming experience. Try the roast crispy rack of pork – the crackling is astonishing, crisp and almost biscuit-like. The meat itself is rich and sweet, cooked to molten perfection. Beer cuisine? The beef rump cooked in brown ale is an unctuous and succulent delight. Or maybe you might fancy something a little less carnivorous? The chilli beetroot risotto is a fiery and heady delight. Proper chips? Yes please.

Ever since landlord and chef Tony Binks turned up in 2006, this stone-built Victorian village inn has become a major hit on the foodie circuit. All his ingredients are sourced locally wherever possible, while once a week he buys a whole pig from a nearby farmer. The shoulder goes for sausages, while the legs go for Sunday lunch.

So is it a pub? Can you expect a decent pint? 'I wouldn't dare change the bar,' said Binks when I visited, 'I'd be strung up'. He's wise in his ways. There are two dining rooms, but the bar is sacrosanct, a community centre, where locals and visitors mix and mingle. Here you might overhear a discussion about vegetables for instance, the virtues of leeks against the windiness of Jerusalem artichokes. Members of The Barrasford Arms Marrow Club hold their regular meetings on the premises. There are darts tournaments and the pub also hosts a quoits team – this is a gastro-pub with equal parts gastro and pub.

The bar is a cosy and comfortable place with framed photos dotting the walls, illustrating the social history of the village: old football teams, long-forgotten hunt meets and a framed *Private Eye* cover featuring Geoffrey Ripon, the former MP for the area. To add to the theme of country comfort, a handful of antlers and the odd stuffed otter's head look down on drinkers. Cask beer? There are normally three on offer. You might like to try the light and sparkling golden ale Sand Dancer from nearby brewery High House Farm. For something darker and more full-bodied, how about Red Kite from Wylam?

The village of Barrasford is in Hadrian's Wall country. This is an area of high moorland dotted with huddled gatherings of woodland. Naturally, it's spectacular for walking, which makes the Barrasford Arms an ideal place to rest and visit after a day yomping the moors. No wonder the marrow men keep coming back.

Opening hours: 12–2 (not Mon), 6.30–11 (midnight Fri); 12–midnight Sat; 12–11 Sun
Food times: 12–2 (not Mon), 6.30-9; 12–3 Sun
Also great for: Country; Pub games

The best **food pubs**

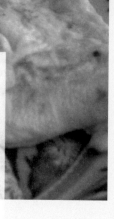

Jalapeno omelettes

'Well I just use two or three free range eggs, beaten in a pan, with some foaming butter, pull with a fork from the outside to the middle of the pan, so that the egg cooks evenly, add a handful of your favourite cheese and four or five slices of pickled jalapenos, with a quick flick of the pan, fold into half, cook until cheese begins to melt, then turn onto a hot plate and eat with a beer for a great breakfast!'

Sophie Dorber, Anchor, Walberswick, Suffolk

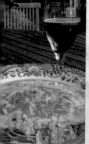

Pub grub

Otley O1 braised locally farmed rabbit (serves two)

2 rabbits

1 white onion, halved

½ bulb of garlic, halved

2 sprigs thyme

½ tsp tomato purée

1 pint O1 ale

½ litre chicken stock

salt

pinch cayenne pepper

flour

oil

Pre-heat oven to 350°F, 180°C, gas mark 4

Cut the rabbits in six: two legs, two shoulders, two saddles; if available use liver and kidneys too. Lightly flour all pieces and pan-fry at a high heat in the oil to get a nice brown colour on all pieces.

Put the rabbit pieces in a ovenproof dish with all other ingredients, bring to a simmer, cover, and cook in oven for approximately 2–2 ½ hours depending on the size of rabbits, and up to 3 hours if using wild rabbits.

Once cooked remove carefully all rabbit pieces, strain the jus and reduce by half. Put the rabbit pieces back in and serve with wilted green vegetables, pan-fried black pudding, pancetta or streaky bacon, and some new potatoes or a chunk of bread to mop up the jus!

Sebastien Vanoni, Bunch of Grapes, Pontypridd, Mid Glamorgan

Bunch of Grapes

Ynysangharad Road, Pontypridd,
Mid Glamorgan, CF37 4DA
01443 402934
www.bunchofgrapes.org.uk

🍺 **Otley O1, seasonal beers; guest beers**

Tom Jones may have grown up across the valley from where the Bunch of Grapes stands but he left for fame and fortune a long time ago. If you're looking for Pontypridd's local hero now look to the Bunch, and the pub's owners, the innovative and passionate brewery Otley.

Built at the start of the 19th century, as a simple alehouse, the Bunch of Grapes was bought by Otley in 2001. It was an unappealing old-school boozer with a colour scheme that hurt the eyes plus a clientele that wasn't too discriminating when it came to the ale. Something had to change and the interior was stripped back to its basics, in the course of which an original fireplace was uncovered. The end result? A clean, modern and comfortable sense of design has been imposed on the place.

There are nine handpumps: Otley's beers naturally appear on cask, joined at the bar by beers from craft brewers including BrewDog, Steel City and Titanic; regular beer festivals are also held. Meanwhile, a goodly selection of world beers and craft ciders helps to fly the flag for righteous drink. The Bunch Beer Academy also features regular talks and beer tastings from noted beer writers who sometimes get to brew in collaboration with Otley. Yet, while the Bunch gets it right in the beer department, it stunningly succeeds when it comes to food.

The menu is new British pub grub with a French twist: the seafood is sustainable and the meat comes from a local butcher with his own abattoir; they also make their own pickled eggs and pork crackling. Try the pancetta and cockles, a delicious riff on a traditional Welsh dish, while whiting in beer batter with chunky hand-cut chips also titillates. Other dishes include home-made burgers and confit belly of Welsh pork. The pub also has its own in-house deli where sausages, burgers and bread can be bought and cooking classes are regularly held by the head chef.

It all works marvellously – regulars enjoy their beer in the front bar, while diners can settle in various nooks and crannies or on special occasions proceed through to the more formal dining area next door. Result: happiness and a great pub.

Though quite what George the ghost makes of it all is far from clear: apparently he's responsible for popping the odd light bulb and moving stuff about. Apart from this, he seems happy with what Otley has done to make this one of the best pubs in the South Wales valleys. Perhaps it's because Otley has given the Grapes back its soul.

Opening hours: 12–midnight; 11–1am Fri & Sat;
11–midnight Sun
Food times: 12–2 (3.30 Sun), 6.30–9.30
Bar menu: 12.30–7.30 (not Sun)
Also great for: Beer range

The best food pubs

Cricket Inn

Penny Lane, Totley, Sheffield,
South Yorkshire, S17 3AZ
0114 236 5256
www.relaxeatanddrink.com

🍺 **Thornbridge Wild Swan, Lord Marples,
Hopton, Kipling, Jaipur IPA**

. . . .

Even though it's classed as a Sheffield suburb, Totley is disarmingly rural. The Peak District is a couple of fields away, which makes the inn a popular pitstop for walkers; fell runners have also been known to stop in for sustenance. And summer weekends bring the thwack of leather on willow from the adjoining cricket pitch.

Totley is also one of the more affluent suburbs of the city, home to various footballers as well as other members of Sheffield's 'glitterati'. There's an accompanying smartness about the Cricket – formerly an old boozer it's now a place of slate flagstones and shaker-style paint-covered wood surfaces, a chalked-up blackboard menu and, in the main high-ceilinged area, long refectory-type tables of the sort normally seen in city noodle bars. However, this is also a real pub featuring real food and beer, which helps to give it a strong local trade of people dropping in for a pint (it's also popular with families).

The Cricket Inn is run in partnership with Thornbridge, which means that a selection of beers from one of the UK's most innovative brewers is available. For beginners there's the light and fragrant Wild Swan, a refreshing pale ale; connoisseurs demand the brewery's much-awarded Jaipur, a spicy, juicy, hoppy India Pale Ale. Lord Maples and Hopton are also available,

plus the brewery's bottled beers such as St Petersburg. You'll drink well here.

You also eat well. The menu contains a collection of hearty and robust dishes, many of which have beer recommendations. The steak and ale pie is divine, while those with an appetite might like to plump for the plate of sausages, black pudding and Yorkshire pudding all dowsed in gravy made with Sheffield icon Henderson's Sauce. If that's too much, pub snacks include pork crackling, real whitebait and great chips fried in beef dripping.

There is a wonderful lack of pretension and a sense of inclusion in this former farmhouse that became a pub when the 3½ mile Totley train tunnel was built in the 19th century. It was also handy for another reason: the room with the canteen-style tables was used as a temporary mortuary whenever tunnel workers were killed in accidents. Apparently, its coolness was a big plus. Inevitably, there's a ghost. Walkers, kids, locals, 'glitterati' and ghosts: the Cricket Inn welcomes everyone.

Opening hours: 11–midnight
Food times: 12–2.30, 5–9; 12–9.30 Sat; 12–8 Sun
Also great for: Railway

Crown

Old Hereford Road, Pantygelli,
Abergavenny, Gwent, NP7 7HR
01873 853314
www.thecrownatpantygelli.com

🍺 **Draught Bass; Rhymney Best Bitter;
Wye Valley HPA; guest beers**

• •

You dine well in and around Abergavenny – after all, the old Welsh border town is home to one of the UK's most vibrant food festivals and there's bound to be a ripple effect throughout the area's pubs. So given that the Crown is a mere two miles out of town, it's not surprising that one look at the menu will have your taste buds laughing out loud as they get heartily tickled. The grub here is seriously good. Take just two examples: the bubble and squeak is a voluptuous green feast on which sit several slices of tender Welsh Black beef, while a plate of locally made faggots and creamy mash both soothes and nourishes the hungry soul.

However, where the Crown differs from many an establishment that takes the gastro route is that it also steadfastly remains a good pub. You will not be asked 'Are you eating with us' the moment you step through the thick oak front door into the cosy confines of exposed wooden beams, slate floor and whitewashed stone walls; the Crown is as proud of its cask beers as it is of its food. On any given evening the bar will be humming with locals from the surrounding hills discussing the rural scene and washing down their take on country life with pints of the generously malty Rhymney Best or the light and refreshing HPA from Wye Valley Brewery. There are usually three other cask beers on show.

The pub also hosts its own darts team and quiz nights are held; in this age when too many rural pubs chuck out the locals and opt for what the 1930s celebrity landlord and author John Fothergill would have called 'day-trippers' it's heartening to see this encouragement of village life. Meanwhile at the end of the bar there's a small book swap library. This is obviously a place that encourages contemplation and we're not just talking about the spectacular views across the green, hilly valley.

You can't always judge a book by its cover and from the outside the Crown is the pub equivalent of a school science textbook: dull and worthy looking. Even though this three-storeyed old coaching inn reputedly dates back several centuries, it doesn't seem anything special. If it wasn't for the presence of its semi-italicised name in the middle of the frontage that whispers rather than screams out 'pub', chances are you'd carry on straight past on the old Hereford road heading north out of Abergavenny. Don't.

Opening hours: 12–2.30 (not Mon, 3 Sat & Sun),
6–11 (10.30 Sun)
Food times: 12–2, 7–9 (not Sun); no food Mon

Culm Valley Inn

Culmstock, Devon, EX15 3JJ
01884 840354
www.culmvalleyinn.co.uk
🍺 **Beer range varies**

Four miles away on the southern side of the M5 sits Culmstock, a small village that both history and the traffic have passed by. However, those unknowing holidaymakers heading west to Cornwall don't know what they're missing. Under the inspired ownership of Richard Hartley, the Culm Valley Inn has put Culmstock on the map, drawing in both beer drinkers and food lovers.

The Inn was once associated with a different sort of travel – it was a railway hotel on a line that was done away by the Beeching Report in the 1960s. Maybe this led to its decline – I have a tattered second-hand copy of Devon CAMRA's 1981 pub guide in which the previous owner had written 'primitive but friendly' in the margins.

Primitive is the last thing you would say about the Culm Valley Inn these days. Walking into its front bar is like entering a pastiche of a farmhouse sitting room, albeit with an area serving beer and cider on one side. It's rustic and robust in its fittings – heavy thick wooden furniture built from old oak, a log fire and a pleasingly distressed bar frontage at which regulars stand and gossip. This is also a very dog-friendly pub, with the pub's dog eager to play with any canine newcomers.

This rusticity feels almost organic, giving off the feeling that the bar has taken root. However, don't be totally fooled: Cold Comfort Farm this is not. Pass through the bar and you will emerge into a dining area that wouldn't be out of place in a

Chelsea bistro – warm terracotta colours and smart yet casual tables and chairs, while the business of the kitchen can be viewed while you eat.

During busy periods up to 10 cask beers are on offer, all served from barrels kept in a temperature-controlled room behind the bar. West Country beers are favoured with the well-established likes of Glastonbury and Branscombe being joined by newer breweries such as Quercus and Red Rock.

Even though it's noted for its food, landlord Hartley is adamant that he runs a 'proper' pub that happens to provide excellent food. Game comes from local shoots, while meat and cheese are sourced from neighbouring producers. How about rollmops, home-cured on the premises with a wonderful balance of sweet and sour, or maybe a warm spiced octopus salad, offering a hint of Mediterranean cuisine? Other dishes might include Devon red ruby burgers or wild duck outrageously marinated in Campari and Cointreau. Believe it or not this works. Set the sat-nav now…

Opening hours: 12–3, 6–11; 11–11 Fri & Sat; 12–10.30 Sun
Food times: 12–2, 7–9; no food Sun
Also great for: Motorway

The best **food pubs**

It's not all gloom and doom. Despite a riot of headlines that places the pub in the intensive care wing of British life, *Great British Pubs* demonstrates that there still remain a lot of successful pubs, inns and taverns, serving great beer and hearty food while offering the sort of welcome that makes even the briefest of visits into a holiday from the cares of normal life. Yet, the question always hangs in the air: what makes a successful pub? And everyone and their mother seem to have the answer. Smile at the customers, offer cask beers not found elsewhere, sell old favourites, concentrate on food, don't sell food, cut prices to the bone, charge a bit more... the litany of suggestions continues, but the reality is a little more complex. There is no one recipe for a successful pub. All the pubs featured here are successful because their licensees have learnt what works and gets customers through the door. The one thing that they share is that they all offer cask beer, whether it's a couple of handpumps or a bewildering array that stands on the bartop like a phalanx of soldiers. Roger Cudlipp runs the award-winning Tom Cobley Tavern on the edge of Dartmoor (p24). He normally stocks 14 cask beers: 'I started with three but I got a lot of real ale drinkers in and they kept on suggesting beers, then brewers would come in and I gradually saw a niche in the market. I was in the *Good Beer Guide* and it snowballed from there.' Other pubs work on the food side of the business, making a virtue of local produce – at the Barrasford Arms in Northumbria (p207) landlord/chef Tony Binks buys a rare breed pig from a local farm every week. The shoulder is used for sausages and the legs for Sunday lunch. Some pubs organise beer dinners or offer beer matching on their food menu. Then there is entertainment in the shape of music, beer festivals, walking clubs, film shows and traditional pub games. For Simon Daws at the Royal Oak in Prestbury (p178), the ambience is important: 'My personal ideal would be a pub where the bar is the engine room, where locals mix with newcomers and where youth feel comfortable drinking with the older generation.... as happens so much in Ireland. A visit to the pub should conjure up thoughts of camaraderie, humour and general relaxing conversation both with people you know and don't know.'

What makes a successful pub? Just ask one of the successful licensees featured within these pages.

George Hotel

High Street, Lower Brailes,
Oxfordshire, OX15 5HN
01608 685223
www.thegeorgeatbrailes.co.uk

🍺 **Hook Norton Hooky Bitter, Hooky Gold, Old Hooky; guest beer**

• •

Across the road in the sleepy village of Lower Brailes the church tower clock is about to strike 9pm and I am told to stop and listen. There's the sound of a bell and then the same bells start playing Auld Lang Syne, a metallic yet charming sequence of chimes. Apparently, most hours are celebrated by a similar parade of clanging tunes.

The George is a near neighbour of the church (some speculate that there's a secret tunnel between the two), a low-slung, gold Cotswold stone Georgian inn that has been with Hook Norton since the 1890s. Rooms, good food and beer: that's the simple secret of its success.

Inside the bar, I order a pint of Old Hooky and note the wooden beams criss-crossing the low ceiling, beneath which sit a couple in the corner, exchanging confidences in between finishing puddings. It's a clean and light space, featuring washed and bleached out wood fittings, though the bare stonework about the fireplace offers an element of earthiness.

Time to eat: a plate of pan-fried bream balanced on a pile of noodles. It is outstanding as the softness of the noodles link arms with the light spiciness of the fish and wander on down the street in a happy mood. A sight of the blue cheese and spinach risotto was also enough to make me consider vegetarianism.

It's quiet tonight but I'm told that the pub is home to a dominoes team. 'They've got travelling reserves and supporters,' says a man at the bar nursing a glass of Hooky Bitter. Puzzlement starts to cross his face, even though I suspect he's told strangers about this before. 'It's really important.' The pub also supports an Aunt Sally team that plays in the Banbury league. Oh and there's a post office twice a week as well.

The George's sign with its fashionable lower case G might look like an archetypal gastro-pub, but there's more to it – this is an inn in the full sense of the word, offering good food, drink and sleeping time that the monks of the middle ages would have been proud of.

Opening hours: 10–3, 5–11; 10–midnight Sat; 10–10.30 Sun
Food times: 12–2, 7–9; 12–3, 7–8.30 Sun
Also great for: Bed & breakfast

Rat Inn

Anick, Hexham, Northumberland, NE46 4LN
01434 602814
www.theratinn.com

🍺 **Caledonian Deuchars IPA; Draught Bass; guest beers**

· ·

Local beef braised in local beer; confit of duck leg; rillette of Craster kipper (very local). You eat well here – it's a place where Northumberland's produce goes from field to plate in a brief matter of miles.

Fancy a pint of ale to go with your meal? Wylam, Hadrian & Border and Mordue's are just a few of the breweries that appear alongside regular tapsters Caledonian Deuchars IPA and Draught Bass (they've got a local who's been drinking it there for 50 years I'm told and they don't want to disappoint such loyalty).

Stomach and throat soothed, what about the eyes? Tradition with a daub of modern style is how the bar might be described – a shaded, cosy place that is warmed by the fire from a cast iron range when winter comes. Cosy corners, oak settles, wooden flooring and beams crossing the ceiling complete the homely pub experience. Amongst the darkened beams of the ceiling there hangs a collection of old chamber pots that the pub is famous for. One of them is a wartime pot with a picture of Hitler inside. The inscription says: 'flip your ashes on old nasty.' Meanwhile in the dining room there are inset carvings of rats around the edge of the flooring and painted on the tiles around the fireplace. Outside in the summer, the garden gives drinkers a view over the Tyne Valley with the shimmering silver of the river visible.

Surely there are not many pubs named after one of our least favourite mammals. No one really knows how it came about its name, though many are the speculations. I talk with landlady Karen Errington, who shrugs and says 'Some say that it was a regular meeting place for all the local rat catchers; others that the largest rat ever seen was caught here.' There's also the tale of a local bloke who ratted on Jacobite sympathisers when Bonnie Prince Charlie's men came through in 1745.

You may never know the real reason for the name but instead console yourself with a good pint and a nourishing plate of local food. Sometimes it pays to just eat and drink.

The best **food pubs**

Opening hours: 12–3, 6–11; 12–11 Sat & Sun
Food times: 12–2, 6–9; 12–3 Sun; no food Mon

Stagg Inn

Titley, Kington, Herefordshire, HR5 3RL
01544 230221
www.thestagg.co.uk

🍺 **Hobsons Best Bitter; guest beers**

In 2001 the Stagg Inn was the first British pub to receive a Michelin star, which immediately put it in the vanguard of the gastro-pub movement. Metropolitan food critics trundled their way down narrow country lanes to this solid inn close to the Welsh border. Therefore, you could be forgiven for thinking that all semblance to a pub would have been lost in the years since.

Good grub may be god at the Stagg, but make your way into the compact bar and you're in pub land: this is still a place where locals gather at the bar for an ale or (more likely, given that we're in Herefordshire) a cider, and put the world to rights. There are three cask beers usually available, with Hobsons Best Bitter (a divine drop: crisp biscuity malt character balanced by citrus notes and a dry and bittersweet finish) joined by another from the same brewer as well as guests from the likes of Ludlow Brewery.

Cider takes its rightful place amongst the ranks too, and we're not talking about the stuff that gets sloshed over ice cubes either: ciders and perries from Dunkertons, Westons and Ralph's are either available in bottle or on draught. As you stand at the bar thinking of what to choose from the latter, you might hear one of the locals utter the words 'powerful stuff'.

All this can be enjoyed in the company of an excellent menu. There are several dining rooms scattered about this old hotchpotch of a building –

it was built in the middle ages but then refurbished during the 19th century with add-ons from the 1970s. The bar features a lot of weathered wood, bare brick walls and a stripped wooden floor, while the dining areas seem to be an homage to striped curtains and clean blond wood. A blackboard menu lies in wait at the bar and the choice is agonising given the Stagg's reputation (and it's all locally sourced as far as is possible). Will it be the warm salad of pigeon breast and black pudding? Or the lamb's sweetbreads and fennel purée? Maybe the sea bass goujons with chips and home-made tartare sauce?

Try the latter as I did and you will be rewarded with juicy goujons that go a dream with the chunky, tangy tartare sauce. You can even bring the Stagg home – the pub's home-made (from their own pigs) sausages, black puddings, chorizo and faggots are all available to take away.

The Stagg Inn is a smart place, make no mistake, but with its dedication to good drink, food and service, it still maintains that country pub atmosphere revered throughout the world.

Opening hours: 12–3, 6.30–11.45 (not Sun); closed Mon
Food times: 12–2, 6.30–9 (not Sun); closed Mon

Woods

4 Bank Square, Dulverton,
Somerset, TA22 9BU
01398 324007
www.woodsdulverton.co.uk

🍺 **St Austell Trelawney; guest beers**

. . . .

Woods by name, wood by nature. There's a forest's worth of weathered and worn wood on display in this former bakery which only became a bar and restaurant in 2004. The décor has an elemental, almost living feel with its wooden floorboards and a bar seemingly carved out of oak; the exposed stone of the walls adds an earthy, rock-hewn ambience. The walls are dotted with local photographs plus the odd Victorian-style painting of a nostalgic scene, odd bits of hunting kit and various stuffed animals. Coins and notes are also jammed into the ancient beams and many an unwary newcomer has been caught out trying to pocket the coins caught in a crack in the floor. The bar and dining room nestle cheek by jowl in a companionable way, without any sense of 'us and them'. This leads to many a diner wandering over for a beer when replete and joining in the banter.

The food is legendary, whether a bar snack or a full blown dining experience. For the menu think French meets British cuisine with raw materials sourced from the West Country. Landlord Paddy Groves keeps his own pigs and chickens, while it's not uncommon to find a deer that he has shot ending up on the menu also. Keep it simple? A seared steak salad with a balsamic vinegar dressing or honey roast ham, egg and chips. For something more substantial, crisp confit of duck leg or slow roast belly of pork satisfy all-comers.

Despite its reputation for good grub, drinkers are positively encouraged at Woods. Three cask beers are dispensed, straight from the barrel, with St Austell's Trelawney, Tribute and HSD being fairly regular, though Proper Job and Otter Head also crop up. Prince William turned up several years back and spent a merry hour chatting away with a local. When he had left, the local turned to his mate: 'Nice chap, that posh bloke. Who was he?' It sums up the peerless quality of this Exmoor gem: rogues and royals, drinkers and diners, locals and visitors, children and dogs all merrily rubbing shoulders.

Opening hours: 12–3, 6 (7 Sun)–11
Food times: 12–2.30, 6 (7 Sun)–9.30

The best
pub gardens

What do we want from pub gardens? A sense of leisure; the shiver of pleasure at the greenery and flowers on display; an outdoor environment that provides a faint echo of the need to reconnect with nature; and of course al fresco food and beer. The Castle has a tranquil lawn dotted with shrubs and flower-beds, but also offers a magnificent view over the battlefield of Edgehill where Englishman killed Englishman during the Civil War in the 1640s; a place to take your pint and mull on the futility of war perhaps?

Another Castle Inn, this time on the south coast in Dorset, offers plenty of space, a tumble and a rumble of green space that has been fashioned (but not controlled or manicured) over the past 30 years. Other pubs such as the Great Western Arms try to be creative with the space they have, while Drayton Court in suburban Ealing offers greenness and tranquillity in the city.

Take your pick, here you will find pubs with sumptuous views from their gardens, pubs that offer space for the kids to roam, pubs with rivers at the end of the garden, and pubs whose gardens shine with a general sense of outside and nature. As the 19th century nature writer Richard Jeffries wrote: 'Let us be always out of doors.'

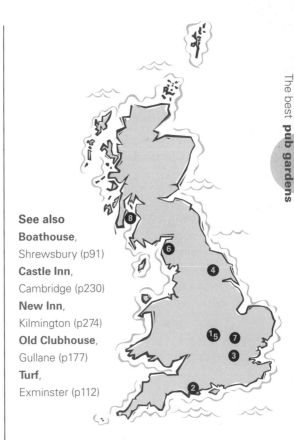

See also
Boathouse, Shrewsbury (p91)
Castle Inn, Cambridge (p230)
New Inn, Kilmington (p274)
Old Clubhouse, Gullane (p177)
Turf, Exminster (p112)

◀ Ferryboat Inn, Thorganby

Castle

Edgehill, Banbury, Oxfordshire, OX15 6DJ
01295 670255
www.castleinnedgehill.com

🍺 **Hook Norton Hooky Dark, Hooky Bitter, Hooky Gold, Old Hooky**

The best **pub gardens**

. . . .

Englishman fought Englishman in the vale that the Castle Inn's garden overlooks. The land below the ridge was the site of the battle of Edgehill, the first major confrontation during the English Civil War. On a warm day, it pays to take your pint of Old Hooky outside and sit in the gardens, a flat, tranquil space dotted with shrubs and bushes, and look out over the battlefield. It's hard to think that thousands of men died in this now quiet part of the Oxfordshire-Warwickshire border. Woodland rolls down the slope and there is a path that will take you into the vale. In fact, there are plenty of paths in the vicinity of the Castle Inn – you're just as likely to come across a group of thirsty ramblers plotting their next moves as you are day-trippers brought out here by the magnificent scenery. And in the distance on a clear day you can see the faint stick-like shapes of the high-rise buildings of Coventry. The city comes to the countryside.

In visual terms, the Castle Inn is a show-stopper. There it is, sitting on a road within the small hamlet of Edgehill, possessing a martial air – turreted towers, one of which is octagonal, battlements, local stone, strong, sturdy, warlike – and looking like it might have been part of the battle. Actually it's an 18th century folly, put up to commemorate the 100th anniversary of the bloody battle. Somewhere near its site, it is said that Charles I unfurled his standard.

Inside, there are two rooms on each side of the bar. The one on the right, with replicas of armour and weapons from the period of the battle, is more of a dining room. Home-made pies are a speciality here including the Boozy Bullock, which is made with a mild; vegetarians are also catered for with imaginative dishes: a green lentil and three bean chilli was on during my visit. The left room is the place to savour a pint of something brewed by the pub's owners Hook Norton. There are usually four cask beers on sale, including Hooky Gold, which delivers light hints of pineapple onto the palate before its dry finish. As if to emphasise the local area's walking possibilities, a group of ramblers discuss the following day's trip, glasses to hand and maps spread on the table.

And out in the garden again looking to the north you fill find yourself thinking of the battlefield. Maybe you should return on Christmas Eve, for it's said that anyone who stands at the top of the inn on that night will see a ghostly re-enactment of the battle on the fields spread out below.

Opening hours: 11.30–11

Castle Inn

nr Lulworth Cove, West Lulworth,
Dorset, BH20 5RN
01929 400311
www.thecastleinn-lulworthcove.co.uk
🍺 Palmers Best Bitter; guest beers

. . . .

Pub gardens come in all shapes and sizes, some offering a compact but well-manicured patch of green with just about enough space to swing a cat, while others might be large enough to stage their own version of the Chelsea Flower Show. The Castle Inn's large garden might not be that extreme in its size (it's about half an acre), but there is a wonderful sense of space and semi-wilderness about it.

It's terraced for a start and full of evergreen shrubs and bushes, offering streaks of colour, and dotted with cherry blossom trees standing around like guests at a garden party. It's landscaped but natural rather than manicured. It's a garden that almost acts as a mirror to the natural beauty of the surrounding Dorset scenery with its rolling hills. 'When we arrived 30 years ago it was just a mountain of weeds,' says landlady Wendy Halliday, 'we didn't realise how big it was. So we built the steps and terraces and that's how it's been ever since.'

From the road the Castle Inn (pedigree: 16th century; former name: the Green Man, though it's had many others) presents a thatch-topped, long whitewashed front to the world, windows peeking out from beneath the fringe-like thatch eaves. It's been around a long time, and given the proximity of the Cove it might have seen smugglers dropping in for a noggin or two. Inside the main bar is open, though still in possession of various individual seating areas; traditional pub décor rules the day with its black wooden beams, horse brasses and photos, and there's a '70s retro survivor in the seashell panels with photos in the middle. The small, cosy lounge bar has several old barrels embedded in the front of the counter. 'They were there when we arrived,' says Halliday.

The sun is shining and it's time to take your glass of beer out into the garden. There are usually five cask beers on (six in the summer) with local lads Palmers and Isle of Purbeck featuring regularly, plus beers from the likes of Sharp's, Dorset Piddle and Plain Ales. Cider drinkers are also served well with a goodly selection from the likes of Westons, Hecks and Orchard Pig. Order some food from the menu, which features a robust selection of pub favourites that are locally sourced. Oh and one other thing: the Castle Inn is extremely dog-friendly. Just look at the website's 'Dog Page'...

The best **pub gardens**

Opening hours: 12–2 (3 Sat), 6–11; 12–3, 6–10.30 Sun
Also great for: Bed & breakfast

Drayton Court

2 The Avenue, Ealing, London, W13 8PH
020 8997 1019
www.fullershotels.com

🍺 **Fuller's Chiswick, London Pride, ESB; seasonal beers**

• •

Leafy, leafy suburbia. Victorian and Edwardian villas and rows of terraced houses flanked by plane trees surround the area in which Drayton Court stands: a hidden corner, just a few minutes walk from the bustle of Ealing High Street. Drayton Court, a late Victorian fantasy of Gothic turrets and towers opened in 1894, an architectural fantasy from a time before the Great War swept away such fripperies (it's ironic that one of the great revolutionaries of the 20th century, Ho Chi Minh, once did a stint in the kitchens here in 1914). Some also whisper about a Masonic temple hidden away below.

As well as being a pub, the Drayton Court functions as a hotel, which is how it started life when it was first built. Inside, there's a large main bar with photos of the building from the early part of the 1900s. There's also a less bustling room to the left of the entrance, with the archetypical shelves of books on the walls.

Yet it's to the back garden that people go when the sun shines, perhaps with a pint of Fuller's much underrated session bitter Chiswick to hand (juicy citrus orange, crisp biscuity malt, a long dry finish). Out here amongst the grass lawn, tables and benches, the flower beds and kids' playing area, it's an ideal place to catch up with friends or just marvel at how getting away from it all is possible even in London. This is the largest pub garden in London, some say the biggest in the country – the kids' area doesn't intrude, while barbecues are a regular event. Whatever the claims for size, there's no getting away from the fact that if you're looking for space where you can enjoy a beer then the Drayton Court offers that extra little bit of rest and recreation.

Opening hours: 11–11 (midnight Wed & Thu; 1am Fri & Sat)

Ferryboat Inn

Ferry Lane, Thorganby,
North Yorkshire, YO19 6DD
01904 448224

🍺 **Beer range varies**

• •

Rural tranquillity is a big draw for those who visit the Ferryboat Inn. It sits on the River Derwent, down to which its spacious green garden rolls, while across the water there is a wetland nature reserve and in the distance the Yorkshire Wolds. It's a magnet for beer lovers who also enjoy watching wildlife or those city dwellers who like to catch their breath and watch the slow pace of the river go by. Flowerbeds add colour during the summer and the fabulous sense of space and nature that is an ideal accompaniment to a glass of two of Yorkshire beer.

Go inside and it's not bad either. There are two drinking areas. The main bar is comfortable and has an air of unchanged calmness. Look at the beam that goes straight through the room: it is reputedly the mast from a ship. An electrician working in the room above had to take some boards up and found a number stamped upon the mast. Then there's a lounge/family room whose French windows open out onto the garden.

'It's like a home with a bar,' says landlady Jackie Williamson. Her mother Olive Rogers has held the license since 1948, and first came to the pub at the age of nine in 1936. In those days farming was the main occupation for the family, with the licensed premises a profitable sideline. Now the farming is gone, but the pub thrives and attracts all manner of awards, including one for its garden a couple of years ago. It was also its local CAMRA branch's Pub of the Year in 2010, while Robert Redford famously pitched up here in 2011.

So what's the attraction (apart from the riverside garden of course)? For a start, it provides the sort of pub atmosphere that many would call 'real'. There is no food apart from robust lunchtime sandwiches, and a minimum of four cask beers on, though there can be up to six. There is no regular beer as such, with the choice continually revolving (as the growing selection of pump clips on the walls demonstrate). The beers show a bias towards local breweries with the likes of Acorn, Leeds, Saltaire and Brown Cow turning up, though ones from further afield such as Durham appear. Westons and Broadoak's ciders are also available. Even though it's down a single-track lane and on the river, the pub is also home to various clubs and has a folk club once a month. The Ferryboat is a regular pub garden of Eden.

Opening hours: 12–4, 7–11; 12–12 Sat; closed Mon (except bank hols)
Also great for: Riverside

The best pub gardens

Great Western Arms

Aynho, Banbury, Oxfordshire, OX17 3BP
01869 338 288
www.great-westernarms.co.uk
🍺 **Hook Norton Hooky Bitter, Old Hooky, seasonal beers**

• •

Great Western? You don't need a degree in rocket science to work out the origins of this popular pub's name. The railway line passes just to the east, while to the west there's a slower and more relaxing mode of transport: the Oxford Canal. Train or narrow boat, the choice is yours, though sadly the trains no longer stop here. The old railway station of Aynho now stands there silent and unused (though probably not unloved by railway enthusiasts), a reminder of a time when railways criss-crossed the whole country. The railway theme continues within with plenty of memorabilia dotted on the walls in the bustling bar area.

For alfresco eating and drinking, there's a delightful courtyard at the back of the pub, an enclosed space with wooden decking, paving, plenty of flowers and even vegetables. Nooks and crannies where horses once stood offer further places to recline and relax. Spend a summer's evening in here and watch the swallows swoop and climb. 'People love them,' laughs landlord Rene Klein, 'I'm not so sure, as I have to clean up after them.' Sometimes a pub doesn't need great expanses of lawn to be able to offer a delightful sense of garden life.

The Great Western majors in food but those who want a pint and a chat are not forgotten. It's a Hook Norton house and offers Hooky Bitter, the magnificent Old Hooky and one of the brewery's monthly specials. There's also an Aunt Sally team – a pub game unique to Oxfordshire. As well as being the guv'nor, Klein is also head chef, leading a team that offer a robust and hearty selection of dishes such as home-made game terrine for starters and grilled chicken and scallops served with potato rosti as a main dish. Those who eschew meat are not forgotten either: the Thai Masaman curry is a popular choice.

Green fingers? The front of the Great Western, solid, farmhouse, 19th century perhaps, seems to be its own homage to the Green Man – the frontage is swaddled with a mass of ivy, the greenery holding the pub in its warm embrace. You might want to do the same.

Opening hours: 11–11
Also great for: Pub games

Kirkstile Inn

Loweswater, Cumbria, CA13 0RU
01900 85219
www.kirkstile.com

🍺 **Cumbrian Legendary Melbreak Bitter,
Grasmoor Dark, Loweswater Gold;
guest beers**

What can you say about the setting of the Kirkstile Inn except 'wow'. It really is jaw-dropping. And then there's the garden – it's not massive and doesn't have loads of flowers, trees or anything that would be at home in the Chelsea Flower Show, but it's the 'wow factor' views of the wild elemental scenery that make it a magnificent pub garden. With glass in hand, never have the words drinking in the scenery been more appropriate.

The Inn's not bad either. The 16th century building is coolly monochrome with white walls topped with a grey slate roof. The jaunty yellow doors provide a splash of colour that picks up the sunlight glancing over the mass of Melbreak, towering behind it like some guardian spirit. This exceptional landscape is exactly why people flock to the Lake District and the Kirkstile really is a bit jammy in its location, set between Loweswater and Crummock Water. Whether you walk, boat or fish, it's tough to beat this spot. There are also rooms to stay in.

It's not half bad if you like your food and drink too. Inside the hostelry is warm and welcoming – low slung beams give it a sense of antiquity and rustic nobility while the tough Lakeland winters are dealt with by cheery open fires. The walls are simply whitewashed and hung with agricultural implements and local scenes.

The pub prides itself on using good local producers. Lunch can be simple (ploughman's, jacket potatoes) or a little more adventurous – black pudding and haggis balls in thyme breadcrumbs and whisky onion marmalade. Come evening, you could tuck into rib-sticking Cumberland tatie pot (lamb stew with vegetables, potato and black pudding) or Moroccan style salmon – to give just a rough idea of the imaginative choices.

Beer is big here as well; after all, the Kirkstile has its own brewery, Cumbrian Legendary Ales, which brews in Hawkshead. Loweswater Gold is the big bartop favourite, an ale brushed with gold and shimmering with tropical fruit notes. Guest ales come from the likes of Yates and Coniston. Children are welcome and dogs can stretch out in the bar areas (though not between 6 and 10pm). But if the weather is kind and the sun is slanting over Melbreak, the garden is, without doubt, the place to be, so you can simply drink in the view.

Opening hours: 10–11; 10–10.30 Sun
Also great for: Brewery taps

The best **pub gardens**

Lordship Arms

42 Whempstead Road, Benington,
Stevenage, Hertfordshire, SG2 7BX
01438 869665
www.lordshiparms.co.uk

🍺 **Black Sheep Best Bitter; Crouch Vale Brewers Gold; Taylor Landlord; guest beers**

• •

The Lordship Arms is one of those delightfully no-nonsense places. Clean and shipshape on the inside and smart and solid on the outside, it sits in the Hertfordshire village of Benington. Husband-and-wife team Alan and Daphne Marshall have run it since 1993. There's a large and lovely beer garden out the back with a wide expanse of lawn festooned with pub tables – it's the sort of colourful space which is just asking for you to go out there pint in hand. There's a large area laid to lawn, herbaceous borders, rose beds and a vegetable plot at the bottom, which often supplies potatoes for the pub's menu. And as if to emphasise the beery connection with the garden, used hops are delivered by Crouch Vale Brewery to be used for mulching. Meanwhile, out front the wide forecourt can also become very decorative at certain times when the pub plays host to classic car rallies and everyone oohs and aaahs over the classic cars and motorbikes.

Then there is the beer. Alan Marshall is a keen CAMRA member and, as you might imagine, his cellar is his pride and joy – the sight of the Lordship Arms' eight handpumps alone is enough to bring tears to a beer lover's eyes. Alongside the regulars, you will find a selection of five ever changing guest beers, including a mild, stout or porter (at the time of writing offerings have included Thornbridge's Seaforth, Dark Star's Saison and Redemption's Hopspur). Conscious that all this choice might cause a headache, the pub also offers 'beer tapas', a trio of ales served in 1/3rd pint glasses. So, really, you can try the lot – and many do.

Food is solid nosh that soaks up the alcohol. Lunches might see you tuck into a ploughman's, a range of baguettes, sandwiches and burgers or bratwurst in a bap. Every Wednesday evening they go a bit wild and throw their delicate beer-tasting tastebuds to the wind with a curry night – no bookings, just first come, first served. And Sunday lunch is a bit of a tradition too with hordes trekking from all around for a good solid plateful.

And while you're nursing your pint before going out into the garden, take a look around the interior once more: old phones, switchboards and the odd call box are a reminder of Alan Marshall's previous life as a BT engineer. You could say that they provide a talking point…

Opening hours: 12–3, 6 (7 Sun)–11

The best **pub gardens**

Ormidale Hotel

Knowe Road, Brodick, Isle of Arran,
North Ayrshire, KA27 8DQ
01770 302293
www.ormidale-hotel.co.uk

🍺 **Arran Ale, Blonde; guest beers**

· ·

This solid no-nonsense Victorian building was built in the 1850s as the summer house of popular landscape painter George Hering and his adopted daughter Marion Adams-Acton (who later on wrote under the name of Jeanie Hering). It was converted into a hotel in 1935 and has been in the same family since then. Hering obviously knew a good view when he saw one – the hotel is set in seven acres of wooded grounds with stunning views to Goat Fell. There's a gorgeous sense of space and tranquility about the gardens, a delicious add-on to the charms of the Ormidale, which is just five minutes from the beach and a short hop from the ferry. Shrubs, flowerbeds and sculpted hedges all bring a touch of the Garden of Eden to the grounds.

The pub may appear all solid and no-nonsense from the outside, but there's a delightful sense of play at work here. They love their music for a start; the place likes to rock. Sundays and Wednesdays are live music nights with anyone welcome to join in the mix of folk, rock, blues and country. Come Friday and Saturday, the place really lets its hair down with its famous disco, held in the large airy conservatory, with music from the '60s to the present. On the other hand for those of a quieter disposition, Tuesday hosts a pop quiz while the field opens out on Thursday for the Ormidale general knowledge quiz.

This sense of unleashing the merry inner child extends outside into the spacious grounds where the children's play area has traditional rope swings, made from old pier ropes – these are sturdy enough even for rotund adults to regain that heady sense of youth.

All that exercising of mind and body works up an appetite and the Ormidale won't let down the tastebuds either: the menu, scrawled on two blackboards, offers a good choice of traditional and less traditional dishes (some imaginative vegetarian choices too). If you've worked up a thirst, local brewery Arran is represented with couple of its beers at the bartop. As the name might suggest, the Blonde is pale in colour with a floral, gently citrusy nose while the palate combines a soft, grainy maltiness with delicate hints of citrus fruit.

Quizzes, gardens, discos, beer. After all this fun and frolics, you may well need a rest. Fortunately, seven comfortable bedrooms (in summer only) complete the picture.

Opening hours: 12.30–2.30 (summer), 4.30–midnight;
12–midnight Sat & Sun

The best **pub gardens**

The best
family pubs

The pubs highlighted in this section welcome kids, along with mum and dad, but they are pubs first and foremost so don't expect to be assailed by legions of noisy clowns emerging from pools of multi-coloured balls like monsters from the deep.

The Green Man in Eversholt is a civilised oasis of calm that provides the family a chance to rest after the rigours of going on safari at neighbouring Woburn Abbey, while the Castle Inn has the largest beer garden in Cambridge – and is next to Castle Hill up which a stroll after lunch will do everyone a power of good. Meanwhile children with a powerful imagination and a love of pirates (be they Long John Silver or Johnny Depp) will warm to the Spyway in Dorset – it celebrates a local man who turned his hand to piracy but yet still managed to die in his bed (there's also a play area in the delightful garden).

Good food, the warmth of a welcome, and space outside in which to run off steam mark out these family pubs – and let's not forget the crèche and play area at the Florence in Herne Hill, which displays jars of sweets on its bar alongside the pumps for its beers brewed on site. Children in the pub might be a contentious issue for some but after all they are the customers of the future.

See also
Bell, Wendens Ambo (p118)
Blue Bell Inn, Halkyn (p55)
The Bridge, Dulverton (p94)
Pigs Nose Inn, East Prawle (p247)

◀ Florence, Herne Hill

Castle Inn

38 Castle Street, Cambridge, CB3 0AJ
01223 353194
www.thecastleinncambridge.com

Adnams Southwold Bitter, Broadside, Explorer, Ghost Ship, Lighthouse, seasonal beers; Taylor Landlord; guest beers

• •

Sometimes a family-friendly pub doesn't need a fairground, a surfeit of turkey twizzlers (call for Jamie Oliver!!) or even a magician – sometimes it's happy being merely a place where families can hang out and relax. A place where children can discover that pubs are not dens of iniquity, but where their parents go to chat with friends and enjoy a drink and a plate of food. A place where people behave like civilised adults and pass on these values to their children.

The Castle Inn is such a place and on sunny days families flock to the suntrap of a garden behind this popular city pub that sits next to Castle Mount. Or in the words of landlord John Halsey, 'It's a whacking great pub garden, the largest in Cambridge and it's busy in the summer but not in the winter, though I have seen people sitting out there in the rain on November 5th'. Halsey's a genial soul who has led a not-so-secret life as an original member of The Rutles (he was Barry the drummer and until recently still took time out to tour with the band and its founder Neil Innes).

I visited the Castle many years ago when it was a Benskins pub. I cannot report on what the beer was like, but I do have a vague memory of a ham (hams?) hanging up behind the bar.

A sign of a landlord's devotion to Spain perhaps? The ham (and Benskins) is long gone and the Castle presents a comfortable interior over two floors, full of nooks and crannies, a comfortable and welcoming place, especially on cooler days after a long morning looking around Cambridge (the centre is a brisk walk down the road). On the food front, children enjoy smaller versions from the excellent menu (Halsey: 'We're not a gastro pub, we do bar meals'), which includes the likes of chip butties, burgers, baps and a Sunday roast. Meanwhile grown-ups can contemplate the excellent cask beers from Adnams, as well as guests from other brewers further afield, such as Mill Green and Old Chimneys. There are normally up to nine cask beers available. Afterwards everyone can work off lunch with a perambulation up the neighbouring Castle Mount.

Opening hours: 11.30–3, 5–11; 11.30–11.30 Fri & Sat; 12–11 Sun
Also great for: Pub gardens

Florence

131–133 Dulwich Road, Herne Hill,
London, SE24 0NG
020 7326 4987
www.florenceherne hill.com

**Florence Bonobo, Weasel, Beaver;
guest beers**

• •

Families are made friends with at the Florence.
There's a dedicated crèche/play area at the back
of the pub, with a TV on the wall, various toys
scattered about and even a blackboard on which
youngsters can try their hand at art. It's a bright
and breezy sort of place that allows kids to let off
steam in their own inimitable way. And as if to
further encourage families, there's also a loyalty
card, 'Mum's the word', which mothers in the
area are encouraged to sign up for. Young children
get their own menu of course – macaroni cheese,
or even a veggie sausage with fries – while the
older children can turn to the same menu as their
mum and dad: grown up food such as char-grilled
squid or chicken and chilli lasagne. So far so
family, but is the Florence a pub?

It has definite gastro leanings and a very non-
boozer sense of its own style. On the outside
its past as a Victorian-era red tile corner street
pub is still apparent, a survivor of the hundreds
that once stood throughout London. It's had a
fresh lick of paint and there's an awning over the
pavement chairs and tables – the Florence has a
newness and fashionability that is well defined.

Go inside and it's all clean lines, with a décor
that owes more to IKEA than the Dog & Duck:
freshly sanded wooden floor, smart furnishings
and plenty of light. Booths, bar stools and tables
provide the seating options. But before you
dismiss it out of hand, it also has its own microbrewery (with kit visible to the public) and up to
three of its ales are always on sale at the long
stylish bar (along with bottled world classics).
Beaver is their take on American Pale Ale, a
bittersweet, fresh and fruity beer that moves
adeptly to a pleasing bitter finish. There is also
Bonobo and Weasel.

Some might shy away from the Florence's pitch
for the family crowd, but parents who enjoy the
ambience of the pub, a pint of beer and a good
plateful of food should not feel that they have to
go to themed 'family' pubs. The Florence offers a
good family environment plus great beer and food
– the crèche is just one aspect of its appeal. Why
should mum and dad have all the fun?

Opening hours: 11.30–midnight (1am Fri); 11–1am Sat;
11–midnight Sat
Also great for: Brewpubs

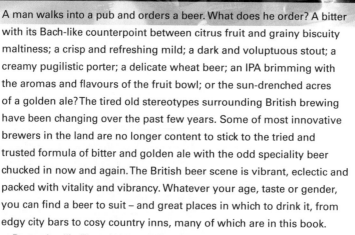

A man walks into a pub and orders a beer. What does he order? A bitter with its Bach-like counterpoint between citrus fruit and grainy biscuity maltiness; a crisp and refreshing mild; a dark and voluptuous stout; a creamy pugilistic porter; a delicate wheat beer; an IPA brimming with the aromas and flavours of the fruit bowl; or the sun-drenched acres of a golden ale? The tired old stereotypes surrounding British brewing have been changing over the past few years. Some of most innovative brewers in the land are no longer content to stick to the tried and trusted formula of bitter and golden ale with the odd speciality beer chucked in now and again. The British beer scene is vibrant, eclectic and packed with vitality and vibrancy. Whatever your age, taste or gender, you can find a beer to suit – and great places in which to drink it, from edgy city bars to cosy country inns, many of which are in this book.

Nick Otley, managing director of the Otley Brewing Company

Breweries like Thornbridge, Otley, Dark Star and Kernel are challenging people's perception of what beer is with some stunning brews – try a black IPA or an American-influenced pale ale or even a collaboration brew that like-minded brewing souls have worked together on. The more established family brewers are also tuning into the new brewing zeitgeist – for instance, Fuller's have resurrected old recipes and come up with stunning beers. And at the same time, the brewers are also getting younger and funkier: the guys that man the mash tuns at Thornbridge look like a rock band. 'When someone asks you what you do for a living, there's nothing better than saying "I make beer",' says Thornbridge's Simon Webster. Next thing to do: go down the pub and drink some.

Green Man

Church End, Eversholt,
Bedfordshire, MK17 9DU
01525 288111
www.greenmaneversholt.com

🍺 **Sharp's Doom Bar; guest beers**

. . . .

Green Man? Surely a pub with this name would be paying homage to the ancient pagan god of the woodlands? Surely the place would be overrun with branches and leaves and attract all manner of disciples. Maybe it's a mini Glastonbury complete with the smell of incense and the hum of chanting? Afraid not. The church is directly opposite and a reminder of the longstanding relationship between the pub and the pulpit, but that's as spiritual as it gets, which is no bad thing.

The Green Man (the pub that is) started life in the 18th century under the intriguing name of Go Further, Fare Worse, but was completely rebuilt in the Victorian era when the village was part of the estate of the Duke of Woburn. Now, the Green Man is an integral part of Eversholt life, and just as importantly for the families who make their way to Woburn's nearby safari park, it's a civilised place to relax and eat after a day spent in the company of lions. Civilised is the word that springs to mind when considering the Green Man. Can you be civilised with kids in tow? Of course you can (if I had a penny for every time a landlord said to me that it's the parents who need to behave I wouldn't be rich but I'd have a fair few pennies).

So why take the family? Food for a start. Adults will enjoy substantial and traditional dishes off the menu, while the young ones can plump for the Little Green Menu, two courses that include the likes of sausage, beans and chips followed by ice cream. Then there's a patio and garden where children can let off steam, in a most civilised way of course.

Inside, you could say that the décor mixes and mashes up clean modern lines with traditional pub features such as an inglenook fireplace and stone flooring. For the grown-ups in need of a glass of beer after the day spent with the wild animals of Woburn, there's Sharp's Doom Bar with guest beers from the likes of Fuller's, Bath and Wharfebank. Every year during the May Bank Holiday weekend, there's also a Real Ale and Sausage festival alongside various village events such as a fête.

As I said all very civilised.

Opening hours: 12–2.30 (not Mon), 6 (5 Fri)–11; 12–11 Sat & Sun

The best **family pubs**

Rose & Crown

Perry Wood, Selling, nr Faversham,
Kent, ME13 9RY
01227 752214
www.roseandcrownperrywood.co.uk
🍺 **Adnams Southwold Bitter; Harveys
Sussex Best Bitter; guest beers**

The Rose & Crown at Perry Wood has the feel of
a pub straight from a fairy story. Set deep in the
heart of 150 acres of magical Kentish woodland
in an area of outstanding natural beauty, it was
once a woodcutter's cottage and you could well
imagine Snow White charming the birds here.
It's picture perfect for the part: whitewashed and
clad in greenery on the outside; inside all cosy
and traditional with an open fire, hops festooned
over the beams and walls decorated with horse
brasses, corn dollies and old black and white
photographs.

Fairy stories often have a dark edge though
and maybe best not to tell younger children
about the time when, back in 1889, an argument
broke out in the tap room between Hammond
John Smith, James Foster and James Packman
over who could cut an acre of corn the fastest.
The next day Smith was found dead and Foster
and Packman were arrested for his murder.
Smith, it seems, decided to hang around the
Rose & Crown where his spirit is blamed for
mischief in the kitchen (apparently he has a
penchant for the ladies).

If the weather closes in, head instead to the
many traditional games on offer. The pub once
had a famous dartboard – in the 1980s it held
the Guinness World record for a darts match

marathon. Darts are joined by dominoes, cribbage
and Shut the Box.

But really, unless the weather is foul, you want
to enjoy the setting here. Walking the woods is
always good for raising a thirst for the great beers
on offer, including Harveys' peerless Sussex
Best Bitter. Footpaths meander all around the
pub, leading to an old windmill and an Iron Age
earthworks. There's a pub walk leaflet outlining
a pleasant circular stroll and there's a popular
Treasure Hunt walk for children. There's also bat
and trap – bring a crew, book the pitch. Eco-
conscious parents will heartily approve of the
pub's green credentials. Alongside composting
and recycling, the owners encourage wildlife
around the pub with bird boxes, log piles and
wildlife-friendly planting.

The kitchen uses local produce wherever
possible and tends towards solid traditional pub
fare with jacket potatoes, filled rolls, steak and
mushroom suet pudding plus the occasional foray
into international territory with the likes of paella.
Friendly staff complete this pub in the woods'
happy ever after…

Opening hours: 11.30–3, 6.30–11 (not Mon); 12–3,
7–10.30 Sun

Spyway Inn

Askerswell, nr Bridport, Dorset, DT2 9EP
01308 485250
www.spyway-inn.co.uk
🍺 **Otter Bitter, Ale**

. . . .

Dorset's coastline was prime smuggling territory during the boom years of the 18th century. Take the kids and enchant them with tales of mysterious lights flashing their message onwards and occasional bloody clashes between revenue men and smugglers. Two centuries on, the romance lingers even if the truth was probably much more mundane. Many smugglers found their end on the gallows, but not Isaac Gulliver, who died in his own bed, a rich and respectable man thanks to a government pardon. The Spyway Inn's name pays homage to him, being hidden away, close to where Gulliver had a farm on Eggardon Hill; it was upon here he planted a clump of pines that could be seen from the sea and used as a sighting point.

This comfortable and award-winning inn dates from Gulliver's tumultuous time, but sadly cannot claim status as his former local as it only became a pub in 1845. Then it was called the Three Horseshoes and a blacksmith's forge was attached. The forge went in the 1960s, and the name of the pub changed in 1975, when the then owners understandably decided to make something of the smuggling theme.

Smuggling yes, but theme is very underplayed. There's information on Gulliver on display in the cosy, snug front bar. If there is any real theme on display it's that of a comfortable country inn offering good ale and food with the benefits of being set amidst beautiful rolling countryside.

The front bar has a lived-in feel, giving it the ambience of a den or a hideaway perhaps, especially on inclement days. Horse brasses dot the old wooden beams while there's an old halter on the wall next to the bar; watercolours of local scenes (for sale) join the old photographs elsewhere. Otter Bitter and Ale are the beers, while summer months see local cider West Milton on draught. Beyond the bar, there's a view towards Askerswell Down, upon which the Dorchester road runs. This is a landscape of green, trees, lanes, fields and honeysuckle draped cottages.

If you're hungry for food, rather than views, then the Spyway possesses two comfortable dining rooms where the menu can include fresh fish, the pie of the day (chicken and mushroom, steak and kidney) and other comfortable dishes; there's also a children's menu. Outside, there's a glorious garden that captures the sun in the summer, while the play area makes sure that youngsters won't go bored. And at the end of the day, all the best family pubs make sure that grownups and children are well-catered for – the Spyway Inn is one of them; me hearties.

The best **family pubs**

Opening hours: 12–3, 6–11

Steam Packet Inn

Harbour Row, Isle of Whithorn,
Dumfries and Galloway, DG8 8LL
01988 500334
www.steampacketinn.biz
🍺 **Taylor Landlord; guest beers**

Happy holidays make for happy families and the countryside that surrounds the the harbour village of the Isle of Whitehorn offers plenty of reasons to be cheerful: secret gardens, an ancient saint's cave, natural history plus this beautiful village at the southern end of this beautiful peninsula in Dumfries and Galloway. After exploration comes contemplation and the Steam Packet makes for a comfortable and civilised family landfall.

With a glass of Fyne Ale's Jarl in your hand you can watch the boats bob up and down, sail in and out and generally immerse yourself in the life of a small Scottish island port. Or you might want to try something else: there are usually five cask beers on offer, including ones from Scottish breweries such as Sulwath, Orkney and Ayr.

Even though landlord Alastair Scoular takes pride in sourcing local produce, especially fresh seafood and fish, the Steam Packet is most definitely a pub: 'We are more an old fashioned pub than a restaurant and I am uncomfortable with the term gastro-pub.' This is commendable as all too often one sees pubs in well-visited areas turfing out the locals and becoming near restaurants. The Isle's beautiful location certainly brings in the tourists, which has its own effect on the way the pub presents itself to the outside world. In the winter it has feel of a predominantly local pub, while the summer sees an influx of visitors, many with children in tow (some of the dishes on the menu are offered in half portions and there is also a children's menu). All of which enables the Steam Packet to maintain a balance: 'The remoteness and rural nature of the pub means we have to try and appeal to many different markets so I would say that we multi-task a lot. We also focus a lot on local produce due to the problems of deliveries etc and this is also true of the beer – I can only sell a beer if it can be delivered to me!'

The Steam Packet? Good cask beer, a pleasing pub menu, atmospheric coastal ambience plus plenty of friendliness towards the family. In reality this is a pub for all seasons.

Opening hours: 11–11 (1am Fri; 12.30am Sat) summer; 11–2.30, 6 (5 Mon)–11, 11–midnight Fri & Sat winter; 12–11 Sun
Also great for: Seaside

Travellers Rest

Slaley, Northumberland, NE46 1TT
01434 673231
www.travellersrestslaley.com

🍺 **Black Sheep Best Bitter; Caledonian Deuchars IPA; guest beers**

. . . .

Children are welcome at the Travellers Rest, but then so are food-lovers and those with a penchant for good cask beer. The fact that kids are welcome (rather than tolerated) is only part of the offering. Go there in the summer and they'll probably want to make their way out to the safe adventure playground at the bottom end of the beer garden; here they'll find swings, a slide and an aerial runway – for parents who fancy a proper pub but also want their kids to be happy this is heaven.

So it's a pub and the fact that kids are allowed in is incidental. Inside, the flag for proper pubs is flown by flagstone floors, black beams crossing the ceiling, a solid wooden bar, log fire in the winter and even some church pews to park oneself on. The open-plan bar has several separate areas and there's a restaurant – the emphasis is on local produce where possible. Milk and cream comes from a neighbouring farm, as does a lot of the meat. Steaks are popular here, though you can't beat the steak and Black Sheep Bitter pie. Four cask beers are sold, with the regular duo of Black Sheep and Deuchars joined by beer from local craft breweries. Mordue's Geordie Pride (gold in the glass with a long bitter finish) is one favourite, though other guests will include beers from Wylam, Allendale and Consett Ale Works.

The Travellers Rest is a former farmhouse from the 16th century that became an inn in 1850 – it occupies a lonely spot, a mile outside the village of Slaley, which itself is south of Hexham. The countryside around and about is moorland, a traditional agricultural area with plenty of rural charm. So it's a gorgeous location too – and given its name you would hope that it offers accommodation and it does. Everyone is welcome here.

Opening hours: 12–11; 12–10.30 Sun

The best **family pubs**

The best
entertainment
pubs

There might be a band in the Flowerpot on a Friday night; its singer strutting like Jagger on a stage in a sound proofed room next door to the bar (where you can enjoy good beer if you're just here for a pint). Or, if you're sitting in the Babbity Bowster in the Merchant City area of Glasgow, then Saturday afternoon brings in the musicians – pints, fiddles and guitars in hand and an uplifting selection of Irish and Scottish folk tunes. On the other hand, local am-drams might want to stage a play in the garden on a summer's eve – check out the Driftwood Spars, a Cornish gem that spans all the arts with both music and theatre featuring throughout the year (in the summer of 1971 a young band called Queen took the stage here – wonder what happened to them?). Like the Flowerpot, there's a brewery onsite.

Morris men are an integral part of many a pub scene, but for something different on the dancing front you should be in the Cumberland Arms when the rapper dancers rehearse in the room upstairs (or maybe they'll be performing outside). Meanwhile, Louis Armstrong is commemorated at a Dover pub of the same name and syncopation rules. The British pub is a stage upon which all take their turn to entertain and bedazzle us.

See also
Alma Inn,
Linton (p116)
Barton Inn,
Barton St David (p79)
Gurnard's Head,
Treen (p196)
Thatchers Arms,
Mount Bures (p86)

◀ Driftwood Spars, St Agnes

Babbity Bowster

16–18 Blackfriars Street, Merchant City,
Glasgow, G1 1PE
0141 552 5055

🍺 **Caledonian Deuchars IPA;
Kelburn Misty Law; guest beers**

· ·

Babbity Bowster? This name of this pub in the prosperous Merchant City area comes from an old Scottish dance (rather than a fluffy Beatrix Potter character as it might suggest) – so if you're of a terpsichorean bent just ask one of the staff or friendly regulars and you'll find out more. Just hope that you won't be given a demonstration. You could also argue that the pub's name invokes the central position that music plays at the Babbity. On any given Saturday afternoon, walk in for a pint and musicians will be beavering away, heads down, pints to hand, jamming and jousting on a series of Scottish and Irish folk tunes. The rest of the week is no slouch either as a cast of regulars and delighted visitors all help to create and sustain the buzzy, bustling atmosphere that infuses one of Glasgow's liveliest cask beer joints.

Unlike for most of us, the years have been kind to Babbity Bowster, though it wasn't originally meant to be the sort of place where folk came to drink beer and enjoy good cheer. The building was originally a family home for a tobacco merchant, designed by the renowned 18th century architect Robert Adam; it's now the sole survivor of a whole street created by Adam during Glasgow's Georgian boom-time. It's only been a pub since the 1980s, but carries its relative newness (in terms of the venerability of many historic pubs)

with ease. Take a look around and admire its clean and open sense of space, the comfortable seating and the lively, confident ambience. There's also a sheltered beer garden with flower boxes and shady trees which makes for a welcome pleasure in summer.

Deuchars IPA and Kelburn's Misty Law are regulars at the bar, and served by air pressure, that rare survivor of Scottish ale dispensation. Guests include the likes of Harviestoun's gorgeously golden Bitter & Twisted. Traditional Scottish grub such as stovies, cullen skink and haggis with neeps and tatties feature on the menu and fill a substantial hole. Meanwhile, those after something a bit more fancy on a similar theme can make their way up to the Schottische, the restaurant on the first floor.

Opening hours: 11–midnight; 12.30–midnight Sun

Cluny

36 Lime Street, Ouseburn, Byker,
Newcastle upon Tyne, Tyne & Wear, NE1 2PQ
0191 230 4474
www.thecluny.com

🍺 **Beer range varies**

. . . .

The Cluny hides its light beneath a trinity of transport links: a road bridge, the Metro bridge and a mainline rail bridge. Traffic roars backwards and forwards high in the sky above the Ouseburn valley, a historical area a mile or so out of Newcastle city centre that acted as the cradle of the city's industrial revolution. Nowadays, the arts and crafts crowd drive the economy of the area making for a liberal vibe that draws in students and others who want to escape the famously frenetic pace of Newcastle's city centre nightlife. The Cluny acts as their recreational centre: part bar, part gig venue.

Ah, the music. The Cluny has developed an enviable reputation as a place where those in search of bands that might be big one day (or were once big) can come and be entertained. For those with a nostalgia for the past, old school rockers such as Wishbone Ash, Stackridge, the New York Dolls and The Animals have shown their faces at the Cluny, but younger bands also see it as an important venue, while established acts occasionally turn up in search of a more intimate venue than they are used to. The hall is to the back of the bar, but rest assured if you want to just come in for a chat and a pint of good beer, once the doors are shut nothing can be heard. There is a real sense of fusion in the way the Cluny operates two different styles of pub.

As befits a place that has made its home in a former whisky bottling plant (the brand was called the Cluny), this is a hip and happening post-industrial bar that just happens to think like a pub, which is why there is an excellent selection of cask ales (up to eight on most days), world beers and artisanal ciders and perries. Here in its L-shaped bar with its pinewood floor, exposed brickwork and raised areas and corners, drinkers come to chill out or maybe have a drink in anticipation of the musical evening ahead. Good hearty grub is also offered at the Cluny, with the lamb burger a particular favourite: moist and meaty and full of flavour, while the real chips are fluffy and funky.

This all makes for an energetic and lively place that all too often spills out onto the green outside when the weather is fine. It's also a place for people watching as ale fans, students and hoary old rockers sip their pints of Harviestoun Bitter & Twisted or an offering from a local brewery and mix and match. Musical and social harmony reigns at the Cluny.

Opening hours: 12–11 (1am Fri & Sat and when holding live music events)

The best **entertainment pubs**

Cumberland Arms

James Place Street, Ouseburn,
Newcastle upon Tyne, Tyne & Wear, NE6 1LD
0191 265 6151
www.thecumberlandarms.co.uk

🍺 Wylam Rapper; guest beers

• •

The Cumberland Arms is a two-roomed Victorian treasure that overlooks the Ouseburn valley. As well as being renowned for its selection of beers and ciders, it is the unofficial home of top rapper dancers the Newcastle Kingsmen. Rapper dancing? Dismiss all thoughts of gangstas and think instead of the traditional sword dance prevalent in the northeast that originated in the pit villages. It's fast-moving and involves a group of five dancers linked by flexible swords of spring steel (the 'rappers'). When they're in action at the Cumberland the sound of their shoes on a wooden floor and the scrapings of a couple of fiddles make for a noisy and exhilarating affair.

Go into the public bar on the left and the walls bear witness to the passion of the dancers with various plaques and swords dotted about. There's a a small lending library in this part of the pub, but library-like silence is unlikely, especially when they practise upstairs. The Cumberland is also a popular live music venue, with gigs upstairs or traditional folk sessions in the back bar.

When the sun comes out, there's an outdoor terrace overlooking the River Tyne; this provides just the spot for whiling away a couple of hours with glass in hand. A lot of people have the same idea, as the pub is home to a mixture of traditional pub fans, rapper fanatics, locals and those that work in the arts and crafts workshops down below.

Beer is the drink of the house. Connoisseurs plump for pints of Jarrow Bitter with its gentle aroma of tangerine, or the fresh and flowery Jetsam from Hadrian Border; there are normally up to six cask beers available. Fancy a cider? Then this is also the place for you. The Cumberland Arms has won awards for its ciders and perries (there are usually up to six available) with Somerset scrumpy sharing bar space with local craft ciders.

As for food, modernist and traditional share space on the menu: anyone for hot spicy wraps, homemade tortillas or belly pork Pad Thai? Ham and eggs or a fish finger sandwich take a more traditional route. Whether you're there for the rappers, the wraps or just the real ale, the Cumberland Arms has something for everything – a shining example of the pub on the hill.

Opening hours: 4–11 Mon; 12–11 (midnight Wed, Fri & Sat)
Also great for: Cider

Driftwood Spars

Quay Road, Trevaunance Cove, St Agnes,
Cornwall, TR5 0RT
01872 552428
www.driftwoodspars.com

🍺 **Driftwood Red Mission, Lou's Brew;
St Austell Tribute; Sharp's Doom Bar;
Skinner's Betty Stogs; guest beers**

• •

It's a pub, it's a restaurant, it's a hotel, it's a rock venue. It's got its own brewery and local actors put on plays in the garden. Meanwhile, surfers drift in from Trevaunance Cove just a few minutes away, rock fans stream in to catch bands before they get famous. Tourists descend from St Agnes to eat in the restaurant and try beers that they've never come across before (and I'm not talking about Doom Bar). And then there are the locals. The Driftwood Spars is many things to many people.

The pub only became a pub in the years after the Second World War, while it started rocking in the 1960s. I wonder what Queen thought about it. That's the band not the monarch. Famously they played here in the summer of 1971 before it all went stratospheric for them. Did Freddie Mercury

have a pint of Devenish? Rod Stewart didn't play here but his Maggie May was supposedly written about a local girl. More recently, other bands that have strutted their stuff at the Drifty include rockers Reef and Aussie folk duo Angus and Julia Stone. There's a gig every Friday night, while in summer it's both Friday and Saturday. Rock on.

Driftwood Spars was originally built in the 17th century. There are three bars, on different levels. Ships' spars cross the ceiling (hence the name). Granite fireplaces provide warmth in the winter and a sense of timelessness in the summer. Nautical notes make up the rest of the décor on the whitewashed stone walls. Go to the bar and try one of the three cask beers brewed on site. Lou's Brew, named after the landlady, is a citrus-edged bitter that drinks lighter than its 5% abv. There is always another Driftwood beer on, along with a trio of fellow Cornish beers. Food is locally sourced. Catch of the day or a gourmet burger perhaps? And once you've stopped rocking, either climb up the hill to St Agnes or better still book ahead and stay the night. Like I said, the Driftwood Spars is many things to many people.

Opening hours: 11–11 (1am Fri & Sat)
Also great for: Sporting

The best **entertainment pubs**

Flowerpot

23–25 King Street, Derby, DE1 3DZ
01332 204955

🍺 **Blue Monkey BG Sips; Marston's Pedigree; Oakham Bishop's Farewell, seasonal beers; Thornbridge Jaipur IPA; guest beers**

On the corner of a busy road, to the north of Derby's city centre, you will find the Flowerpot, its upper storey painted a bold and striking plum colour. It's an early 20th century neighbourhood pub, once owned by local brewery Offilers.

In the building next door the pub continues, redbrick, taller, untidier, its lower half plastered with posters advertising past, present and future rock concerts, its doors firmly shut until the evening when the crowds come. The Flowerpot is a hybrid: a traditional cask beer pub with an attached brewery (it was Headless Brewing but it's now Black Iris) out at the back and firmly on Derby's cask beer circuit; it's also a lively venue for rock bands who either continue to relive their tumultuous youths (Eddie & the Hot Rods, former Marillion singer Fish) or are well-drilled ensembles eager to pay tribute to their heroes (the Smyths, The Jamm, Fred Zeppelin). There's something for everyone here.

The Tardis springs to mind. From the outside, you might think a front bar and a saloon and that's it, but once inside there's a whole world to discover. Front of house has the air of a cosy terraced house parlour, the kind of place that belongs to another age. On the wall, old tobacco ads share space with an ancient school photograph and above the mantelpiece there's a framed copy of Derby County's fixtures for the season 1914/15, surrounded by adverts for local pubs including the New Flowerpot, as it was once called. Poignancy attaches itself to this last artefact – how many of those games were ever played?

The bar starts on the left hand side. A sextet of handpumps offers beer from the likes of Oakham, Thornbridge and Black Iris (whose beers were due to make their debut at the time of writing). Follow the bar into another room. Here books line a shelf, and above there is a row of beer bottles. Through here turn into another large room, overlooked by three racks of casks, offering beer straight from the barrel (there are usually a minumum of 10 cask beers available). Other breweries regularly seen also include Acorn and Burton Bridge. All this beer stimulates appetite and the pub's menu goes for a robustly hearty and straightforward mix of pub grub. Sandwiches, hot cobs, smothered chips, bangers and mash and gourmet burgers all spring forward for the drinker's attention; there are also plans to introduce Derbyshire dishes.

Whether you're someone who likes to mix music and ale, or just in for a quiet pint (next door's concert hall is expertly soundproofed), the Flowerpot is a place to while away the blues.

Opening hours: 11–11 (midnight Fri & Sat); 12–11 Sun

Louis Armstrong

58 Maison Dieu Road, Dover,
Kent, CT16 1RA
01304 204759

🍺 **Hopdaemon Skrimshander IPA;
guest beers**

· ·

As you might think from the name, jazz swings
at the Louis Armstrong. The pub was once
called the Grapes but the name was changed
thanks to then landlord Robert 'Bod' Bowles, an
accomplished jazz musician and Armstrong fan.
Interviewed a few years back, his widow Jackie
Bowles said: 'We changed it in 1971 the year
after Louis Armstrong died. There was another
pub in Dover called The Grapes and jazz was such
an important part of what we were about that we
thought Louis would be much more fitting.'

Jazz might rule the roost here, but rock, pop
and blues also tread the boards; there's even a
regular slot for world music. Musicians en route
to Europe on tour often contact the pub and ask
if they can play a slot – this unpretentious
Dover pub a short walk from the train station
is a thriving centre of live music.

Yet, it's also a pub where four cask beers are
regularly available. So if you're in for a spot of
syncopation or a regular fix of rhythm and blues,
this is the place where you can have it with a pint
of Kentish ale to hand. Hopdaemon's Skrimshander
IPA is the regular drop at the bar – aromatic and
bittersweet, with bold hop notes and a dry finish.
Other breweries joining in the fun include Gadds',
Goacher's and Whitstable. You drink your beer to
the sound of music. The stage is in the bar area,
which was once the usual saloon and public bar,
but was knocked through by Bowles. Basically,
it's a traditional pub with live music.

The décor is comfortably scruffy with old jazz
posters on the wall plus quite a lot of images
of Armstrong as you would expect. Outside it's
end of terrace, though double fronted; red tiles
and red brick, a central gable; it has the air of
a Victorian villa. Its former name is chiselled in
stone at the front. There's a faded and battered
painting of Armstrong hanging there as well.

Sometimes the spirit of a particular pub is hard
to track down. Is it in the architecture or in the
people who drink there? Is it in its location,
whether town or village? With the Louis Armstrong
I would hazard a guess that its spirit is in the
music that continues to be played within its
confines week after week, a continuing memorial
to the endeavours of its late landlord whose
daughters now run the show.

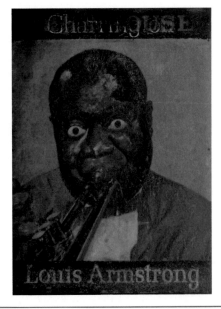

Opening hours: 2–late; 7–late Sun

Old Fire House

50 New North Road, Exeter, Devon, EX4 4EP
01392 277279

🍺 Otter Amber, Bitter, seasonal beers; guest beers

· ·

Come the weekend and the Old Fire House starts to rock. Down in the main bar, on a platform where drinkers sit during the rest of the week, you will hear and see bands from across the southwest, drawing in those who fancy a spot of blues, jazz or folk. And if that's not enough, one of the pub's regulars serenades Thursday night drinkers with a spot of Spanish guitar in the small courtyard; if it's too cold he plays inside. The mood of the Old Fire House is entirely appropriate for music as well. Inside it's dark and cosy with an underlying theme of dark wood, exposed stone walls and fairy lights draped over the bunches of dried hops that hang from the ceiling. As six o'clock comes, the lights also dim and candles are lit on drinkers' tables.

There's a sense that you could be sitting in a bar in Paris or Brussels, such is the delicious moodiness that the Old Fire House's lighting policy creates.

Beer is a big draw here as well. There can be up to eight beers on, all of them drawn straight from the cask and mainly coming from brewers in the region, though interlopers such as Elland and Banks & Taylor are very welcome. On my visit, Elland's Born to be Mild – chocolate, coffee, blackcurrant with chocolate powder in the finish alongside a crisp biscuitness – was a delicious reward for an afternoon traipsing round the shops. Cider and perry drinkers are not forgotten either – there are four handpumps dispensing cider from the likes of Sandford, while Hogan's award-winning perry is also available in bottle. The bistro-style food includes an array of home-cooked dishes such as fish cakes, chilli and cauliflower cheese, while a blackboard advertises a selection of pizzas.

The Old Fire House is a bit of a Tardis. From the outside, in the partially covered courtyard, it seems likely that it'll be small and crowded. Not so. There's another area on the second floor, and during special occasions the baronial hall-like top room is opened up. Here, though, due to the distance from the cellar, there is no cask beer, though bottled beers are sold. Or you could just go downstairs with your glass and get a refill.

This is a popular place with students and those who want to combine a good selection of cask beer with a lively music scene. And for those interested in history it is close to the spot of the catastrophic 1887 Theatre Royal fire in which nearly 200 Exonians lost their lives. A poignant event to mull as you sip your beer.

Opening hours: 12–2am (3am Fri & Sat; 1am Sun)
Also great for: Cider

Pigs Nose Inn

East Prawle, Kingsbridge, Devon, TQ7 2BY
01548 511209
www.pigsnoseinn.co.uk

🍺 **Otter Bitter; South Hams Devon Pride, Eddystone; guest beer**

• •

You need to travel down the deep and narrow country lanes of the South Hams to get to the small village of East Prawle. A mile away the sea crashes against the ancient rocks of Prawle Point, the most southerly part of Devon. This is beautiful coastal country and a mecca for walkers. The Pigs Nose sits in the centre of the village, an ancient former smugglers' inn that has also done time as a petrol station and hotel. Now it's an award-winning traditional rural pub that has gained a reputation for its regular roster of rock gigs. In the hall that adjoins the pub, you can often find the likes of The Animals, Curiosity Killed the Cat and Chris Farlowe turning up to strut their stuff to both appreciative villagers and those who negotiate the narrow lanes from further afield.

Landlord Peter Webber used to be a tour manager for rock bands in the 1980s and he obviously knows how to put on a good show.

The pub itself is a delightful place, with a low-ceilinged bar off which there are a couple of rooms. One of them is named the 'Snog' and its walls are covered with all manner of graffiti, while there's also a pool room on the other side of the bar. The pub itself is a clutter of artefacts including old black and white photos on the wall, ancient farming implements, bugles, Toby jugs, horse brasses and the odd barometer. There's a comfortable anarchy about the complete lack of a theme in the knick-knacks on display. Most licensees' collections celebrate an obsession or a hobby, but the Pigs Nose's display just seems to be there. The pub also possesses a friendly and quirky sense of its own value. As I sit there with a glass of South Hams light and refreshing Devon Pride (brewed in the nearby village of Stokenham), one of the pub's two dogs wanders over to say hello. Meanwhile, Peter Webber enjoys a pint and a chat at the bar, a microphone in his hand. I never find out what it was for!

Outside there's a group of men dressed in berets and blue and white striped tops, all with strings of garlic around their chests. Comedy Frenchmen. 'We're from Nottingham,' one of them explains to me, 'and we come and camp on Dartmoor every year. Last year we were dressed as Mexicans.' Their presence seems to sum up the friendly and quietly comfortable anarchy of the Pig's Nose – a pub that offers excellent beer, good food, an offbeat environment and the occasional chance to rock the night away.

Opening hours: 12–2.30, 7–11 (not Sun in winter)
Also great for: Family; Seaside

The best
pub games

All across the country, pubs put on nights dedicated to games that have entertained the pub-going yeomanry of these isles down the centuries – many of them with their roots firmly embedded in the medieval japes of maypoles, church ales and licensed tomfoolery. Some, however, go back even further. It is claimed that quoits, as played at the Charles Bathurst up on the Yorkshire Moors, goes back all the way to ancient Greece (a cert for the Olympics perhaps?). Darts and pool? Mere upstarts coming late on the scene: darts in the 19th century and pool only reaching these shores in the 1960s. Skittles is a West Country favourite – at the Ring O'Bells on a game night you'll be witness to the passion that this game invokes. The lazy man's cricket, or Bat and Trap, can be seen in its Kentish heartlands at the King's Head in Canterbury, while they play all manner of games at the Lewes Arms: pea-throwing, Toad in the Hole and the mysterious Dwyle Flunking. For those of a more sedate persuasion there's a Crown Green Bowls pitch at the back of the Nursery – and the pub isn't bad either, being a perfect survivor of 1930s pub architecture and serving local ales from Hydes. Game on.

See also
Barrasford Arms, Barrasford (p207)
Batemans Brewery Visitor Centre, Wainfleet All Saints (p41)
Great Western Arms, Aynho (p224)
White Lion, Fewcott (p123)

◀ Quoits pitches at the Charles Bathurst, Arkengarthdale

Charles Bathurst

Arkengarthdale, Richmond,
North Yorkshire, DL11 6EN
01748 884567
www.cbinn.co.uk

🍺 **Black Sheep Best Bitter, Riggwelter;
Taylor Landlord; Theakston Best Bitter**

. . . .

Stand outside this 18th century inn and breathe in the views – 360 degrees of rolling moor, dotted with sheep. Arkengarthdale is Yorkshire's most northerly dale – it's starkly and stunningly beautiful. This valley was once the centre of a thriving lead mining industry, but tourists have now replaced the miners – with people flocking to walk the Dales and enjoy the market towns that lie dotted about. Locals also come here to enjoy a game of quoits – the pub has a team in the local league.

Landlord Charles Cody once told me that he was a quoits fanatic and firmly believed that the success of the pub owed a lot to the game. 'The pub was derelict and shut when we came here in 1997,' he recalled, 'but I reintroduced quoits as soon as we moved in, building four clay pitches. It's a strong local game with a local feel and very much in keeping with the style of this area. I believe that the miners played the game, but it probably died out with the closure of the mines.'

The Charles Bathurst is named after an important figure in the erstwhile mining industry and is a rambling place, deceptively large (there are 19 bedrooms), showing off its history in various levels and additions. It is comfortably stylish, soft cream paintwork meeting mellow wood floors, soft stonework and silvery slate.

They take their food very seriously here with provenance a big deal – lamb, beef and game are all locally sourced and fresh fish is delivered from Hartlepool six days a week. The menu is written up above the fireplace and changes depending on what comes in from market. It's pretty upmarket on the whole: supreme and confit of guinea fowl with sweet potato and cardamom puree with Madeira jus gives a flavour. But the lunch menu also offers more straightforward fare (hot and cold baguettes with hand-cut chips for example).

The beer is also good – you might want to have a Black Sheep Riggwelter. And then go and have a look at the quoits pitch. Some aficionados claim that quoits is nowt less than an Anglicised version of discus-throwing and insist the game's ancestry can be traced back to ancient Greece. With this in mind, there has even been optimistic talk of trying to get the game into the Olympic arena. But for now it stays firmly localised, solid, secure in its place – just like the Charles Bathurst really.

Opening hours: 11–midnight

Jug & Glass

Main Road, Lea, Matlock,
Derbyshire, DE4 5GY
01629 534232
www.jugandglasslea.co.uk

Banks's Mansfield Cask Ale; Copper Dragon Golden Pippin; Marston's Pedigree; guest beers

. . . .

The Jug & Glass is at one end of a row of stone built cottages, standing on the road that passes through Lea, a solid, reassuring presence, a traditional village inn, a place where locals gather and enjoy their sense of community whilst having a few pints. It was built in 1778, apparently by Florence Nightingale's uncle, though it didn't start selling ale until the 1820s. Lea is part of a parish that also includes three other settlements – and the Jug & Glass is the sole pub. So is this an icon of splendid rural isolation? After all, walkers pass through the area, popping in for a pint before continuing on their way through the Derwent Hills. Truth to be told, the Jug & Glass's position is not so black and white – yes you can tick the box marked rural but it's not truly isolated. Matlock is only a short drive away (as are other urban areas) but I would imagine that this adds to the attraction. Not only do they have a good local trade but people, hearing about the pub, will make an effort to visit it.

And if they visit on the right night they will be able to watch skittles. The pub's team is in the Ripley and District Skittles League and during the season the pub will be heaving on home match nights as locals concentrate and try to knock over a set of nine wooden pins. The pitch is outside and the game is very similar to West Country skittles. And if you so desire, you can follow the fortunes of the team as their results are posted up on a notice board in the pub (alongside other notes from the locals, including a 20-something who advertises his skills as a mole-catcher).

There are three rooms in the Jug & Glass, with the bar and the tap being the main area for enjoying a glass of well-kept beer. The décor is pub traditional and includes photographs of local football teams through the years. There is also a restaurant whose menu inclines towards home-made dishes using locally produced materials where possible. As for cask beer there are usually seven available with guests coming from both the likes of locals Whim and Buxton, and from further afield.

Skittles, good food and beer, molecatchers and even its own cricket team – the Jug & Glass is that great example of the rural pub as a social service.

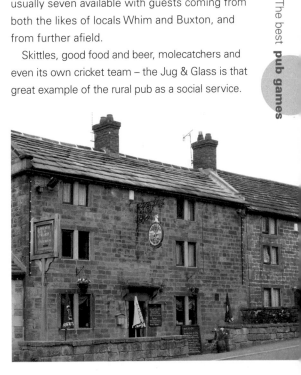

Opening hours: 12–2, 6–11; 7–11 Mon; 12–11.30 Fri & Sat; 12–9 Sun

The best **pub games**

King's Head

204 Wincheap, Canterbury, Kent, CT1 3RY
01227 462885

🍺 **Greene King IPA; Harveys Sussex Best Bitter; guest beer**

• • • • • • • • • • • • • • • • • • • •

You'll find the Grade II listed King's Head ensconced deep in the heart of the conservation area of Wincheap in ancient and beautiful Canterbury. In this part of town the Romans made their wine and the name Wincheap apparently comes from the Old English for 'wine market'. So it's a naturally auspicious location for a pub and the traditional, oak-beamed 15th century building seems imbued with the very essence of joviality and bonhomie.

This sense of good nature stretches over into the King's Head's sporting instincts as it plays host to its own Bat and Trap team, which takes part in a local league during the summer months. Even though variations of the game have been played all over England, it's currently a game that is very much identified with Kent (it's nicknamed 'the lazy man's cricket' – the ball springs out of a trap and you hit it). Other games also feature strongly here with the usual lively darts and bar billiards as well as the quieter and more cerebral cards, crib and chess.

Locals and visitors alike are unanimous in their praise for this traditional inn, lauding its friendliness and wholehearted welcome, whether staying for a few nights or simply dropping by for a quick pint. Harveys Sussex Best and Greene King IPA are staples at the handpumps plus a constantly changing guest beer sourced from micro-breweries around the country.

The décor is very traditional, with gleaming copper pans dangling from heavy beams. Half-timbered walls are whitewashed in-between; beer mats snake around the walls and garlands of hops swoop around the bar, as they should (wine might have been here first but hops and beer are what we associate Kent with). Outside there's a seating area, swathed in greenery, which has the feel of a secret garden.

If all this sport on show makes you feel that you would rather watch than indulge, then major events are shown at the bar on the TV screen, perhaps the only thing that's changed in this pub's long history of keeping people happy.

Opening hours: 12–2.30, 4.45–midnight; 12–midnight Fri & Sat (11.30 Sun)

Lewes Arms

1 Mount Place, Lewes, East Sussex, BN7 1YH
01273 473152
www.thelewesarms.co.uk

🍺 **Fuller's London Pride, ESB; Gale's Seafarers Ale, HSB; Harveys Sussex Best Bitter; guest beers**

· ·

Walk into the Lewes Arms and ask if they do pub games and the answer will be yes. Do you want the details, will probably be the gist of the next sentence. Take a deep breath. This late Georgian back-street pub organises an annual World Pea-Throwing Championship, spaniel racing, an annual marble tournament, stool ball (whatever that is), Dwyle Flunking and Toad in the Hole (it also has an annual panto). The latter game involves trying to throw a round lead disc (they used to be coins) into a hole in the middle of a small, slightly sloping table. According to Arthur Taylor in the magisterial *Played At The Pub*, this game had all but died out in the 1990s but the town of Lewes oversaw its much-welcomed revival. As for Dwyle Flunking, it involves people getting soaked in stale beer and looks very silly – its origins go back as far as 1966, though there have been claims over the years for a more antiquated background.

The Lewes Arms hit the headlines back in 2006 when Greene King was its owner. As well as the cask beers of the Suffolk brewery, the Arms sold Harveys Sussex Best Bitter, which is brewed a few minutes away. The storm broke when Greene King announced that they would be dropping Harveys from the pub and many of the locals started a boycott. A website was formed, a media campaign took place and Harveys was eventually reinstated.

This was a fantastic example of pub community taking action. The pub is now owned by Fuller's, who have wisely kept Harveys on the bar top.

As the bloody-minded action of the locals demonstrates, the Lewes Arms has its army of regulars. Yet it's also friendly and open to all who come through its doors. There are three drinking spaces, supplied by a central bar – lots of plain wood and a comfortable sense of permanence about the fixtures. There's a compact room on the right of the entrance with a couple of stools and window seats, while the other two drinking areas are equally convivial – the walls feature information and pictures of Lewes' November 5th bonfires. Food is pub grub using locally sourced produce with chillies a speciality. Given the amount of games on view at the Lewes Arms, perhaps they could apply for their own Olympic Games.

Opening hours: 11–11; 11–midnight Fri & Sat; 12–11 Sun
Also great for: Community

HOOK NORTON BREWERY

THE STAR INN

Pub games

Think pub games and what springs to mind? Teenagers popping pool? The desultory throw of darts? Elderly men shuffling cards? Visit a West Country pub during the skittles season and match nights will see the beer flowing and the bar crowded with skittlers (as they're known) all having a good time. The roots of games such as skittles, Aunt Sally, shove ha'penny, quoits and Bat and Trap are firmly embedded in English history. The styles and names of the games might vary from county to county, but the verve and vigour with which they're played echo across the land as they have done for centuries. In comparison, darts (c. 19th century) and pool (c. 1960s) are positive upstarts.

Aunt Sally – a game that involves throwing sticks at a skittle on a post – reputedly has its origins in the English Civil Wars. Quoits avows an even more venerable past with some claiming that it is no less than an Anglicised version of Ancient Greece's discus throwing. Skittles can't claim such classical origins but still has a highly respectable family tree dating back to the middle ages. These games are not just quaint anomalies in the odd rural backwater either. Skittles, quoits, Bat and Trap and Aunt Sally all interest enough players to maintain leagues in which dead-serious players compete. The rules vary as well: West Country skittles with a long alley is only played in, surprise, surprise, the West Country, but there are different versions available to pub-goers around Northampton and the East Midlands. Northampton's version of skittles involves a hooded table of smallish skittles, at which you throw a wooden 'cheese'. The variations mirror the regional differences that we find in beer styles across the country. Games like these are a welcome reminder of a time when our forebears had to make their own entertainment and the pub, tavern or inn was at the centre of their social universe.

Aunt Sally being played at the Star Inn, Sulgrave

Nursery

258 Green Lane, Heaton Norris,
Cheshire, SK4 2NA
0161 432 2044
www.hydesbrewery.co.uk

🍺 **Hydes Light Mild, Owd Oak, Original
Bitter, Jekyll's Gold, seasonal beers;
guest beers**

• •

A pub's devotion to its chosen sport comes
in many guises. Some have dartboards, well-
chalked blackboards to their side and a worn
rubber mat on the floor; others have skittle alleys
(though take a tour around the West Country
and see how many have become restaurants),
where the rumble of the balls can be heard on
league nights. Then there's the Nursery in south
Manchester suburbia. Not only was the pub an
HQ for Stockport County football team when they
played nearby, but if you go to the back of this
immaculately preserved example of a 1930s pub,
you'll see an equally immaculate bowling green
where crown green bowls is played. Show-offs.

The pub's not bad either. It was built in the
late 1930s, a magnificent multi-room example
of inter-war pub design. In the lounge there is
banquette seating, a tile-surround fireplace above
which stands a mirror, and well-spaced out tables
that give a sense of room and security – this is
a pub ambience designed to make people feel
totally at home. Elsewhere there is the old smoke
room with wood panelling giving it the air of a
committee room, and a rare example of a vault
bar with its own entrance, in other words the
northern version of a public bar with dartboard,
sturdy tables and chairs and wall mounted

seating. Coming across the Nursery for the first
time you would half expect to hear the voices of
Neville Chamberlain or Winston Churchill coming
from an ancient wireless, such is the spell that
is cast. It's no great surprise to discover that the
pub has been a regular in the *Good Beer Guide*
for a quarter of a century and was CAMRA's
National Pub of the Year in 2001.

The Nursery is owned by Mancunian brewers
Hydes and is a fine showcase for their beers,
which includes a smooth easy drinking mild.
There are usually a couple of guest beers with
Wigan-based AllGates a regular visitor. Food is
good value, hearty and traditional.

Good things come in threes: with the Nursery
you have the fantastic survival of a more
traditional pub design, some great beers from
Hydes and the chance to watch the fireworks fly
when the bowls start moving across the green.

Opening hours: 11.30–11 (11.30 Fri; midnight Sat);
12–11.30 Sun
Also great for: Heritage

The best **pub games**

Ring O'Bells

High Street, Ashcott, Bridgwater,
Somerset, TA7 9PZ
01458 210232
www.ringobells.com
🍺 **Beer range varies**

• •

Game? As I can testify after one evening watching a couple of teams battle it out in this traditional village pub on the Polden Hills, West Country skittles is more of a full-out battle.

A ladies team was playing that night and I watched one of the players (mild mannered administrator by day and ferocious skittler at night) have a go. She held a cannonball sized chunk of tropical hardwood in a menacing manner, took careful aim, shifted her weight and hurled the ball towards the waiting skittles. The ball rumbled like distant thunder as it hurtled down the alley then – with a reverberating sonic boom – the majority of the pins fell and scattered. If you're heading out for a quiet drink on a weekday night in the West Country skittles season it would be wise to check that there's no match on. On the other hand, the Ring O'Bells hums and thrives when the skittlers are on the game – and the best panacea for the midweek blues is a pub with happy folk.

The A39 runs through the small village of Ashcott on its way to Glastonbury. Head up in the direction of the church and you'll find the pub, of 18th century origin though much altered over the years. It's been with the same team for nearly 20 years, husband and wife and the wife's brother. Together the three of them have created an essential village local while also winning awards for the quality of their cask beers – even when

the skittlers aren't in town you'll find a diverse mix of villagers chatting and drinking in here.

The oldest part of the pub features the bar, around which there are several drinking spaces. Look at the bar and be thankful. It features several humble bar stools: essential parts of pub furniture that are not as visible as they used to be. They're simple unsung objects that allow drinkers to collect at the bar, engage in conversation with all and sundry – they are to be encouraged.

In the middle of a skittles game, you need a beer and the Ring O'Bells doesn't disappoint. Moor Brewery used to be around here and you still get beers from them at the bar, including Merlin's Magic. Isle of Avalon also has a local connection and their beers are very regular; other beers come from West Country breweries such as Cotleigh, Skinner's and RCH. Food is taken seriously, but not to the detriment of drinkers. Pub grub favourites such as steak and ham, and egg and chips delight.

Back at the skittles alley, the pub has four men's and two women's teams, all playing in the local winter leagues, while the summer also sees games as well. Game? Yes please.

Opening hours: 12–2.30, 7–11 (10.30 Sun)
Also great for: Cider

Star Inn

Manor Road, Sulgrave,
Northamptonshire, OX17 2SA
01295 760389
www.thestarinnsulgrave.co.uk

🍺 **Hook Norton Hooky Bitter, Old Hooky,
seasonal beers**

• •

George Washington's ancestral home is in the
village of Sulgrave, so naturally the Star Inn gets
plenty of Americans popping in for a pint. Even
John Wayne got in on the act: after he'd paid his
regards to Washington and had a mosey around
the Manor, he dropped into the Star Inn for a cold
one (apparently his only visit to a British pub).

It was a wise choice and years after the Duke
made his visit, the pub continues to thrive.

Go there most nights of the week and you'll
encounter a laid-back mixture of locals having
their evening constitutional and visitors
(Silverstone is also pretty near) chilling out with
a glass of the local beer from the pub's owners
Hook Norton. However, Thursday nights in the
summer are a bit different and things might be
more frenetic, especially if the pub's Aunt Sally
team are playing at home in the Banbury League.
They take their Aunt Sally seriously out here, as
does Hook Norton who sponsors the local league.

Aunt Sally is an outdoor form of skittles that
involves throwing sticks at a skittle on a post. It
reputedly has its origins in the English Civil Wars
when bored Royalist soldiers in Oxfordshire
found time hanging heavy on their hands. Others,
however, ascribe its origins to a somewhat
unsavoury game called 'throwing at cocks'. This
saw a cockerel tied to a stake by one of its legs
while participants threw a stick at the unfortunate
bird until it was killed. In pragmatic rural fashion
the winner took the bird home for his pot. The (less
bloodthirsty version of the) game has remained
popular in its heartland of Oxfordshire and there
are several leagues. At the Star Inn, the game is
played in the leafy garden at the back of the pub.

As is the case with the majority of old pubs
(the Star started life in the 1700s), the bar was
once two rooms, but Hook Norton carried out
a sensitive refurbishment that still gives you
a couple of different spaces. The ceilings are
low, the flagstones on the floor are worn and
there's plenty of good grub to be had. And come
Thursday nights the Aunt Sally players will troop
in and set themselves up for another evening of
sport. John Wayne would have loved it.

The best **pub games**

Opening hours: 12–3, 6–11; 11–11 Sat & Sun

voted

CAMRA

BEST REAL ALE PUB IN...

...BRITAIN: 2008, 2009

...YORKSHIRE: 2004, 06, 08, 09

...SHEFFIELD: 04, 05, 06, 07, 08, 09, & 10

Opening Hours

MONDAY-THURSDAY: 12 'til 11pm

FRIDAY-SUNDAY: 12 'til LATE (MIDNIGHT)

The best CAMRA award-winners

Everyone likes a a winner, especially if it's a pub. As soon as you enter an award-winning pub, you can tell you're there: framed certificates hang on walls, often accompanied by photographs of beaming licensees, a history of a pub's route to success.

CAMRA has a series of pub awards, going from local level through to regional and culminating with the highest accolade of all, the National Pub of the Year. This selection includes several national award-winners: the Blisland Inn hides itself down small lanes, several miles away from Bodmin, but in 2001 national success turned up at its door (it's also been the local CAMRA branch's Pub of the Year several times since). The Kelham Island Tavern, flooded by the Don in 2007, was national winner two years in a row, currently the only pub ever to have been so. Bang up to date and you'll find the Harp on the southern edge of Covent Garden, 2011's National Pub of the Year, a thriving pub in the heart of London with the air of a neighbourhood pub.

All the pubs here have shone at many levels, many times, though the Bell in Pensax must have some sort of record – it has been awarded its local branch's Pub of the Year 10 times in a row!

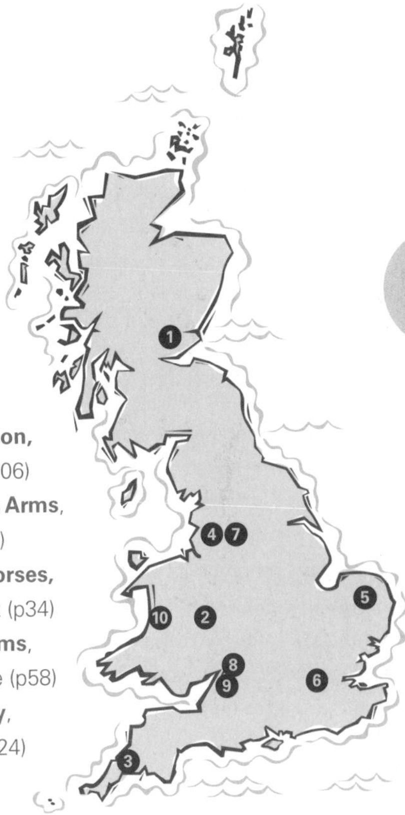

See also
The Anderson,
Fortrose (p206)
Bricklayer's Arms,
Putney (p65)
Coach & Horses,
Weatheroak (p34)
Penrhyn Arms,
Penrhynside (p58)
Tom Cobley,
Spreyton (p24)

Albert Tavern

2 High Street, Freuchie, Fife, KY15 7EX
07876 178863

🍺 **Beer range varies**

• •

150 years after Prince Albert's death in 1861 a Scottish pub named after him won CAMRA's award for best pub in Scotland for the second year in a row. After Albert's death, his heart broken wife (and Queen) would mourn for the rest of her life and cast a pall on the nation – much against his wishes it is claimed. Maybe it would have comforted him to know that the naming of many pubs and taverns after him must have lightened some of the gloom.

The survival of this village pub's name down through the years is no mean feat. It started business as a coaching inn in 1780, and Albert might not have been its first name. You might have to go to Freuchie to do some original research though –which isn't such a bad idea.

So what's the attraction? Outside, it's compact, painted white with black-eyed windows and a covered entry porch of the sort where muddy boots might be left (walkers are lured by the nearby Lomond Hills while the former royal residence Falkland Palace is also close). You could mistake it for an old farmhouse. No frills, no fuss inside, just a warm welcome and traditional décor: beams trace their way across the ceiling of the bar and lounge, while wood panelling offers that indefinable sense of comfort around the bar. This is a village pub used by both locals and travellers, engendering a sense of belonging to the local community. Handpumps don't proliferate like trees in a forest; there are usually four cask beers on offer, ever changing and instructive in their attraction to the palate. On the bar front you might find Hop Back's Summer Lightning or Dark Star's HopHead, or closer to home, Harviestoun's Schiehallion.

Robert Hunter became the landlord in 2005, a former diamond engineer in search of a complete lifestyle change (the pub had already been a National Pub of the Year runner-up in 2002 so he had big boots to fill). After winning the first award in 2010 he was quoting as saying: 'I wanted to do something I always wanted to do, which is run a little pub in the country.' He's succeeded – and how.

Opening hours: 5 (12 Fri & Sat)–midnight; 12.30–midnight Sun

Bell

Pensax, Abberley, Worcestershire, WR6 6AE
01299 896677

🍺 **Hobsons Best Bitter; guest beers**

. . . .

The Bell is obviously doing things right. It has been voted Pub of the Year by its local CAMRA branch 10 years in a row. It has also been voted West Midlands Pub of the Year a couple of times while Worcestershire CAMRA made it their Pub of the Year in 2009. Given that the Bell sits in splendid rural isolation, rather than in the middle of Pensax village ('We've got very few chimney pots,' says chef and bar manager Ian Mercer), this avalanche of awards is even more remarkable – people make an effort to get to this pub. Yet it's all well-deserved, as the Bell is one of those pubs in which it's easy to fall in love with on first visit.

Inside there's a main bar and a snug, with a dining room at the back overlooking fields. The theme of the décor is the usual bric-a-brac that licensees build up over the years and denotes their interests: newspaper cuttings from the first World War, beer bottles, beer mats and ceramic cockerels, the latter being a particular passion. Summer is ideal for the beer garden at the back, while the wood burners are fired up in the winter.

As the awards might suggest, you'll get a decent beer or two here. Hobsons Best Bitter is on all the time, while there are up to five guests – coming from breweries near and far. There might be HPA from Wye Valley, Worcestershire Way from Bewdley, Taylor Best or Exmoor Gold. 'We try to support the local breweries when we can,' says Mercer, 'but we also like to get beers that our customers have tried on their travels.' There is an annual beer festival and several ciders and perries. Food is not ignored either with a menu of home-cooked dishes, including steaks, pasties and curries; chicken, ham and leek pie is a favourite.

As for the Bell's origin, it's late Victorian. It has a black-and-white exterior as is common in this part of the world, stands on a B-road and is surrounded by rolling countryside. There was a pub (and brewery) on this site in the early part of the 19th century, but it was knocked down and rebuilt in 1883 by a prosperous cotton merchant called John Joseph Jones. Jones also commissioned the building of the clock tower at nearby Abberley Hall but he's best known nowadays as the person for whom the phrase 'keeping up with the Joneses' was first applied to.

Opening hours: 12–2.30, 5–11; 12–10.30 Sun; closed Mon
Also great for: Country

Blisland Inn

The Green, Blisland, Bodmin,
Cornwall, PL30 4JF
01208 850739

🍺 **Beer range varies**

The Blisland Inn has been run since the 1990s by Gary and Margaret Marshall, who have turned what was a village local apparently dying on its feet into a must-visit destination. Gary is the man in charge of the beer, a former Royal Navy stoker, who wears loud Hawaiian shirts and shorts even in the bleakest of Cornish winters. His nickname is King Buddha (thanks to a large tattoo on his expansive belly and his jovial nature), which is also the name given to one of the pub's beers.

Beer is a passion for him – up to nine cask beers are regularly available, including King Buddha and one other brewed especially by Sharp's. The other beers are a mixture of Cornish and craft brewers from the rest of the country, and every May Gary organises a Mild Month. It's a lot of beer and the count for the number of different cask beers Gary has sold since taking over is fast approaching 3,000 (naturally there are hundreds of pump clips on display). To make things even more interesting there are also a couple of wooden barrels behind the bar. They were constructed by a retired Nottingham cooper and are usually sent to a local brewery who will fill them up; sometimes a local cider appears in one. You'll eat heartily here too, with home-cooked dishes such as chicken and ham pie and liver and bacon on the menu.

The pub itself is a solidly built, slightly stern stone building from the end of the Victorian era, in front of which flutters the black and white flag of Cornwall during the summer months. The lounge bar has the feel of the old-fashioned parlour rooms some might remember from childhood. Toby jugs hang from the dark wooden beams while the walls are festooned with local village photos. A pair of stag's antlers hang over the fireplace, a reminder of past country pursuits in this wild part of the southwest. Then there are the barometers: Gary collects them and has well over 200.

Unsurprisingly, awards shower down on the Blisland Inn like confetti at a wedding – as well as being Cornwall CAMRA's Pub of the Year several times it was also named CAMRA National Pub of the Year in 2001. Visit it most days and this robust village pub will be vibrant with enthusiastic drinkers, which is all the more astounding as it lies hidden away down the narrowest of country lanes, miles from the town of Bodmin, without the faintest hope of 'passing trade' – if you're going make sure you're not the driver…

Opening hours: 11.30–11; 12–10.30 Sun

Crown

154 Heaton Lane, Stockport,
Greater Manchester, SK4 1AR
0161 480 5850
www.thecrowninn.110mb.com

🍺 **Beer range varies**

. . . .

Here is the English pub in a nutshell: 'It's gone all sunny,' says the friendly barmaid as I sit there with my pint. A man at the bar takes a sip of his and responds: 'I was working at Cheadle today and it was hailing down. You can't trust our weather.' The staple of pub conversation: the state of the weather. And then someone else chips in: 'We might have a good summer.' Guffaws all round. Every pub has an eternal optimist.

The Crown is a traditional pub, where people talk to each other as they drink their beer. It's in an incongruous position though. There it is, engraved windows, an old Boddingtons sign picked out in stone. Traditional. While above is a massive railway viaduct and in the air the constant drumming sound of a motorway. Yet, step inside and the soundtrack morphs into the murmur of voices at the bar and the ticking of a clock, while the landscape is dark chestnut brown-coloured wood, fitted benches, several rooms and a bar that can offer up to 16 cask beers (the blackboard numbers them and the licensee is obviously of a superstitious bent as 12a sits between 12 and 14). Breweries from both the locality and further afield are offered – Blue Monkey, Castle Rock, Moorhouse's, Spitting Feathers and Hawkshead being just a small example of names on the bar. Food is basic pub grub and filling, but the beer is the big draw here.

The room at the back of the bar could once have been a private place – the wall features panels where beer was served; the bells that remain at the backs of the benches no doubt there to call for service. Now, the door is gone but the room still offers a nook-like sense of seclusion. A couple of other rooms across the corridor offer a similar feel.

There's a timelessness and sense of endurance about the Crown, as if it's been like this forever, which in some ways it has. It was built in the 18th century, did time as a brewhouse in the 1820s and survived the building of the viaduct in the early years of the railway age. It also survived the great pub purges of the 1960s when snugs and tap rooms vanished as breweries knocked their properties through. In the mid-1990s it began to offer a larger than normal range of cask beers and it's been a regular name on the CAMRA roll of award-winners ever since then.

Opening hours: 12–11; 12–10.30 Sun
Also great for: Motorway; Railway

Fat Cat

49 West End Street, Norwich,
Norfolk, NR2 4NA
01603 624364
www.fatcatpub.co.uk

🍺 **Adnams Southwold Bitter; Fat Cat Bitter,
Honey Cat, Wild Cat; Fuller's London Pride;
Woodforde's Wherry; guest beers**

• •

If you're going into the Fat Cat for a swift one,
make sure you know what you want in your
glass. Sometimes there can be up to 30 cask
beers on offer – dispensed by handpump or
served straight from the cask; additionally, there
are great lagers from Europe, Belgian fruit beers
and other craft beers from around the world.
Ditherers should beware when let loose in this
cornerstone of the Norwich cask beer scene. At
least you won't need to worry about having to
choose food as well: sustenance is confined to
lunchtime, when filled rolls and pies are available.
Eat before you go is the best advice.

The pub was originally called the New Inn, a
Victorian redbrick corner boozer that was pretty
down in the dumps when bought by Colin and
Marjie Keatley in 1991. After a six-month period of
renovation, which including ripping things up and
starting all over again, it re-opened under its new
name of the Fat Cat. Apart from recreating a tap
room and making the place more comfortable,
one of the boldest physical expressions of its
philosophy was the fact that were 12 handpumps
on show, including a regular mild. The pub was in
the *Good Beer Guide* within a year.

Since then, the beer choice has grown, and
grown men and women are known to groan with

ecstasy at the sight of all those beers. Inside
there's a solid central bar, gleaming with brass
fittings and ceramic handled handpumps, while
the walls are dotted with a rash of nostalgic signs
for long lost pubs (though very few will mourn the
passing of Watneys).

The Fat Cat (which styles itself as a free
mouse) and the Keatleys received their reward
for their foresight and hard work in 1998 when
they were announced as CAMRA's National Pub
of the Year; they won the award again in 2004,
making them the first pub to have picked up the
prestigious gong twice.

As if running one of East Anglia's most popular
pubs wasn't enough (there's also a sister pub
in Ipswich under the same name), the Fat Cat
brewery was set up in 2005 elsewhere in the
city. Its beers, obviously available at the pub, also
keep winning awards. Given the financial ups and
downs of the past few years, this is one Fat Cat
we can all agree to like.

Opening hours: 12–11 (midnight Thu–Sat)

Harp

47 Chandos Place, Covent Garden,
London, WC2N 4HS
020 7836 0291
www.harpcoventgarden.com

🍺 **Dark Star Hophead, seasonal beers; Harveys Sussex Best Bitter; Sambrook's Wandle; guest beers**

. . . .

What illustrious neighbours the Harp has. It sits in a small side street on the southern edge of Covent Garden, while the Garrick lurks just around the corner. The National Portrait Gallery is a mere block away and English National Opera's Coliseum is within hailing (or should that be singing?) distance. These days the Harp is a bit of an illustrious institution itself: in 2011 it was awarded CAMRA's prestigious National Pub of the Year award.

So let's have a look at this city centre gem. In front of its multi-coloured mullion windows (the image of a harp picked out in each of them) sit hanging baskets, a burst of floral colour guaranteed to enliven the gloomiest of days. Below the windows, a blackboard leans against the wall offering passers-by details of the pub's award-winning sausages and the day's cask beers. Even though the Harp lies in the heart of London, you'll find that it retains the feel of a friendly neighbourhood local as regulars come and go, greetings exchanged, companions all. Here a man in overalls, holding his pint, talking on a mobile, there a more gentrified chap, white scarf and smart suit, maybe off to the Coliseum later?

Inside there's a single long room, one side dominated by the bar (upstairs has more of the air of a gentlemen's club). Hundreds of handpump labels dot the old mahogany-brown gantry, a faded and weathered piece of Victoriana. The labels offer an historical record of the Harp's dedication to cask beer, a sign that its current champion status has been long in the offing. Victorian oil paintings of long-forgotten folk hang on the walls, maybe a friendly nod to the Portrait Gallery down the way. The bar staff are young and friendly, happily offering samplers of any of the eight cask beers on display – a bibulous challenge to any beer fan with time on their hands. Harvey's superlative Best Bitter is a regular, and is usually joined by three brews from fellow Sussex brewers Dark Star.

During its seasonal outing you might be lucky and come across Dark Star's Extra Stout, a goodly drop that brims with chocolate, roast coffee beans and ripe plum notes. If not, then there's always the same brewery's succulent Hophead. There are also several artisanal ciders of the sort you would normally find on a Somerset farm. Food consists of the aforementioned sausages plonked in baguettes – proper sausages, meaty and juicy, an excellent accompaniment to a glass of ale.

One can harp on forever about the Harp but the proof is in the seeing.

Opening hours: 10.30–11.30 (11 Mon); 12–10.30 Sun
Also great for: City

Kelham Island Tavern

62 Russell Street, Sheffield,
South Yorkshire, S3 8RW
0114 272 9463
www.kelhamislandtavern.co.uk

🍺 **Acorn Barnsley Bitter; Bradfield Farmers Blonde; Pictish Brewers Gold; Thwaites Nutty Black; guest beers**

• •

It's definitely a case of lightning striking twice for this Sheffield beer palace. In 2008 the Tavern was CAMRA National Pub of the Year and it made history by scooping the same prestigious award again a year later. And all this for a pub that had to close its doors for six weeks in the wet summer of 2007 when the nearby River Don decided it would break its bank and go for a stroll (the Tavern's near neighbour the Fat Cat – p45 – also suffered a similar fate). In fact it's a miracle the pub is still serving beer at all – it's the sole survivor of an old street of terraced houses and a former factory, all of which have long gone, while in its previous incarnation as a Stone's Brewery house it seemed to have reached the end of the road in 2000 when it closed. Yet, fate took a hand and the pub reopened in 2001 and has since become a leading refreshment spot on the Sheffield 'real ale trail'.

So what's the lightning rod that attracts the accolades? In one word: beer. Beer is very definitely on the menu (along with crusty rolls, though only served at lunchtime). This is the place where novices can discover Acorn's full-bodied and intensely bitter bruiser of a Bitter, roasty, chocolatey and gratifyingly full of flavour for such a low-gravity beer (it's 3.8%). The other 11 cask beers include offerings from the likes of Pictish, Thwaites and the Brew Company (their autumn seasonal St Petrus Stout is gorgeous and luscious). There are also beers from overseas – a sprightly lager from Warsteiner, a fruity Weiss from Kaltenburg and a goodly variety of Belgian classics. Yet, there is more – some pubs offer a similar selection of beers, well-kept and tasty, but fall short with the mood and the feel of a place.

Here the Kelham Island Tavern rises above its competition with a certain ambience. Walk through its door and the word traditional springs to mind: this is a pub interior that can magic away the tensions of the working day. The bar has the feel of a large and comfortable front parlour with plush cushioned chairs and heavy wood furniture. A brace of Staffordshire dogs simper from the fireplace; above them a sign warning against swearing. Brewery mirrors glisten on the yellow walls; and a host of award certificates demonstrate the pub's popularity. As the pub faces southwest, when the sun shines the pub glows. Conversation flows, conviviality flourishes, all accompanied by the great ales on display. And if the Don ever decides to come this way again, I can think of nowhere better to be stranded.

***

Opening hours: 12–midnight
Also great for: Record breaking

Old Spot

Hill Road, Dursley,
Gloucestershire, GL11 4JQ
01453 542870
www.oldspotinn.co.uk

🍺 **Severn Vale Session; Uley Old Ric; guest beers**

• •

Mention the word Dursley to most people and the first thing that springs to mind is the awful family that Harry Potter stayed with in between terms at Hogwarts. Given that JK Rowling has said that she conjured up the name in reaction to much-hated childhood trips to Dursley, it's a bit tough on this unpretentious and lively Cotswold market town. Thankfully, Dursley has a better reputation amongst beer lovers – it is home to the Old Spot, a frequent award winner and former CAMRA Pub of the Year.

Down a side street and behind the bus station, this bustling and spirited free house was bought by Ric Sainty in 1993. He named it after the famous

Gloucestershire pigs while proceeding to offer a spectacular range of cask beers. Sainty sadly died in 2008 but an oil painting of him in the window alcove continues keeps watch over the pub.

Inside its multi-roomed interior, eight handpumps dispense local beers from the likes of Uley (who only brew a couple of miles away) and Severn Vale, plus a sprinkling of others from further afield. The walls are garnished with award plaques, the insignia of long-gone local breweries and venerable relics of those still keeping the faith, such as a framed Adnams ad for their Nut Brown Ale. Jack the pub dog also likes to keep an eye on things. There are regular beer festivals, with the locals encouraged to come up with themes; there are also breweries of the month beer selections and 'meet the brewer' nights, which are exceptionally popular. Trips to beer festivals and Gloucestershire breweries are organised; meanwhile, numerous local charities also receive the pub's support.

Food is hearty and home-cooked, featuring such perennial favourites as sausage and mash, haddock and chive fishcakes, and cottage pie. Due to its many awards the pub's popularity keeps on growing but landlord Steve Herbert still manages to keep a deft balance between the demands of new customers who travel for the food and regulars who like nothing better than to study the beers on display.

Time spent at the Old Spot Inn is time spent well, time spent in discovering a pub that is at one with its community. It's easy to throw various phrases about but this is truly one of those pubs that are at the hub of their local area.

Opening hours: 11–11; 12–11 Sun
Also great for: Motorway

The best **CAMRA award-winners**

Seven Stars

Thomas Lane, Redcliffe, Bristol, BS1 6JG
0117 927 2845
www.7stars.co.uk

🍺 **Beer range varies**

• •

Hidden away down an alleyway in the Bristol parish of Redcliffe, jostled in its narrow den by the St Thomas the Martyr church opposite and a few minutes from the River Avon, the Seven Stars is one of the great survivors of Bristol's pub scene. It has a history as an inn going back to the 1700s and during the late 18th century it was frequented by the notable anti-slave campaigner Thomas Clarkson in his investigation of the city's role in the horrific trade. Somehow it has passed through the centuries little-changed and remains a fine example of an old-style city boozer.

It may be hidden away but Bristol CAMRA's Pub of the Year 2010 is not shy in coming forward. Step inside through a small lobby and you're in a casually distressed, well-worn sort of pub interior

that some companies would pay hefty sums to emulate, but which to the Seven Stars' has come naturally, organically and over time. Wooden floorboards have been trod by generations of beer drinkers, while wooden fittings and furniture give off a sense of comfort and continuity. Music is important here, with regular acoustic sessions plus appearances from the local morris men; the juke box has an interesting selection including the likes of Joy Division, Led Zeppelin in their folky phase and Nick Drake.

The bar sits in the centre of the action, heroic with eight handpumps, all dedicated to the furtherance of West Country cask beer. Butcombe's seasonal porter Old Vic was a rich and creamy drop of darkness in the glass, so good that in the fashion of Oliver Twist I went back for more. Other beers on the counter included Otter Ale, Forge brewery's Litehouse, Art Brew's Art Nouveau and Palmers Tally Ho! – a chestnut brown strong bitter from Dorset, with cocoa and hazelnut on the palate.

Those with a penchant for the apple are not left out either with a small but heartening selection of artisanal ciders and perries. As this is primarily a drinking pub, no food is offered, but there are plenty of places around where you can get something to eat if you so desire.

Bristol is a great beer-drinking city with some marvellous pubs, but the Seven Stars is something special, a place where history and the new combine alongside a great selection of beers to produce a real gem of a place. On arrival at Bristol, make for this place immediately. Oh, and there are discounts on the ales for CAMRA members – how can you lose?

Opening hours: 12–11; 12–10.30 Sun

Ship & Castle

1 High Street, Aberystwyth,
Ceredigion, SY23 1JG
07773 278785
www.shipandcastle.co.uk
🍺**Wye Valley HPA; guest beers**

. . . .

The Ship & Castle. What's in a name? The answer isn't exactly rocket science. For a start the remains of Aberystwyth's medieval castle stand broken and gap-toothed above the bay, so there's the castle. Meanwhile the town's harbour used to heave with ships back in the 19th century. Sailors, no doubt, would have been regulars in the bar, some full of tales of distant shores, while others would have been taking a breather between regular trips down to Bristol. As the coat of arms of the West Country's capital featured a ship and castle, it's a fair chance that the pub's name echoed this link with Bristol.

Time moves on, the sailors are gone and this popular street-corner pub nowadays welcomes in a mixture of students, lecturers and locals, all drawn by the prospect of an ever-changing roster of cask beers, served in a comfortable environment. There are usually five on, with regular crowd-pleaser Wye Valley's HPA (gold in colour, crisp and refreshing on the palate) joined by craft brewers' beers from all over the region. There are also two ciders on draught, from Westons and Gwynt y Ddraig, plus a small but pleasing list of European beers.

Local man Ian Blair runs the Ship & Castle; there's a pleasing sense of continuity in his relationship with the pub: father and grandfather were both regulars. He's also a man keen on getting his customers to taste their beer. 'I introduced a five pump platter – five 1/3 measures served on a circular oak plate – designed to encourage folk to try all the flavours on offer,' he says. As if that's not enough there are two annual beer festivals as well. All of which led the pub to pick up the CAMRA Pub of the Year award for Wales in 2010, as well as local awards.

The pub was totally refitted in 2009 giving it a sense of space and air. The booth-shaped bar has a row of coloured glass panes in the gantry, while the bare brick wall surrounding the fireplace bears a symbol of the pub's enduring relationship with the sea: a ship's wheel. Who's not to know that in the dead of night, when the hubbub of the evening has died down and the bar is silent, that the ghost of some long ago sailor who once frequented the pub returns to remember a haunt he loved so well during Aberystwyth's years of maritime plenty.

Opening hours: 2–midnight (1am Fri & Sat)

The best
at success

The awesome eight. What is it that marks these pubs out as so special? Go back to the very first *Good Beer Guide,* published in 1974 (here's a pub quiz question: what was the name of the brewery that readers were told to avoid like the plague within its pages?*) and you will see seven of these pubs within its pages – and they have reappeared in it every year throughout the tumult and thunder that has rained down on the British pub and brewing industry over the past 40 years. The eighth pub? The Fisherman's Tavern in Broughty Ferry didn't feature in that first edition as its range didn't go as far north as Scotland, but it's been in every edition of the *Good Beer Guide* since then.

The list stood at ten (plus the Fisherman's Tavern) several years back when the *Guide* celebrated its 35th edition – and even more as you go further back in time, but the attritional nature of passing time on the British pub has brought the number low. But for now celebrate the longevity of these hardy public houses. These are pubs that have been consistently serving good ale, without drama, and welcoming their local community for the best part of half a century, if not longer – here's to the next 40 years.

*Answer: Watneys

◀ Square & Compass, Worth Matravers

Buckingham Arms

62 Petty France, Westminster, London,
SW1H 9EU

020 7222 3386

www.youngs.co.uk

🍺 Wells Bombardier; Young's Bitter,
Special; guest beers

. . . .

If the bar counter in the Buckingham Arms
was a painting it would be one created by
Picasso. Languid in its curvature, it's a sensuous
centrepiece that stands out as soon as you enter
the pub. You just want to touch it. To the back of
the counter, there hangs a grouping of mirrors,
helping to create a sense of spaciousness.
Built in the early part of the 19th century,
the Buckingham Arms started off as a shop,
becoming a pub in the 1840s. In the early 1900s
Young's of Wandsworth bought it and it's been
selling their beers ever since.

The Buckingham Arms is one of those rare
London pubs that has survived the last 100 years
or so relatively unchanged. There has been some
refurbishment of course, but stand in the single
room that looks out on to the street and you
still get a sense of how it was a century ago.
Bleached and sanded floorboards contrast with
the dark brown wood fittings, while the wide
windows are divided into a series of small panes,
giving the front a mullioned look.

The cream-coloured wall gives a clue to the
pub's provenance – a selection of quotes about
London coming from a mixture of celebrities:
George VI, Morrissey, Oscar Wilde, Shelley,
Madness. Some might find this a bit pub-by-
numbers, but I think it anchors the pub's sense
of London identity in the heart of Westminster.
Meanwhile on the street, its three-storeyed
façade is easy on the eye, with hanging baskets in
summer adding their own colourful floral tribute.

Even though it's just a stone's throw from
Buckingham Palace, there's a down-to-earth
quality about the Buckingham Arms, a warm and
worn quality that makes you think of London
pubs of yesteryear. This is the sort of place where
you'll find locals whiling away some time with
their newspapers while passing tourists pop in for
their London pub fix.

Five cask beers are usually available, with
Young's Bitter and Special being joined by their
Bedford companion Bombardier. On my last
visit, there were two guest beers: Black Sheep
Best Bitter and Sharp's Cornish Coaster, bringing
both a touch of Yorkshire and Cornwall to this
comfortable bolthole in Westminster.

Opening hours: 11–11; 12– 5 Sat; closed Sun

Fisherman's Tavern

10–16 Fort Street, Broughty Ferry,
Dundee, DD5 2AD
01382 775941
www.fishermanstavern.co.uk
🍺 **Belhaven IPA; Caledonian Deuchars IPA; guest beers**

· ·

Appearances can be so deceptive, especially when it comes to pubs. A cosy and comfortable-looking pub might from the outside seem to offer hospitality, good beer, food and welcome, all enjoyed in a homely, relaxed and – yes – old-fashioned way. Walk in through the door however and the telly is showing racing, the carpet is sticky, the locals stop talking and watch your progress to the bar and the beer in your glass would be better off on a bag of chips.

Thankfully this is not the case with the Fisherman's, which offers a welcoming atmosphere to match its pleasing face to the world. As does its home town of Broughty Ferry, on the eastern outskirts of Dundee, sitting by the banks of the Tay as it turns tidal and empties into the North Sea. There it stands towards the end of the street, a stone's throw from the water and within sight of the local lifeboat house. It's sandwiched within a terrace of old houses that were once fishermen's cottages (to the left the Fisherman's Tavern Hotel continues with the theme of hospitality) and has been a pub since 1827.

There's a spartan simplicity about its cottage-like appearance, offering a promise of cosiness within. It doesn't disappoint. The ceilings are low and there are several drinking areas, one of which has a Victorian fireplace, while another features a coal fire in winter. There are also up to six cask beers on at any one time, coming from the pub's owner Belhaven (itself now owned by Greene King, some of whose beers appear). For some, especially if they've been at the eponymous golf course nearby, St Andrews is the choice of beer when it's on (chestnut brown in colour with hints of caramel and toffee on the palate and a smooth finish), while others enjoy the interplay between the soft floral aroma and crisp cracker-like bite of Deuchars IPA.

The Fisherman's is the only Scottish pub that has appeared in every edition of the *Good Beer Guide* that has featured Scotland (the first one didn't). And this suggests it's a hardy survivor of the Scottish pub scene, a world that has witnessed its fair few ups and downs. So what's the secret? Is there a secret? Perhaps there isn't one apart from the offering of a decent array of cask beers, good pub grub and a comfortable welcome. Sometimes that is all you need.

The best **at success**

Opening hours: 11–midnight (1am Fri & Sat);
12.30–midnight Sun
Also great for: Bed & breakfast

New Inn

The Hill, Kilmington, Devon, EX13 7SF
01297 33376

🍺 **Palmers Copper Ale, Best Bitter, Dorset Gold**

I once received valuable gardening advice at the New Inn. It was late April and the sun had been shining for several weeks. As I sat in the compact front bar, cradling my glass of Dorset Gold, the conversation between several locals turned to runner beans. Don't put them out yet, was the general advice, there'll still be frost to come. I come to the pub for all manner of things, but this is the first time I've found myself in the middle of a *Gardeners' Question Time* moment.

Yet this overheard snippet encapsulates the ambience of this long-serving entry in the *Good Beer Guide*. It is a traditional place where people chat and offer their views on all manner of subjects in the manner of the village parliament that a good local pub can often be. Here you also enjoy a pint of Palmers, while hearty helpings of home-cooked food (nothing too fancy, ploughman's and the like) are served in the long dining area a couple of steps down from the front bar. The décor is traditional: the walls are painted a buttery yellow, an old clock keeps time in the front bar, old photographs tell tales of the village and settle-style seats offer comfort. With a longstanding licensee at the helm and a subtle rather than showy note towards the past, you can see why the New Inn has kept its place in the *Good Beer Guide*.

Outside, take time to admire the thatched Devon longhouse style (also note the old tin sign on the wall for Palmers mineral waters) and then pass into the large and attractive garden with its views over Axe Vale and an attractive willow standing in the centre of the lawn. Obviously the local branch of *Gardeners' Question Time* works overtime in this part of the world.

Opening hours: 11.30–2.30, 6–11; 12–3, 7–10.30 Sun
Also great for: Pub gardens

The best at success

Queen's Head

Fowlmere Road, Newton,
Cambridgeshire, CB22 7PG
01223 870436

🍺 **Adnams Southwold Bitter, Broadside, seasonal beers**

. . . .

There it stands, seemingly a tumble of buildings of different sizes that have been seamlessly fused into one, at the crossroads in the quiet village of Newton, south of Cambridge. Starting off as a farmhouse in the 17th century, it did time as a coaching inn and it might have operated a brewhouse at one time as well. A few notable facts: George V and his cousin Kaiser Wilhelm enjoyed a glass here, as did the Shah of Iran when he was still preening on the Peacock Throne; more pertinently the Queen's Head belongs to that small band of brothers who have been in every edition of the *Good Beer Guide*.

Let's take a look inside. At the bar tradition and timelessness rule the roost: wooden settle,

benches and seats, tiled floor and a stuffed goose (in life, this was Belinda who would patrol the outside of the pub). With the beer, even though the Queen's Head is a free house, it's Adnams' ales all the way. Southwold Bitter and Broadside are on permanently and seasonal choices from Southwold pop up depending on the weather. All are served straight from the cask. 'We think it's the best way to serve cask beer and people seem to like it,' says Robert Short, who runs the pub with his father David. He in turn has been at the bar for 40 years after taking it over from his grandfather. A complete list of all the landlords since 1729 can be seen in the lounge (there's also a games room where devil-among-the-tailors can be played).

When the weather is cold this is one of those rare places where Adnams' gorgeous barley wine Tally Ho can be found, a monumental beer full of Christmas cake and fruit notes all kept in line by a subtle yet assertive peppery, spicy hop character. It's cellared for 14 months so as to deepen the flavour and make it even more delicious.

Food? Famously, the pub serves a soup, a brown soup, or maybe Brown Windsor, though what goes into the pot depends on what's available. The only continuity is the colour brown and a matching colour chart is available for those who partake. There are also made to order sandwiches: beef, ham, cheese, salmon and so on.

There aren't many pubs left like this and Robert Short holds no illusions of what would happen if a brewery or pub company got hold of it. 'They'd knock it through to make more room and put on more beers,' he says, 'but it won't happen as we're not going anywhere.'

Opening hours: 11.30–2.30, 6–11; 12–2.30, 7–10.30 Sun

The best **at success**

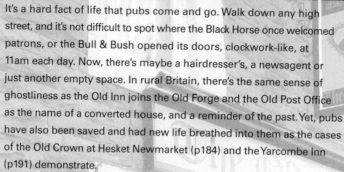

It's a hard fact of life that pubs come and go. Walk down any high street, and it's not difficult to spot where the Black Horse once welcomed patrons, or the Bull & Bush opened its doors, clockwork-like, at 11am each day. Now, there's maybe a hairdresser's, a newsagent or just another empty space. In rural Britain, there's the same sense of ghostliness as the Old Inn joins the Old Forge and the Old Post Office as the name of a converted house, and a reminder of the past. Yet, pubs have also been saved and had new life breathed into them as the cases of the Old Crown at Hesket Newmarket (p184) and the Yarcombe Inn (p191) demonstrate.

Good community pubs are as important to CAMRA as good ale – after all, there is no better place to enjoy cask beer. CAMRA has a lot of experience of pub campaigning, both nationally and locally, and has achieved some notable successes. Here, it offers a compact, six-point plan on how to save a pub.

The community-owned Old Crown, Hesket Newmarket

Media – contact local newspapers, and radio and TV stations to let them know of the threat to a local pub; set up a website or blog and use social networking sites such as Facebook to reach as many people as possible.

Community – contact local people and point out to them the advantages of having a local pub, explain that the pub is more than a place to drink – it might host clubs, music nights, comedy clubs and even a place for young mums to meet in the morning.

Articulate – explain to the wider world why the pub is important. Write letters to newspapers, both local and national; contact your MP and local politicians.

Warmth – many pubs raise money for charities but you can also use this as a way of gaining the pub-saving campaign some publicity.

Involvement – get local businesses involved in the campaign; in rural areas it's mutually beneficial for neighbouring businesses to cooperate.

People – get the local CAMRA branch involved and if a pub needs to be bought follow the example of the Old Crown and try and get villagers to buy a share in the pub. Details of local CAMRA branches can be found at www.camra.org.uk/branches.

Roscoe Head

24 Roscoe Head Street, Liverpool,
Merseyside, L1 2SX
0151 709 4365
www.roscoehead.co.uk

🍺 **Jennings Bitter; Tetley Bitter;
guest beers**

. . . .

In a city that has its fair share of great pubs, it's no mean achievement for the Roscoe Head to have remained in every edition of the *Good Beer Guide*. Pubs have come and gone, beers and breweries vanished, but the Roscoe ploughs on, a stunning example of a city backstreet boozer that has never lost its charm, comfort or dedication to good beer.

It wasn't always a pub, having started life in the 1870s as a three-storeyed private house. This homely aspect is immediately apparent as soon as you walk through the door. The bar is small, with a snug attached to one side, while further relaxation can be taken in a couple of other rooms.

Standing in the Roscoe you can still sense the ghost of the house that once was. Yet, the shadow of previous pub life also remains: old brass bells remain on the fitted benches, a survival of a time when there was a door to this room and meetings could be conveyed, while a bell rung when more pints were needed (according to landlady Carol Ross, whose parents once ran the pub, these bells worked until relatively recently).

At the back, the windowless room is dark though cosy, and those interested in brewery memorabilia will note the old advert on the wall for 'India Pale and Mild Ales' from a long-gone Gateshead brewery. The Roscoe Head is a great example of the pub as a bolthole from the outside world, a place that is not too cramped but still small enough to encourage that great currency of pub life: conversation. It's also hard not to overhear your fellow drinkers, whether they're discussing politics or football or a work colleague's problems.

Oh and the beer. That is after all, what we are here for. There are six cask beers on most of the time, with a couple of regulars; and guest beers like those from local heroes Liverpool One or Belfast's College Green as well as Acorn's Apollo IPA, a creamy, bitter, citrusy India Pale Ale from Barnsley. Grub is unpretentious and hearty: cottage pie, chips and peas; sausage, chips and peas; and egg, chips and peas, though those with a more adventurous palate can opt for chicken curry. Baguettes and butties are also available.

Comfort, conversation, good beer and a decent plateful of food: the Roscoe Head has it all. Long may it continue on its righteous path.

Opening hours: 11.30 (12 Sun)– midnight
Also great for: Community

The best **at success**

Square & Compass

Worth Matravers, Swanage,
Dorset, BH19 3LF
01929 439229
www.squareandcompasspub.co.uk
🍺 Palmers Copper Ale; guest beers

. . . .

Back of beyond, a fair way from anywhere, down country lanes – phrases that sound just about right for the Square & Compass' lonely situation on the Isle of Purbeck (though as the crow flies it's not too far from Swanage). Getting to this Wessex stalwart of the *Good Beer Guide* either requires the use of a car (with a designated driver of course) or a bicycle. Or maybe you would like to let your legs take the strain – there are plenty of walks out here and the South West Coast Path passes by, though a steepish decline towards the sea is needed to reach it. But the Square & Compass offers a mighty reward if you're walking and in need of refreshment.

Located at the intersection of a couple of roads in the village (or maybe should that be lanes?), the Square & Compass is an unchanging point in a forever-changing world and has been owned or run by members of the same family for over a century.

Into the bar you go, except that there's no bar. Instead there's a serving hatch out of which beers are dispensed, straight from the cask. Palmers Copper Ale is the regular (offering a circus like act of juggling between dry grainy biscuit and juicy citrus fruitiness, with an encore of a dry, bittersweet finish), but you will also discover all manner of guests including beers from Hop Back, Wessex and RCH. There is also a goodly amount of artisanal ciders available, including those from Westons and Hecks, as well as one made by owner Charlie Newman. Food is simple but delicious – a selection of home-made pies and pasties and when they're gone they're gone. And you can even nod your head in time to the music: there are regular musical events, while thespians occasionally turn up to tread the boards in the pub's back garden in the summer.

Oh, and I almost forgot, there's a compact museum of fossils in a room next to the main bar with the hatch. Take your pint in and ponder on the antiquity of the rocks on display – the Square & Compass is an appropriate home for them.

Opening hours: 12–3, 6–11; 12–11 Sat, Sun & summer
Also great for: Country

What was the first pub? Who knows. Maybe the folk of the Iron Age gathered in a hut within their lonely hill-forts and drank alcoholic potations. Certainly as soon as the Romans arrived they ordered wayside inns (or *tabernae*) to be built alongside their new straight roads. Chequer boards (hence making the inn sign the Chequers one of the oldest in these isles) were hung outside to indicate that these *tabernae* were places to pop into for a noggin of wine (the Romans were wine drinkers after all) and a bite to eat. The Saxons and all the other tribes that sailed west from over the northern seas brought in toasts and enjoyed nothing better than a good night of wassailing.

Come medieval times, the monks took over, running their own hostelries where weary travellers could stop for a bite and a pint and a quick look at an illustrated scroll. Taverns in the town acted as a home from home for anyone sick of looking at the four walls of their wattle and daub hovel. Coaching inns provided warmth and platefuls of wholesome grub for travellers when crossing countries and borders in comfort was unheard of. Victorian gin palaces made drinkers feel like royalty amid the opulence of engraved glass, polished brass and fluttering gas lamps, much to the dismay of temperance campaigners.

In the 20th century the pub took on a multitude of roles, many of which it still holds onto today: second home, hideaway, social club, beer palace and music centre. Gastro-pubs take the food route (some to the extent that it's difficult to call them pubs), while the latest manifestation is the craft beer house where beer sits proudly at the centre of attention. Two thousand years after the first pubs set up shop, drinkers are still being welcomed into their hallowed confines. Other countries may have the *keller*, *birreria* or bar. But the British have the pub and for that give thanks.

Star Inn

Netherton, Northumberland, NE65 7HD
01689 630238

🍺 **Camerons Strongarm**

. . . .

Sometimes being last isn't all that bad. It might mean bottom of the heap for some, but for others being last confers some sort of badge of honour. Take the Star Inn at Netherton. As the village sits in the shadows of the Cheviot Hills and Scotland's not that far away, it's inevitably been called the Last Pub in England. But if you were coming from the north, wouldn't that be the First Pub in England?

Whichever direction you come from, there's a more obvious reason for celebrating the Star Inn than just an accident of geography. For a start, it's one of the rare survivors who have been in every edition of the *Good Beer Guide*. And the reason for that? 'It's like sitting in someone's front room' say a lot of its champions, referring to the lounge that lays off the compact bar. Front room? Only if your front room has a big brewery mirror hanging over the fireplace then. But is it deserving of its appearance in every edition of the *Good Beer Guide*? Make your own mind up, but I would say yes. There aren't many pubs that have managed to remain unchanged throughout the decades and also get away with selling only one cask beer.

The floor of the front bar has vividly patterned lino, while the wooden panelled walls are a creamy caramel brown. Step through into the lounge (or someone else's front room) and you're presented with an austere yet welcoming ambience. Nothing much seems to have changed for a while. This is one of those pubs that keep a sense of their own continuity, a bit like an aristocratic bloodline. Landlady Vera Wilson-Morton is just the latest member of her family to keep house since her grandfather turned up in the village in 1917 and took over the pub. Not suprisingly the pub is listed on the CAMRA National Inventory of Historic Pub Interiors.

There's little ceremony here. The sole beer, the no-nonsense local bitter Camerons Strongarm, is served in the bar (or maybe you would want to call it a hallway), through a panel in the wall. No food is served, not even crisps or nuts.

This is an isolated area and gets busier at the weekends when the walkers and nature lovers arrive, eager to grab themselves a slice of pub life as it used to be. For that reason opening hours are limited to evenings only and then that's not every night. So choose your time right. This is the last pub in England (perhaps), and you wouldn't want to find it closed…

Opening hours: 7.30–10.30 (10 Wed); closed Mon, Thu & Sun

Star Tavern

6 Belgrave Mews West, Belgravia,
London, SW1X 8HT
020 7235 3019
www.fullers.co.uk

🍺 **Fuller's Chiswick Bitter, Discovery,
London Pride, ESB, seasonal beers**

. . . .

They're talking about dogs at the mahogany bar counter in the Star Tavern. There's a chap whose lurcher is being fed scraps from the plate of another chap who's just enjoyed steak and chips for his lunch and is drawing deeply on his London Pride.

I order a glass of ESB. It's pitch perfect in this famous Fuller's pub: deep booming orange marmalade notes, a bittersweet sweep of refreshment and a dry, dusty finish that sets you up for another one. London Pride, Discovery and a seasonal Gale's beer are also available. I suspect that Pride is the bestseller. Was this what was drunk when – allegedly, and I use the word carefully – the Great Train Robbers organised their caper here in the 1960s, but no one's totally sure that's not just some myth put about by someone who's had too much ESB. With this legend very much in mind, my ears prick up when I accidentally overhear a couple of heavy looking guys in suits on a table across from me talking about 'the boys'. Moments later it transpires they're talking about a building site. You shouldn't always believe everything you see in Guy Ritchie's movies.

The Star has been in the *Good Beer Guide* for 40 years (sounds like a stretch), an unbroken record that's only enjoyed by one other London pub. Why, I wonder? It certainly serves wonderful beer, but I believe that there's another reason for its longevity – built during the Georgian period, this is a pub that has survived the ages of London pub life: the beer shops of the 1830s, the glitz and glass of the gin palace, the Defence of the Realm Act during the first World War, Brewers' Tudor between the wars, the destruction of the Blitz and the war on traditional pubs in the 1960s and 1970s. It has survived.

There are three separate areas: the bar, an adjoining lounge and a back room, all of which feature old prints and handbills on the wall. The feel of the pub is that it has settled into its age with great ease. The décor is cream and reddish brown, lit up by the gilt highlights of mirrors and light fittings. It's a pub that is quietly confident. The best time to enjoy it is in the afternoon between the lunchtime and evening hordes, when there's the quiet buzz of conversation and you get a sense of an oasis in the centre of diplomatic London.

Opening hours: 11 (12 Sat)–11; 12–10.30 Sun

The best **at success**

Great British Pubs
appendices

Great British beer

Beer, specifically real ale, is at the heart of every great British pub and defines what CAMRA is all about. Britain is best known for the style known as bitter, but there is far more to British beer than bitter and especially now, during what is a real renaissance in British brewing. The choice of beer available in pubs is greater than ever and often bewildering so, here is a guide... Taken from the *Good Beer Guide 2012* and written by Roger Protz

❶ Porter & Stout

Porter was a London beer that created the first commercial brewing industry in the world in the early 18th century. Porter started life as a brown beer and became darker when new technology made it possible to roast grain at higher temperatures to obtain greater colour and flavour. The strongest version of porter was dubbed stout porter or stout for short. The name porter was the result of the beer's popularity with the large number of porters working the streets, markets and docks of 18th-century London.

During the first World War, when the British government prevented brewers from using heavily-roasted malts in order to divert energy to the arms industry, Guinness and other Irish brewers came to dominate the market. In recent years, porter and stout have made a spirited comeback in both Britain and the United States, with brewers digging deep in to old recipe books to create genuine versions of the style from the 18th and 19th centuries.

Look for a jet-black colour with a hint of ruby around the edge of the glass. Expect a dark and roasted malt character, with raisin and sultana fruit, espresso or cappuccino coffee, liquorice and molasses. The beer should have deep hop bitterness to balance the richness of malt and fruit.

❷ Mild

Mild was once the most popular style of beer in Britain but it was overtaken by bitter in the 1950s. It was developed in the 18th and 19th centuries as a less aggressively bitter style of beer than porter and stout, and was primarily drunk by industrial and agricultural workers to refresh them after long hours of arduous labour. Early milds were much stronger that modern interpretations, which tend to fall in the 3% to 3.5% category, though Rudgate's Dark Ruby Mild at 4.4% is more in keeping with earlier strengths. Mild is usually dark brown in colour, due to the use of well-roasted malts or roasted barley, but there are paler versions such as Banks's Mild, Timothy Taylor's Golden Best and McMullen's AK. Look for rich malty aromas and flavours, with hints of dark fruit, chocolate, coffee and caramel, with a gentle underpinning of hop bitterness.

❸ Old ale

Old ale is another style from the 18th century, stored for months or even years in wooden vessels where the beer picked up some lactic sourness from wild yeasts and tannins in the wood. As a result of the sour taste, it was dubbed 'stale' by drinkers and the beer was one of the components of the early blended porters. In recent years, old ale has made a return to popularity, primarily due to the popularity of Theakston Old Peculier and Gale's Prize Old Ale.

Contrary to expectation, old ales do not have to be especially strong and can be no more than 4% alcohol. Neither do they have to be dark: old ale can be pale and bursting with lush malt, tart fruit and spicy hops. Darker versions will have a more profound malt character, with powerful hints of roasted grain, dark fruit, polished leather and fresh tobacco. The hallmark of the style is a lengthy period of maturation, often in bottle rather than cask.

4 Barley wine

Barley wine dates from the 18th and 19th centuries when England was often at war with France and it was the duty of patriots, usually from the upper classes, to drink ale rather that French claret. Barley wine had to be strong – often between 10% and 12% – and was stored for as long as 18 months or two years. The biggest-selling barley wine for many years was Whitbread's 10.9% Gold Label, now available only in cans. Fuller's Vintage Ale (8.5%) is a bottle-conditioned version of its Golden Pride and is brewed with different varieties of malts and hops every year. Expect massive sweet malt and ripe fruit of the pear drop, orange and lemon type, with darker fruits, chocolate and coffee if darker malts are used. Hop rates are generous and produce bitterness and peppery, grassy and floral notes.

5 IPA

India Pale Ale changed the face of brewing in the 19th century. The new technologies of the industrial revolution enabled brewers to use pale malts to fashion beers that were pale bronze in colour. First brewed in London and Burton-on-Trent for the colonial trade, IPAs were strong in alcohol and high in hops to keep them in good condition during long sea journeys. IPA's life span was brief, driven out of the colonies by German lager. But the style has made a spirited recovery in recent years, brewed with great passion in both Britain and the U.S. In Chicago, Goose Island's IPA is arguably the finest American interpretation of the style while in Britain Marston's Old Empire and Meantime's IPA are just two modern versions of the style arousing new interest. Look for a big peppery hop aroma and palate balanced by juicy malt and tart citrus fruit.

6 Burton ale

As the name suggests, the origins of Burton Ale lie in Burton upon Trent, but the style became so popular in the 18th and 19th centuries that most brewers had 'a Burton' in their portfolio and the expression 'gone for a Burton' entered the English language. Bass at one time had six different versions of the beer, ranging from 6% to 11.5%: the stronger versions were exported to Russia and the Baltic States.

In the 20th century, Burton was overtaken in popularity by pale ale and bitter but it was revived with great success in the late 1970s with the launch of Ind Coope Draught Burton Ale. But when

Allied Breweries broke up, the beer moved first to Tetley's in Leeds and then J W Lees in Manchester, where it's brewed in small batches but is worth seeking out: it's based on the recipe for a once-famous bottled beer, Double Diamond Export. Other Burton Ales exist under different names today: Young's Winter Warmer was originally called Burton. Bass No 1, brewed occasionally, is called a barley wine but is in fact the last remaining version of a Bass Burton Ale. Look for a bright amber colour, a rich malty and fruity character underscored by a solid resinous and piny hop note.

7 Pale ale

The success of IPA in the colonial trade led to a demand for beer of a similar colour and character in Britain. IPA, with its heavy hopping, was considered too bitter for the domestic market, and brewers responded with a beer dubbed pale ale that was lower in alcohol and hops. Pale ale was known as 'the beer of the railway age', transported round the country from Burton-on-Trent by the new railway system. Brewers from London, Liverpool and Manchester built breweries in Burton to make use of the local, mineral-rich water to make their own versions of pale ale. From the early years of the 20th century, bitter began to overtake pale ale in popularity and as a result pale ale became mainly a bottled product. A true pale ale should be different to bitter, identical to IPA in colour and brewed without the addition of coloured malts. It should have a spicy, resinous aroma and palate, with biscuity malt and tart citrus fruit. Many beers are called bitter today but are in fact pale ale, Marston's Pedigree being a case in point.

8 Bitter

Towards the end of the 19th century, brewers built large estates of tied pubs and they moved away from beers stored for months or years and developed 'running beers' that could be served after a few days of conditioning in the pub cellar. Bitter was a new type of running beer: it was a member of the pale ale family but was generally deep bronze or copper in colour due to the use of slightly darker malts, such as crystal, that gave the beer fullness of palate. Best is a stronger version of bitter but there is considerable crossover. Bitter falls into the 3.4% to 3.9% band, while best bitter is 4% upwards, though a number of brewers dub their ordinary bitters 'best'. A further development of bitter comes in the shape of extra or special strong bitter of 5% or more: Fuller's ESB and Greene King Abbot being well-known examples. With ordinary bitter, look for spicy, peppery and grassy hop character, a powerful bitterness, tangy fruit and juicy/nutty malt. With best and strong bitters, malt and fruit character will tend to dominate but hop aroma and bitterness are still crucial to the style, often achieved by 'late hopping' in the brewery or adding hops to casks as they leave for pubs.

9 Golden ale

Golden ales have become so popular, with brewers of all sizes producing them, that they now have their own category in the Champion Beer of Britain competition. Exmoor Gold and Hop Back Summer Lightning launched the trend in the early 1980s and other brewers quickly followed suit in a rush to win younger drinkers away from mass-produced lagers to the pleasures of cask beer. The style is different to pale ale in two crucial ways: golden ale is paler, often brewed with lager malt or specially produced low temperature ale malt and, as a result, hops are allowed to give full expression, balancing sappy malt with luscious fruity, floral, herbal, spicy and resinous characteristics.

While brewers of pale ale tend to use such traditional English hops as Fuggles and Goldings, imported hops from North America, the Czech Republic, Germany, Slovenia and New Zealand give radically different hop notes to golden ale. As a result, golden ales offer a new and exciting drinking experience. They are often served colder than draught bitter and some brewers, such as Fuller's, have installed cooling devices attached to beer engines to ensure the beer reaches the glass at an acceptably refreshing temperature.

🔟 Wheat beer

Wheat beer is a style closely associated with Bavaria and Belgium and the popularity of the style in Britain has encouraged many brewers to add wheat beer to the portfolios. The title is something of a misnomer as all 'wheat beers' are a blend of malted barley as well as wheat, as the latter grain is difficult to brew with and needs the addition of barley, which acts as a natural filter during the mashing stage. But wheat, if used with special strains of yeast developed for brewing the style, gives distinctive aromas and flavours, such as clove, banana and bubblegum that make it a complex and refreshing beer. The Belgian version of wheat beer often has the addition of herbs and spices, such as milled coriander seeds and orange peel – a habit that dates back to medieval times.

⑪ Fruit/speciality beers

Brewers have become restless in recent years in their quest for new flavours. The popularity in Britain of Belgian fruit beers has not gone unnoticed and now many home-grown brewers are using fruit in their beer. Others have gone the extra mile and add honey, herbs, heather, spices, and even spirit – brandy and rum feature in a number of speciality beers. It's important to dispel the belief that fruit and honey beers are sweet: both fruit and honey add new dimensions to the brewing process and are highly fermentable, with the result that beers that use the likes of cherries or raspberry are dry and quenching rather than cloying.

⑫ Scottish beers

Historically, Scottish beers tend to be darker, sweeter and less heavily hopped than English beers: a reflection of a colder climate where hops don't grow and beer needs to be nourishing. The classic traditional styles are Light, Heavy and Export, which are not dissimilar to mild, bitter and IPA. They are also often known as 60, 70 and 80 Shilling Ales from a 19th-century method of invoicing beers according to their strength. A Wee Heavy or 90 Shilling Ale is the Scottish equivalent of barley wine. Many new brewers in Scotland produce beers that are lighter in colour and with more generous hop rates.

How beer is brewed

Before you can raise a pint in the pub, enormous skill and the finest natural ingredients come together in the brewery to turn barley malt, hops, yeast and water into beer. Here, the brewing process is followed at Harveys, Lewes.

◀ 1
Malt – partially germinated barley – is stored at the top of the brewery. Harveys uses the classic Maris Otter variety.

4 ▶
Head brewer Miles Jenner checks the temperature of the mash as brewing gets under way. Temperature is crucial to allow malt starch to turn into fermentable sugar.

◀ 2
Malt is added to a hopper ready to be ground into grist. The grist is then dropped into the mash tun to start the brewing process.

◀ 5
At the end of the mash, the grain is 'sparged' or sprinkled with hot liquor to wash out remaining malt sugars.

3 ▶
Pure water, known as 'liquor', has percolated through the chalk downs of Sussex before reaching the brewery. Hot liquor is mixed in the mash tun with the malt grist.

◀ 6
The wort or sugary extract runs out of the mash tun into a receiving vessel where it is checked en route to the copper.

7 ▶

The hop store: Harveys uses traditional hop varieties from farmers in Sussex and surrounding counties.

8 ▶

The copper, where wort is vigorously boiled with hops: the boil extracts acids and tannins from the hops that add aroma and bitterness to the beer.

◀ 9

Some of the hops are added late in the boil for additional aroma and flavour. 'Late hopping' restores any aroma lost earlier during the boil.

◀ 10

After the boil, the hopped wort is cooled and transferred to a fermenting vessel. Yeast is 'pitched' or blended into the wort to start fermentation.

11 ▶

To keep the yeast working busily, turning malt sugar into alcohol, the fermenting beer is roused or oxygenated from time to time.

12 ▶

Beer is racked into casks in preparation for the final destination: the pub cellar where it enjoys a vigorous second fermentation.

◀ 13

In the racking hall, finings are added that will clear the beer of yeast and protein in the pub cellar.

14 ▶

And finally... checking the quality of the finished beer in the pub. Another perfect pint is poured!

Index

Index by region

England

Bedfordshire
Green Man, Eversholt, 233

Berkshire
Bell, Aldworth, 182
Bounty, Cookham, 93

Cambridgeshire
Cambridge Blue, Cambridge, 15
Castle Inn, Cambridge, 230
Queen's Head, Newton, 275
Brewery Tap, Peterborough, 42

Cheshire
Bhurtpore Inn, Aston, 14
Brewery Tap, Chester, 141
Nursery, Heaton Norris, 255
Sutton Hall, Sutton, 143

Cornwall
Blisland Inn, Blisland, 262
Seven Stars, Falmouth, 109
Blue Anchor, Helston, 32
Witchball, Lizard, 171
Driftwood Spars, St Agnes, 243
Gurnard's Head, Treen, 196

Cumbria
Old Crown, Hesket Newmarket, 184
Watermill Inn, Ings, 87
Kirkstile Inn, Loweswater, 225
Beer Hall, Staveley, 138
Plough Inn, Wreay, 121

Derbyshire
Fountain Head Inn, Branscombe, 82
Brunswick, Derby, 33

Brewery Tap – Derby's Royal Standard, Derby, 142
Flowerpot, Derby, 244
Jug & Glass, Lea, 251

Devon
The Fountain Head, Branscombe, 82
Culm Valley Inn, Culmstock, 212
Pigs Nose Inn, East Prawle, 247
Old Fire House, Exeter, 246
Turf, Exminster, 112
Duke of York, Iddesleigh, 81
New Inn, Kilmington, 274
Ye Olde Cider Bar, Newton Abbot, 61
Beer Engine, Newton St Cyres, 31
Dolphin Hotel, Plymouth, 67
Tom Cobley, Spreyton, 24
Bridge Inn, Topsham, 151
Waterman's Arms, Totnes, 203
Yarcombe Inn, Yarcombe, 191

Dorset
Spyway Inn, Askerswell, 235
Anchor Inn, Seatown, 104
Castle Inn, West Lulworth, 221
Square & Compass, Worth Matravers, 278

Durham
Surtees Arms, Ferryhill, 187
Rat Race Ale House, Hartlepool, 131

Essex
Thatchers Arms, Mount Bures, 86
Bell, Wendens Ambo, 118

Gloucestershire & Bristol
Red Lion, Ampney St Peter, 161
Boat Inn, Ashleworth, 90

The Apple, Bristol, 54
Seven Stars, Bristol, 268
Three Tuns, Bristol, 50
Zerodegrees, Bristol, 145
Old Spot, Dursley, 267
Royal Oak Inn, Prestbury, 178

Hampshire
Bat & Ball, Waterlooville, 174
Black Boy, Winchester, 64

Herefordshire
Barrels, Hereford, 40
Victory, Hereford, 60
Bridge Inn, Kentchurch, 95
Alma Inn, Linton, 116
Stagg Inn, Titley, 216

Hertfordshire
Lordship Arms, Benington, 226
Woodman, Wildhill, 190

Kent
King's Head, Canterbury, 252
Louis Armstrong, Dover, 245
Railway Hotel, Faversham, 129
Butcher's Arms, Herne, 166
Lifeboat Ale & Cider House, Margate, 105
Rose & Crown, Perry Wood, 234

Lancashire
Taps, Lytham, 188

Leicestershire
The Pub, Leicester, 21

Lincolnshire
Signal Box Inn, Cleethorpes, 169
Batemans Brewery Visitor Centre, Wainfleet All Saints, 41

Greater London

Star Tavern, Belgravia, 281
George Inn, Borough, 155
The Rake, Borough, 22
Royal Oak, Borough, 75
Black Friar, City of London, 150
Gunmakers, Clerkenwell, 69
Freemasons Arms, Covent Garden, 176
Harp, Covent Garden, 265
Drayton Court, Ealing, 222
Euston Tap, Euston, 127
Old Brewery, Greenwich, 159
Dove, Hammersmith, 99
Florence, Herne Hill, 231
Southampton Arms, Kentish Town, 23
White Horse, Parsons Green, 25
Tom Cribb, Piccadilly Circus, 179
Cask Pub & Kitchen, Pimlico, 16
Bricklayer's Arms, Putney, 65
Buckingham Arms, Westminster, 272

Greater Manchester

Britons Protection, Castlefield, 152
Marble Arch, Manchester, 47
Port Street Beer House, Manchester, 74
Stalybridge Station Refreshment Rooms, Stalybridge, 133
Crown, Stockport, 263

Merseyside

Baltic Fleet, Liverpool, 29
The Philharmonic, Liverpool, 160
Roscoe Head, Liverpool, 277

Norfolk

Fat Cat, Norwich, 264
King's Head, Norwich, 71

Northamptonshire

Star Inn, Sulgrave, 257

Northumberland

Barrasford Arms, Barrasford, 207
Rat Inn, Hexham, 215
Ship Inn, Low Newton, 36
Star Inn, Netherton, 280
Olde Ship Inn, Seahouses, 108
Travellers Rest, Slaley, 237

Nottinghamshire

Victoria, Beeston, 134
Canalhouse, Nottingham, 98
Kean's Head, Nottingham, 70
Olde Trip to Jerusalem, Nottingham, 168

Oxfordshire

Great Western Arms, Aynho, 224
White Lion, Fewcott, 123

Shropshire

Six Bells Inn, Bishop's Castle, 37
Three Tuns, Bishop's Castle, 49
All Nations, Madeley, 28
Boathouse, Shrewsbury, 91
Cock Hotel, Wellington, 183

Somerset

Ring O'Bells, Ashcott, 256
Barton Inn, Barton St David, 79
Old Green Tree, Bath, 73
Star, Bath, 163
Black Horse, Clapton in Gordano, 119
Queens Arms, Corton Denham, 200
The Bridge, Dulverton, 94
Woods, Dulverton, 217
Rose & Crown, Huish Episcopi, 162
Halfway House, Pitney, 20

Staffordshire

Burton Bridge Inn, Burton upon Trent, 43
Coopers Tavern, Burton upon Trent, 153

Suffolk

Nutshell, Bury St Edmunds, 167
Butt & Oyster, Pin Mill, 96
King's Head, Laxfield, 158
Triangle Tavern, Lowestoft, 189
Lord Nelson, Southwold, 106
Anchor, Walberswick, 194
Cherry Tree Inn, Woodbridge, 195

East Sussex

Evening Star, Brighton, 44
Lewes Arms, Lewes, 253

West Sussex

Royal Oak, Friday Street, 185
Hare & Hounds, Stoughton, 84

Tyne & Wear

Centurion, Newcastle upon Tyne, 126
Cluny, Newcastle upon Tyne, 241
Crown Posada, Newcastle upon Tyne, 154
Cumberland Arms, Newcastle upon Tyne, 242

Warwickshire

Castle, Edgehill, 220
George Hotel, Lower Brailes, 214

West Midlands

Bartons Arms, Birmingham, 149
Vine, Brierley Hill, 51
Olde Swan, Netherton, 35
Beacon Hotel, Sedgeley, 30

Wiltshire

Red Lion, Cricklade, 201

Worcestershire

Mug House, Bewdley, 100
Cider House, Defford, 56
Walter de Cantelupe, Kempsey, 122
King & Castle, Kidderminster, 128
Bell, Pensax, 261
Coach & Horses, Weatheroak, 34

Good Beer Guide 2012

Editor: Roger Protz

The *Good Beer Guide* is the only guide you will ever need to find the right pint, in the right place, every time. It's the original and best-selling guide to around 4,500 pubs throughout the UK. Now in its 39th year, this annual publication is a comprehensive and informative guide to the best real ale pubs in the UK, researched and written exclusively by CAMRA members.

£15.99   ISBN 978-1-85249-286-1

London's Best Beer, Pubs & Bars

Des de Moore

This is the essential guide to beer drinking in London. This practical book is packed with detailed maps and easy-to-use listings to help you find the best places to enjoy perfect pints in the capital. Laid out by area, find the best pubs serving the best British and international beers wherever you are.

£12.99   ISBN 978-1-85249-285-4

Good Bottled Beer Guide

Jeff Evans

A pocket-sized guide for discerning drinkers looking to buy bottled real ales and enjoy a fresh glass of their favourite beers at home. The 7th edition of the *Good Bottled Beer Guide* is updated and redesigned to showcase the very best bottled British real ales now being produced, and detail where they can be bought. Everything you need to know about bottled beers; tasting notes, ingredients, brewery details, and a glossary to understand more about them.

£12.99   ISBN 978-1-85249-262-5

Edinburgh Pub Walks

Bob Steel

A practical, pocket-sized travellers' guide to the pubs in and around Scotland's capital city. Featuring 25 town, park and costal walks, *Edinburgh Pub Walks* enables you to explore the many faces of the city. Featuring walks in the heart of Edinburgh, as well as routes through its historic suburbs and nearby towns along the Firth of Forth, all accessible by public transport.

£9.99   ISBN 978-1-85249-274-8

Lake District Pub Walks

Bob Steel

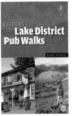

A pocket-sized, traveller's guide to some of the best walking and best pubs in the Lake District. The 30 walks are grouped geographically around tourist hubs with plenty of accommodation, making the book ideal for a visitor to the Lakes. The book is fully illustrated, with clear Ordnance Survey mapping and written directions to help readers navigate the routes.

£9.99   ISBN 978-1-85249-271-7

Cider

Photography by Mark Bolton

Cider is a lavishly illustrated celebration of real cider, and its close cousin perry, for anyone who wants to learn more about Britain's oldest drink. With features on the UK's most interesting and characterful cider and perry makers, how to make your own cider, foreign ciders, and the best places to drink cider – including unique dedicated cider houses, award-winning pubs and year-round CAMRA festivals all over the country

£14.99   ISBN 978-1-85249-259-5

It takes all sorts to Campaign for Real Ale

CAMRA, the Campaign for Real Ale, is an independent not-for-profit, volunteer-led consumer group. We promote good-quality real ale and pubs as well as lobbying government to champion drinkers' rights and protect local pubs as centres of community life.

CAMRA has 125,000 members from all ages and backgrounds, brought together by a common belief in the issues that CAMRA deals with and their love of good quality British beer and cider. From just £20 a year – that's less than a pint a month – you can join CAMRA and enjoy the following benefits:

A monthly colour newspaper informing you about beer and pub news and detailing events and beer festivals around the country.

Free or reduced entry to over 140 national, regional and local beer festivals. Money off many of our publications including the *Good Beer Guide* and the *Good Bottled Beer Guide*.

Access to a members-only section of our national website, **www.camra.org.uk**, which gives up-to-the-minute news stories and includes a special offer section with regular features saving money on beer and trips away.

The opportunity to campaign to save pubs under threat of closure, for pubs to be open when people want to drink and a reduction in beer duty that will help Britain's brewing industry survive.

Log onto **www.camra.org.uk** for CAMRA membership information.